Well-Being and Extended Working Life

Most European countries have experienced labour market reforms at varying times leading to extended working life and a postponement of retirement age. This book provides a gender perspective on the impact of extended working life on the different dimensions of well-being, the factors which can limit extended working life, and the working conditions of older workers.

Over the course of 11 chapters the book explores factors that can limit access to paid work or affect working conditions for older workers, including care for dependent individuals, negative stereotypes surrounding aged workers and poor health. It also investigates differences in working conditions for older workers by gender compared to other groups of workers and across European countries including case studies from Austria, France, Spain, Poland, Croatia, Albania and Turkey.

This book will be of interest to all scholars and students of social policy, sociology, gender studies and labour studies more broadly.

Tindara Addabbo (University of Modena & Reggio Emilia) is a Full Professor of Economic Policy and Coordinator of the Doctoral Research Course in Labour, Development and Innovation at the Department of Economics Marco Biagi. She publishes on the gender impact of public and social policies, employment and wage discrimination by gender, income distribution, well-being, quality of work.

Patricia Carney (Health Service Executive) is a Senior Researcher at the Department of Public Health HSE Midlands and a trained health economist. She publishes on the health, social and economic impacts of informal care for older people on different factors of well-being, infectious disease epidemiology, determinants of health inequalities, health and well-being and the life course.

Áine Ní Léime (Assistant Professor in Ethics, Business and Society at the school of Business and Economics University of Galway) is Former Chairperson of COST Action IS1409 Gender and Health Implications of Extended Working Life in Western Countries (2015–2019). Her recent publications focus on gender, older workers, retirement and extended working life.

Jeroen Spijker (Centre d'Estudis Demogràfics-CED, Spain) is a "Ramón y Cajal-13" Research Fellow. He obtained a BA in 1994 in Sociology and Human Geography from Massey University, New Zealand and a Master in 1997 and PhD in 2004 in Spatial Sciences (specialisation Demography) from Groningen University, the Netherlands. He has published on a wide range of topics in the field of demography, including population ageing, elderly care, family formation after divorce and widowhood and how the recent economic crisis in Catalonia and Spain has affected the health of the 50+.

Siniša Zrinščak (University of Zagreb) is a Full Professor and Head of the Chair of Sociology at the Faculty of Law. Previously, he taught Comparative and European Social Policy at the Department of Social Work (Faculty of Law, University of Zagreb). He publishes mainly on religious and social policy changes in post-communism, Europeanisation and gender.

Gender and Well-Being

Series editors: Christina Borderias and Bernard Harris

The aim of this series is to enhance our understanding of the relationship between gender and well-being by addressing the following questions:

- How can we compare levels of well-being between women and men? Is it possible to develop new indicators which reflect a fuller understanding of the nature of well-being in the 21st century?
- How have women and men contributed to the improvement of individual well-being at different times and in different places?
- What role should institutions play in promoting and maintaining well-being?
- In what ways have different social movements contributed to the improvement of well-being over the last 300 years?

The volumes in this series are designed to provide rigorous social-scientific answers to these questions.

Books in the series:

Gender Inequalities, Households and the Production of Well-Being in Modern Europe
Edited by Tindara Addabbo, Marie-Pierre Arrizabalaga, Cristina Borderías and Alastair Owens

Gender, Law and Economic Well-Being in Europe from the Fifteenth to the Nineteenth Century
North Versus South?
Edited by Anna Bellavitis and Beatrice Zucca Micheletto

Well-Being and Extended Working Life
A Gender Perspective
Edited by Tindara Addabbo, Patricia Carney, Áine Ní Léime, Jeroen Spijker and Siniša Zrinščak

https://www.routledge.com/Gender-and-Well-Being/book-series/ASHSER1313

Well-Being and Extended Working Life

A Gender Perspective

Edited by Tindara Addabbo,
Patricia Carney, Áine Ní Léime,
Jeroen Spijker, and Siniša Zrinščak

Routledge
Taylor & Francis Group
LONDON AND NEW YORK

First published 2023
by Routledge
4 Park Square, Milton Park, Abingdon, Oxon OX14 4RN

and by Routledge
605 Third Avenue, New York, NY 10158

Routledge is an imprint of the Taylor & Francis Group, an informa business

British Library Cataloguing-in-Publication Data
A catalogue record for this book is available from the British Library

Library of Congress Cataloging-in-Publication Data
Names: Addabbo, Tindara, editor.
Title: Well-being and extended working life : a gender perspective / edited by Tindara Addabbo, Patricia Carney, Áine Ní Léime, Jeroen Spijker and Siniša Zrinščak.
Description: Abingdon, Oxon ; New York, NY : Routledge, 2023. | Series: Gender and well-being | Includes bibliographical references and index. | Identifiers: LCCN 2022023812 (print) | LCCN 2022023813 (ebook) | ISBN 9780367702649 (hardback) | ISBN 9780367702663 (paperback) | ISBN 9781003145325 (ebook)
Subjects: LCSH: Retirement age--Europe. | Older women--Employment--Europe. | Older people--Employment--Europe. | Well-being--Europe. | Age and employment--Europe.
Classification: LCC HD7108.4.E85 W45 2023 (print) | LCC HD7108.4.E85 (ebook) | DDC 331.3/98094--dc23/eng/20220525
LC record available at https://lccn.loc.gov/2022023812
LC ebook record available at https://lccn.loc.gov/2022023813

ISBN: 978-0-367-70264-9 (hbk)
ISBN: 978-0-367-70266-3 (pbk)
ISBN: 978-1-003-14532-5 (ebk)

DOI: 10.4324/9781003145325

Typeset in Goudy
by MPS Limited, Dehradun

Contents

Figures

Tables

Contributors

Tindara Addabbo (University of Modena & Reggio Emilia) is Full Professor of Economic Policy and coordinator of the Doctoral Research Course in Labour, Development and Innovation at the Department of Economics Marco Biagi. She publishes on the gender impact of public and social policies, employment and wage discrimination by gender, income distribution, well-being, quality of work.

Sabrina Aouci (National Retirement Fund of Public Social Security – CNAV), Researcher at the Ageing Research Department of the CNAV since 2007. She holds a PhD (2015) in Sociodemography, Paris Ouest Nanterre La Défense University and a Master of Sociodemography «Change in contemporary societies» (2006), Paris Ouest Nanterre La Défense University. Her main research interests include Transition from work to retirement; Risk of economic, professional, social and family fragility observed in the transition to retirement; Retirement intention and the postulate of "free choice" in retirement decisions.

Hande Barlin (Gebze Technical University) is a member of faculty at Economics Department. Previously she designed and implemented development, empowerment and social integration projects and carried out research on regional development and European economics. Currently, her academic work concentrates on health economics, labour economics, ageing and social inclusion.

Amand Blanes Llorens (Autonomous University of Barcelona – UAB) is a Researcher at the Centre d'Estudis Demogràfics and Lecturer at the UAB. He has a degree in History and Political Science and a PhD in Demography from the Autonomous University of Barcelona. His main research topics are in the field of demography, including population ageing, health, morbidity and mortality, elderly dependency and he is an expert in population and household estimations and projections.

Patricia Carney (Health Service Executive) is a Senior Researcher at the Department of Public Health HSE Midlands and a trained health economist. She publishes on the health, social and economic impacts of informal care for older people on different factors of well-being, infectious disease epidemiology, determinants of health inequalities, health and well-being and the life course.

Ivana Dobrotić (University of Zagreb) is an Associate Professor of Comparative Social Policy and an Associate Member of the Department of Social Policy and Intervention at the University of Oxford. She recently completed a Marie Skłodowska-Curie Individual Fellowship at the University of Oxford as a PI of the InCARE project investigating parenting leaves and childcare policies' development in Southeastern Europe. Her research interest is in the field of comparative social policy, with a particular interest in care and paid work, gender, social and spatial inequalities. She is a Steering Committee member of the *ECPR Standing Group on Gender and Politics* and co-editor of the *Annual Review of Leave Policies & Related Research*.

Antía Domínguez-Rodríguez (University of A Coruña) is a Lecturer and Researcher at the Department of Sociology and Communication Sciences. She obtained a BA (2009) in Statistics from Salamanca University, a BA (2010) in Sociology from Basque Country University, a Master (2013) in Territorial and Population Studies (specialisation Demography) and a PhD (2018) in Demography (on "Health and the last years of the working life") from the Autonomous University of Barcelona. Her main topics are demography and ageing, family, health and retirement.

Jacques-Antoine Gauthier (Life course and inequality research center (LINES) at the University of Lausanne) is a Senior Lecturer in sociology. His current researches focus on modelling and analysing longitudinal, life-course data. The central focus of his research is the construction of individual life trajectories, especially during major transitions such as partnering and parenthood. He is also interested in the development of multidimensional sequence analysis techniques and in the visualisation of longitudinal data.

Michaela Gstrein (WPZ) An Economist and experienced Project Leader, she is currently part of the WPZ Research team. Previously worked at the Austrian Institute for Advanced Studies (IHS Vienna) applied research group. She has participated in many interdisciplinary local and international research projects, taking the role of coordinator or partner. Her interest lies in the field of gender studies, quality of life, statistics, women and family-related economic issues, benefits and transfers, female labour market activity, WLB and pension outcomes, social security, demography, economic growth and employment in the EU as well as social cohesion and integration.

Barbara Haas (Vienna University of Economics and Business – WU) is an Associate Professor of Sociology and Senior Lecturer at the WU. She publishes on the gender impact of changes in employment (education, low income and sustainability) as well as on international welfare state comparisons (gendered labour markets and social policy).

Nicky Le Feuvre (University of Lausanne, Switzerland) is a Professor of Sociology at the University of Lausanne in Switzerland. She obtained her PhD from the University of Aston in Birmingham and worked for several years as Director of the Interdisciplinary Gender Studies Centre in Toulouse (France). She has undertaken a large number of cross-national comparative studies of women's career paths and employment patterns, particularly in highly qualified occupations (law, medicine, academia, etc.). She is currently leading the NORFACE DIAL project *Dynamics of Accumulated Inequality for Seniors in Employment* (DAISIE).

Michaela Kobler-Weiß (Vienna University of Economics and Business – WU) is an Assistant to the Rector's Council, assigned primarily to the Vice-Rector for Academic Programs and Student Affairs. Her main research areas include the social dimension in university settings, employment discrimination by gender and status, impact of educational attainment on job security and employability.

Nilufer Korkmaz Yaylagul (Akdeniz University, Turkey) is an Associate Professor of the Gerontology Department. Previously she implemented projects about social exclusion and informal care and service usage of older immigrants. She has a particular interest in informal care and ageing in a gender perspective.

Áine Ní Léime (Assistant Professor in Ethics, Business and Society at the school of Business and Economics University of Galway) is Former Chairperson of COST Action IS1409 Gender and Health Implications of Extended Working Life in Western Countries (2015–2019). Her recent publications focus on gender, older workers, retirement and extended working life.

Murat Anil Mercan (Gebze Technical University, Turkey) is a Professor at Gebze Technical University. His research interests include labour economics and demography and he published several articles in these subjects. He is also a Management Committee Member of Cost Action IS1409 Gender and Health Impacts of Policies Extending Working Life in Western Countries.

Jim Ogg (National Retirement Fund of Public Social Security – CNAV) is Head of the Ageing Research Unit. He has a background in sociology and has published widely on family life and ageing. He was Deputy Editor of the journal *Ageing & Society* from 2009 to 2016 and is currently Editor of the journal *Retraite et société*.

Julie Rochut (French Public Retirement Scheme), Researcher, Ageing research Department, French Public Retirement Scheme (since 2015). She holds a PhD (2010) in Economics, School of Advanced Studies in the Social Sciences (France) and Lausanne University (Switzerland) and a Master of Science (2005) in Economics Paris Sorbonne University. Her main research interests include Labor Economics, Health Economics, Applied Econometrics

Thierry Rossier (Copenhagen Business School in Denmark) is a Postdoctoral Research Fellow. He obtained a PhD in social and political sciences from the University of Lausanne. His research focuses on elites and social inequality, economics and the economists, political activism, and quantitative methods in the social sciences.

Adila Sahbegovic (Managing Authority of the European Social Fund in Austria, Federal Ministry of Labour, Social Affairs, Health and Consumer Protection). Her main research interest includes social inequalities, employment patterns, labour market development, gender differences and diversity, equality and gender mainstreaming, gender wage gaps, the reconciliation of work and private life as well as well-being and career progression.

Elena Sarti (University of Modena & Reggio Emilia) is a Research Assistant at the Department of Communication and Economics. Her research interests are on well-being evaluation and distribution, quality of work, employment and wage discrimination by gender, health economics, human development and econometric methods for policy evaluation.

Jeroen Spijker (Centre d'Estudis Demogràfics-CED, Spain) is a "Ramón y Cajal-I3" Research Fellow. He obtained a BA in 1994 in Sociology and Human Geography from Massey University, New Zealand and a Master in 1997 and PhD in 2004 in Spatial Sciences (specialisation Demography) from Groningen University, the Netherlands. He has published on a wide range of topics in the field of demography, including population ageing, elderly care, family formation after divorce and widowhood and how the recent economic crisis in Catalonia and Spain has affected the health of the 50+.

Nadia Steiber (Institute for Advanced Studies, Vienna) is a Senior Researcher (since January 2018). Her main research interests include social inequality in labour market outcomes, quality of work, work motivation, labour supply, youth unemployment, retirement decisions, ageing societies, the social consequences of economic downturn, work-family links, work-life balance, women's work and employment, intergenerational social mobility and well-being.

Debra Street (State University of New York at Buffalo) is a Professor of Sociology at the State University of New York at Buffalo. She researches public policies associated with health and income security over the life course, with particular attention to outcomes for vulnerable populations. Street is a *Fellow* of the Behavioral and Social Sciences division of the *Gerontological Society of America* and has received the *SUNY Chancellor's Award for Excellence in Teaching* and the *CISP Contributions to International Education* award.

Piotr Szukalski (University of Lodz, Poland) obtained his PhD in economics at the University of Lodz, where he works in the Department of Demography. He has published over 200 articles and chapters related to social gerontology, intergenerational relations and family issues. His research interests are in how intergenerational relations are affected by social and family change.

Izabela Warwas (University of Lodz, Poland) Associate Professor in the Department of Labour and Social Policy. Her scientific interests focus on the issues related to human resources management, age and diversity management. Author and co-author of 130 publications. She has participated as a coordinator, specialist on evaluation and expert in several dozen European and national projects.

Boris Wernli (University of Lausanne, Switzerland) is a Professor at the Institute of Social Sciences of the University of Lausanne. He is Head of Surveys at the Swiss Centre of Expertise in the Social Sciences (FORS). He has a particular interest in survey methodology and data analysis and has published widely on political behaviour, contemporary family arrangements and the life course.

Justyna Wiktorowicz (University of Lodz, Poland) – PhD in economic sciences, a Researcher at the Department of Economic and Social Statistics at the Faculty of Economics and Sociology. She publishes on the situation of older people on the labour market, especially in the context extending working life, education, competencies, age, and knowledge management and evaluation.

Megi Xhumari (University of Tirana, Albania) is a Part-time Assistant Lecturer at the Department of Social Policy and Social Work, and a Psycho-social Programme Coordinator at Bethany Social Services, a Civil Society Organization in Tirana. She has ten years of experience as a researcher, social worker and psychotherapist in various national/international organisations in Albania, Western Balkans and USA.

Merita Xhumari (University of Tirana, Albania) is a Professor of Social and Public Policy, with 35 years of experience. She has 25 years of experience as a researcher in various national/international projects in Albania and Western Balkans. Author of the university textbook "Process and Institutions of Social Policy" (in Albanian); of monograph "Pension Trajectories in Western Balkans 1990–2010", and co-author of many published studies.

Siniša Zrinščak (University of Zagreb) is a Full Professor and Head of the Chair of Sociology at the Faculty of Law. Previously, he taught Comparative and European Social Policy at the Department of Social Work (Faculty of Law, University of Zagreb). He publishes mainly on religious and social policy changes in post-communism, Europeanisation and gender.

Preface

In the burgeoning social science literatures on population ageing, later life work and well-being, one constant has been the persistent and predictable inequality in lived experiences and outcomes among different subgroups in national populations. Such inequalities among older workers and aged people reflect the consequences of complex interactions among varying family forms, health status, social hierarchies (including gender, the main focus of this book, but also race, social class and other social statuses) and nation-specific public policies. For both women and men, the best predictor of high-quality employment opportunities and financial security at older ages is first having a good education, a good job and good benefits (whether employer-provided or public) at younger ages, and then being fortunate enough to avoid very heavy unpaid caregiving responsibilities throughout the adult life course. Obviously, not everyone arrives at older ages with such built-in life course advantages.

The policy trajectories for most 21st-century initiatives to extend working lives and meet older people's retirement income needs have been built on the gendered foundation of 20th-century employment and pension policies. Those mid-20th-century policy foundations were predicated on the norms reflecting male breadwinner/female homemaker models that assumed full-time lifetime employment for men, upon whom women would depend for much (in many cases all) of their access to financial resources in later life. How the experience of later life has … and yet, has simultaneously not quite … changed! The legacy of gendered social policies has implications for today's older people, even while countries tweak policies to extend working lives. Although the importance of women's labour force participation, the inequities of gender norms that still relegate to women the primary responsibility for unpaid care, and gender pay gaps throughout the life course are well-documented, 21st-century policy initiatives have yet to fully address the disadvantages many women experience, whether in terms of later life employment, or the gendered outcomes that undermine their capacity to establish or sustain well-being at older ages.

In **Well-being and Extended Working Life: A Gender Perspective**, a distinguished group of social scientists take on the task of documenting and analysing how recent employment and pension policy initiatives have, in limited instances, contributed to improved chances for well-being across a number of dimensions, including health and income security. However, the analysis also establishes that social policies have not gone nearly far enough to honour women's lifetime contributions to their societies by ensuring a dignified, adequately-resourced, old age and, in some instances, have actually undermined the potential for that outcome. The first half of the book provides analysis comparing European countries on a range of social policies, social and cultural circumstances and well-being outcomes for women and men. The second half provides detailed case studies that explore the interaction of nation-specific economies, labour markets, welfare state types and social norms with policy changes that improve or undermine well-being, using a gender lens. These country-specific chapters provide important windows into differences that arise from having a similar "problem" – population ageing and the assumption that later life work must be expanded – yet having different cultural norms and policy practices associated with varied economies and welfare state regimes to provide insights into gendered outcomes arising from unique national circumstances.

While concern about the worldwide population ageing juggernaut was the policy catalyst to extend working lives and contain public pension costs, other equally profound and less predictable social forces suggest that other policy turning points may have been reached. Although these events are too recent to fully realise and analyse using a gender and well-being lens, their profound impact on international experiences is already well-established. The enveloping social disruption of the global COVID-19 pandemic demonstrated that affluent governments CAN initiate large-scale interventions to improve the well-being of their populations. The catastrophe of a European war may have as yet unforeseeable and unintended consequences on the national economies and social policies that contribute to later life work and well-being and evolving gender relations within countries. In sum, the holistic approach of this book provides an invaluable empirical and conceptual foundation that can support future research that incorporates its analytic rigour and gender-sensitive policy recommendations as countries establish their "next" welfare states in the wake of international disorder.

Debra Street

Acknowledgements

This book is based on the work of COST Action IS1409: "Gender and health impacts of policies extending working life in western countries". COST (European Cooperation in Science and Technology) is a funding agency for research and innovation networks. COST Actions help connect research initiatives across Europe and enable scientists to grow their ideas by sharing them with their peers. This boosts their research, career and innovation. The editors would like to thank all the Authors that contributed to this book, the Editorial Assistants at Routledge, Taylor and Francis for their guidance and insight, the Gender and Well-Being series editors for their inspiring comments and the wider membership of COST Action IS1409 for stimulating exchanges on the topic of gender and health impacts of policies extending working life. This book provides a detailed exploration of the working conditions and the well-being implications for older workers and their families in a set of European countries characterized by different policies on ageing at work, different welfare systems and employment conditions. This would not have been possible without input from each Author that contributed to this volume.

EUROPEAN COOPERATION IN SCIENCE & TECHNOLOGY

Funded by the European Union

1 Introduction to Well-being and Extended Working Life: A Gender Perspective

Tindara Addabbo, Patricia Carney, Áine Ní Léime, Jeroen Spijker, and Siniša Zrinščak

Extended working life

Extended working life (EWL) refers to a set of policy measures that are designed to encourage and/or compel people to work past traditional state pension age. This age ranges mainly between 60 and 65 across different countries, in some instances, is gender-specific and is sometimes lower for workers in high-risk job groups, or workers with a high grade of disability. EWL policies have been introduced and strongly promoted by international agencies including the Organisation for Economic Cooperation and Development (OECD) and the European Union as one of the main policy responses to population ageing. The OECD has been particularly vigorous in promoting these policies, recommending that countries adopt them in 2006 and then publishing scorecards that monitor to what extent countries have done so (OECD, 2006, 2013, 2015, 2017, 2021). Typical EWL policies include raising state pension age, increasing the number and duration of contributions necessary to qualify for contributory state pensions, the removal of mandatory retirement age and sometimes flexible working policies which allow people both to receive state pensions and to earn money (OECD, 2017).

While an average 65-year-old is expected to live almost twice as long as was the case a century ago (Spijker & MacInnes, 2013; Human Mortality Database, 2022), not everyone ages at the same rate or in the same way and in some instances delaying retirement may have a detrimental impact on individuals with poorer health. The ageing population and those aged over 50, often the subject of national and international ageing surveys (Kenny et al., 2010; Schröder, 2011; SHARE, 2019), are not a homogenous group as demonstrated by the literature (Ma & Nolan, 2017; Murphy et al., 2015; Aassve et al., 2012; Achdut et al., 2015; Ahrenfeldt et al., 2018; Fontaine and Haywood, 2018; Gannon et al., 2018; Halmdienst & Winter-Ebmer, 2014).

There has been some critique of EWL policies on the basis that they may adversely affect well-being in terms of economic security and health of different groups of older workers. For example, extending working life is likely to exacerbate existing gender inequalities in relation to workforce participation and pensions (D'Addio, 2015; Ginn & Macintyre, 2013; Ní Léime et al., 2017). In

DOI: 10.4324/9781003145325-1

addition, there is still an expectation that women will be involved in unpaid care work, so they may not be free to engage in paid employment (Lewis, 2006; Ní Léime & Street, 2017). EWL policies have also been criticised for focusing excessively on cost-containment, being simplistic and one-size-fits-all (including raising state pension age) (Moulaert & Biggs, 2013; Ní Léime et al, 2020). This means that differences based on type of occupation and health are not taken into account and that people engaged in physically demanding work may be disadvantaged by being required to work for longer. There is evidence that individuals employed in manual type work are more likely to develop chronic conditions associated with musculoskeletal problems earlier than those in other occupations (Marmot, 2010; Carr et al., 2018; Swanberg et al., 2020). Another group of workers who may be adversely affected by EWL policies are those in low-paid precarious occupations (Lain, 2012; Kanfer, et al., 2020; Kim, et al., 2018). If these workers lose their jobs, it may often be very difficult for them to find alternative employment in their 50s or later, due to age-related discrimination.

Changing workforce characteristics

In Europe the proportion of older people in the general population has been on an upward trajectory in recent decades. This is due to increases in life expectancy, particularly at older ages, coupled with sustained below-replacement fertility rates (Rechel et al., 2013). This changing labour force demographic coincides with the changing role of women with respect to overall participation in the workforce and the level of commitment to work outside the home.

In addition to the aforementioned factors influencing change in labour force demographics, a range of social factors over the last decades have also played their part. Better health care, increased accessibility to education and changing cultural attitudes with respect to women's participation in the workforce have all contributed to the tide of transformation in labour force participation (LFP) (Gros, 2019).

Examining LFP data for the EU28 from 2000 to 2019, the number of years women dedicated to paid employment has increased from an average of 29.2 years in 2000 to an average of 33.9 years in 2019 (Eurostat, 2022). This increase coincides with an increase in the total number of women participating in the labour force at all ages, with the increase in participation rates most notable for those between the ages of 55 and 64 (Gros, 2019). However, one has to take the heterogeneity across European countries on the expected duration of working life into account (i.e. the number of years a person aged 15 is expected to be in the labour force throughout his or her life) with regard to the gender gap to the disadvantage of women. In 2019, the duration of working life was on average 33.9 years for women and 38.7 years for men in EU28 countries. The duration of working life for women ranged from 27.3 years in Italy to 41.1 years in Sweden. In the case of men, it ranged from 34.5 years in Croatia to 43.3 years in the Netherlands (Eurostat, 2022).

Examination of impacts of EWL policies by gender

The different role that women play in social reproduction activities has been found to impact their probability of EWL, their working conditions in EWL and their likelihood of retiring early and calls for specific public policies and company-level solutions to improve work-life balance. The quality of their EWL is also affected by gender inequalities related to their more discontinuous work trajectories over the life course and the gender pay gap which disadvantages women with negative effects on their retirement income.

Caring for grandchildren or dependent older people is found to reduce the probability of extending working life, reduce the hours of work provided by carers and increase the likelihood of early retirement (Burr & Colley, 2019; De Preter et al., 2013; Reeuwijk et al., 2013; Porcellato et al., 2010; Szinovacz and Deviney 2000).

De Preter et al. (2013) investigated retirement trends across Austria, Germany, Sweden, Belgium, Spain, Italy, France, Denmark, Greece, Switzerland and the Netherlands using SHARE data. The authors show that women have a significantly higher probability of retiring early than do their male counterparts. Likewise, according to results from the English Longitudinal Study of Ageing (ELSA), exit patterns were also found to be heavily affected by traditional gender roles in England (Van der Horst et al., 2017). Further evidence on this is provided by Burr & Colley (2019) through in-depth interviews with older carers in the United Kingdom. The women interviewed described the impacts of their caring role on their current working life and ability to participate in the labour force. Many had to reduce their working hours outside home, reduce their career aspirations and would be more likely to retire earlier rather than extend their working life. A qualitative study of 30 Dutch 60–64-year-old employees investigated predictors of early retirement and recommended employers improve the work environment to make EWL possible by introducing effective solutions to facilitate work-life balance and motivate employees to extend their working lives (Reeuwijk et al., 2013). Edge et al. (2017) literature review highlights the importance of workplaces adapting to provide flexible arrangements to enable women to balance the demands of work with the domestic and caring responsibilities they face, in order for women to have a healthy EWL.

Contents of the book

This book is innovative in its focus on gender and in the fact that it involves in-depth empirical analysis of working conditions in individual countries and a conceptual chapter, thus moving beyond a simple review of EWL policies to consider the relevant issues in a fine-grained, nuanced manner, with the potential to inform policy recommendations. This book also offers a holistic analysis of EWL considering the impacts of working conditions, grandparental care, health and attitudes to older workers. The timing of the book is important;

with its publication coinciding with the effect of pension reforms being experienced, after the reforms have been in situ for a sufficient period of time. The reforms have mainly been redesigned to extend the working life by delaying the age at which people become eligible for a pension.

Looking more closely at these issues in various social contexts, the book explores factors that can limit access to paid work or worsen working conditions for older workers, including care for dependent individuals, stereotypes of ageing or bad health (exacerbated by the recent economic crisis). It also investigates differences in working conditions by gender for older workers compared to other groups of workers and across European countries characterised by different policies on ageing at work, welfare systems and employment conditions. The book is not confined to exploring the working conditions of older workers, but also considers the effects that extending working life has on specific dimensions of well-being (health, life satisfaction, subjective well-being (SWB) as well as unpaid care work for family members). In the context of care, one chapter proposes a care model to facilitate transitions between employment, care and pension in a gender-sensitive way. In order to represent the essence of change experienced in countries across Europe, a wide range of countries is examined throughout this book. The countries have been chosen in terms of policy reform, culture, welfare systems and employment conditions in order to investigate the impacts of a range of policy reforms.

The book examines the working conditions of older workers and the effects that extending working life has on specific dimensions of well-being. A first focus in the book concerns the probability of later employment comparing those aged from 50 to 64 and 65+ (Chapter 2). It also examines the limits encountered in different phases of the life cycle in matching working time and care needs (Chapter 3). The book explores methodological and analytical challenges to map factors that differentiate the employment experiences of older (50+) workers in the European context (Chapter 4), and to what extent ageing and age discrimination can impact on mental health and job satisfaction (Chapter 5). The book also includes six country-specific studies, with several focusing on Eastern European countries. Chapter 6 assesses the impacts of EWL on different dimensions of well-being in Albania from a gender perspective referring to the impacts of social security reforms, labour market policies, education and training. Factors that can limit access to paid work or negatively affect working conditions for older Polish workers such as care for dependent individuals are explored in Chapter 7. The relationship between employment and bad health is explored during the Great Recession in Spain (Chapter 8) and during the COVID-19 pandemic in France (Chapter 10). The book also investigates gendered differences in SWB in Turkey (Chapter 9). The final chapter discusses the relations between active ageing policy ideas and social policy reforms in Croatia (Chapter 11).

Gstrein in Chapter 2 discusses how gender, health and life satisfaction relate to extended working lives in European countries by analysing the Eurofound's European Quality of life survey (EQLS). Limitations to EWL, that translate to involuntary early retirement, have been shown to be more widespread in Continental Europe countries which are characterised by strict employment protection legislation, facing economic recessions, with a very low probability for older people to find a new job. On the other hand, voluntary early retirement is more likely to occur in countries characterised by generous early retirement provisions. In these instances, early retirement is more attractive for retirees and encourages firms to push employees towards early retirement as found by Dorn & Sousa-Poza (2010) in 19 industrialised countries[1] using data from the 1997 International Social Survey Program (ISSP). By estimating logistic regressions on the probability of being employed on European Quality of Life microdata for a more recent period (2018/19), Gstrein analyses the impact of health and life satisfaction on the probability of working in later life (measured as being employed), controlling for gender, health, education, family status, size of the household of the respondent and her/his income and through different years.

Haas et al. (Chapter 3) analyse data on a set of European countries using the 2010–2012 European Social Survey (ESS) investigating the reasons for the mismatch between preferred and actual working hours in different phases of the life cycle. The authors draw comparisons between the occurrence of over and underemployment, including also those individuals who are out of the labour force. These data are unique to the ESS and enable analysis of the mismatch between actual and preferred working time to analyse underemployment related to involuntary early retirement. Haas et al. find evidence of involuntary early retirement for older workers with a low occupational status and that the higher the social class position, the less likely people are to experience a mismatch between the actual and preferred employment participation at the end of the employment career. A high occupational status helps to extend paid working life, due to better health and more attractive job conditions. Early retirement is also more affordable for workers in highly skilled jobs. This suggests that a substantial share of early retirement is due to a *lack of employment opportunities* for older workers. The analyses further identified the following risk factors for the experience of involuntary retirement (underemployment): employment histories that involve late-career job loss, unemployment, illness or disability. Women are more likely to have interrupted paid work trajectories preventing them from retiring at their preferred age: either they have to extend working life to make up for missing social security contributions (involuntary work) or they have difficulties in re-integrating into the labour market upon job loss (involuntary retirement).

According to the European Foundation for the Improvement of Living and Working Conditions, Eurofound (2017), there are substantial differences across European countries in the policies that support sustainable working environments. Rossier et al. (Chapter 4) draw on the sixth wave of the European Working Conditions Survey (EWCS) to analyse how working conditions of those aged 50+ differ by gender and with respect to other age groups of workers in the Czech Republic, Ireland, Italy, Sweden, Switzerland and the United Kingdom, countries characterised by different gender regimes, labour market structures and extending working life policy initiatives. Older workers' satisfaction in their jobs is indeed found to differ when compared to younger workers and by gender showing a higher work satisfaction among employed men and women aged 50+ in the Czech Republic, similar work satisfaction according to age group in Ireland; higher satisfaction only for women workers aged 50+ in Switzerland and the United Kingdom; and for men aged 50+ in Italy and in Sweden. The chapter highlights the differences in the impact of factors affecting other dimensions of working conditions with a special focus on the policies aimed at extending working lives in each national context.

In Chapter 5, Addabbo and Sarti focus on the impact of different variables related to personal characteristics and working conditions on job satisfaction, with particular attention to what happens for younger (<50 years old) and older (50+) age groups by using the EWCS for the year 2015 for 35 European countries. Multivariate model results show that work-life balance and wage levels remain important factors for both job satisfaction and mental health, as well as working conditions (explored through job demand and job hazard composite variables). Age discrimination decreases job satisfaction and mental health especially for those who are aged 50+.

Specific attention is provided by Xhumari and Xhumari (Chapter 6) to the impact of EWL on different dimensions of well-being in Albania, a country characterised by a lower level of quality of life and work satisfaction than for the EU28 countries on average and showing a sharp decrease in labour market participation among workers aged 50+. Xhumari and Xhumari use the EWCS, 2015 and the EQLS, 2016, for this purpose, in which Albania participated for the first time. In the context of the impact of recent labour market reforms, the analysis concerns the perceptions of people in the 50–64 age group, who report particularly high levels of job insecurity and the expected adequacy of their income in old age. Moreover, in recent years standards of living have also decreased for those in the 50+ age group, especially among women.

The impact of care work on the supply of labour is investigated by Wiktorowicz et al. (Chapter 7). The authors use the 2015 wave of the Social Diagnosis Survey on the conditions and quality of life in Poland to analyse the extent to which care for dependent people in the family can affect access to paid work by gender by taking into account the heterogeneity in the country in terms of cultural factors and different public care policies for older people. They find that caring responsibilities are a barrier to extending working life in the case of women, and also by place of residence whether in the countryside or in small- and medium-sized towns. Finally, this chapter also questions the role of social policies and organisations in extending economic activity. The authors conclude that only a minority of employers (23%) confirm offering additional unpaid leave to meet the need to care for dependent persons.

Other limits to EWL are related to poor health status (see among others Leijten et al., 2015; De Wind et al., 2013, 2014; Demou et al., 2017; Mortelmans & Vannieuwenhuyze, 2013; Olesen et al., 2012). Domínguez-Rodríguez et al. (Chapter 8) focus on the interaction between self-rated health and employment for older workers during the global financial crisis with a specific focus on Spain, which was deeply affected by the crisis. Questions raised in the chapter include whether the economic crisis has penalised people with poorer health in their LFP; and whether changes in female LFP were also associated with factors other than health during the economic crisis. Results showed that, while the trend in labour force activity among men remained stable and increased for women due to a cohort effect, the probability of economically active men and women being employed declined between the two periods. Moreover, health status had a strong independent effect on being employed during the economic crisis, whereby a poor health status affected employment status more among men than women, possibly because men are more likely to exit through retirement while women have a greater economic need to continue working.

Barlin et al. (Chapter 9) reflect on a specific group of older workers in Turkey with the aim of identifying their motivations for extending working life beyond public sector retirement age by means of qualitative analyses on workers aged 60+ from three different cities in Turkey based on purposive sampling. Various aspects of working life and working conditions, including work-life balance on SWB and life satisfaction, are also considered in this chapter. Working in later life contributes to SWB through enhancing self-realisation, competence, autonomy and independence, feeling useful, active living, perceived positive health effects, job satisfaction, financial relief, socialisation and taking part in public life. Motivations for working, work experiences and plans regarding working life interact. Positive experiences motivate participants to work. However, negative experiences lead participants to determine a time frame to quit working. Gender differences in working in later life are mostly related to the domestic and public domain. Consequent to the different levels of engagement of men and women in domestic life and public space throughout the life course, they have developed different perspectives and lived experiences in self-realisation, independence, being active and feeling useful.

In Chapter 10, Aouici et al. analyse working conditions and retirement behaviour from a gender perspective in France, paying particular attention to the inherent difficulties that older French women face in balancing work and family commitments that have been exacerbated during COVID-19 pandemics. Pandemics brought about a deterioration of working conditions (increase in work intensity, time pressures and stress) for older women employed in jobs characterised by physical and/or psychological constraints. Older workers are also found to be more vulnerable to illness and to the deadly and debilitating effects of COVID-19.

Finally, Dobrotić and Zrinščak (Chapter 11) analyse reforms in the area of active ageing in Croatia through a gender equality lens with particular attention to the policy ideas driving the different policies and reforms and their gender impact. The narratives of key political parties and social partners are examined by analysing Parliamentary debates in the field of pension reform, employment and family policies. The chapter argues that the active ageing ideas have entered social policy debates, but mainly as part of narrow, labour market-oriented reforms that aim to change the pension system by extending working lives. However, these have been happening in the context of a collapsing economy and a very low employment rate. Gender equality arguments have not been central and/or have been employed in an instrumental way, used either to "defend" features of the "old" system, or argue for policy instruments that could serve employment-oriented or demographic goals.

Policy recommendations

Policy recommendations are discussed for each chapter with some referring to cross-European data and others (Chapters 6 to 11) relevant to individual countries only.

Haas et al. in Chapter 3 highlight the occurrence of disequilibrium between preferred and actual working time by analysing ESS data across European countries. They show how this misallocation of working time is related to the level of education and, for underemployment, is also more common in countries with constraints in terms of low wages, high unemployment rates and a lack of part-time jobs. The discrepancy in preferred and actual allocation of time is more present in the eastern and southern parts of Europe than in the Continental and Nordic countries. In order to achieve a better match between preferred and actual working hours, the authors suggest introducing policies to lower the conflict between paid work and care through providing affordable and attractive child and elder care facilities. They also recommend that safe, high-quality part-time jobs be provided that could contribute to a smooth transition into employment or retirement.

Chapter 4 analyses EWCS data to investigate the implications of working conditions for possibilities of extending working life across European countries. For workers in some countries including the Czech Republic, Italy and Ireland, challenging physical and emotional work tends to lead to early exit from work. This suggests that policies such as flexible working and alternative work for those in physically demanding jobs would facilitate workers to extend their working lives.

Addabbo and Sarti in Chapter 5 investigate the determinants of job satisfaction and mental health for younger (<50 years old) and older (50+) age groups and found that work-life balance and wage levels play an important role in shaping job satisfaction and mental health, as well as working conditions. Therefore, policies to improve work-life balance and controlling job demand can result in higher well-being in terms of both mental health and job satisfaction. The higher impact of age discrimination for employees aged 50+ suggests that attention needs to be paid to the prevention of age stereotyping and discrimination, by implementing dedicated inclusive policies at the workplace, and support to employers and managers in the development of age-management practices.

Chapter 6 focuses on EWL policies in Albania. The authors argue that EWL policies should encompass employment policies, including training opportunities and flexible working. They recommend that women be given more supports to enable them to combine employment with caring and other unpaid contributions to the family to prevent them from having to exit early to retirement.

This includes improving access to childcare and introducing child and family benefits as part of the social protection system. They also recommend the provision of more lifelong learning to advance job skills and flexibility for older workers as they approach retirement and the implementation of an integrated system for social protection, employment, education and vocational training policies.

The findings of Chapter 7 based on Polish data confirm the need to implement measures that would support people of pre-retirement age in their decisions to continue their professional careers, especially in rural areas and small- and medium-sized towns. Since women in Poland provide the bulk of unpaid care for older people, there is a need to increase the provision of such care by the state and employers to enable women to continue working, if they so desire. The chapter also highlights the fact that there is no public discussion about care facilities, particularly for older people, and that the concept of EWL is not addressed in social policy documents.

In Chapter 8, findings from Spain showed substantial differences in LFP according to health status at the end of the economic crisis there (2014). The authors recommend that special attention be paid to those working in sectors that are most vulnerable during times of economic crisis and especially those with a poor health status who are economically active.

Chapter 9 explores the motivations of workers in Turkey for extending their working lives and the contribution of EWL to subjective well-being. The authors found that the main motivations for continuing to work in later life were financial necessity and job satisfaction. They found that especially for workers in physically demanding jobs, it was very important to have flexible working options in order to cope with such demands. They identified many positive outcomes to working later – including improving physical and mental health, autonomy and independence. The authors recommend that the positive implications of extending working life be disseminated. Men and women perceive different benefits to extending working life; they recommend that policies should be gender-differentiated to account for this.

Aouci et al. in Chapter 10 draw comparisons between pre-COVID-19 pandemic and current working conditions of the population aged 50+ in France and their retirement behavior. Their analysis identifies older women as a particularly vulnerable segment of the labour force due to their higher likelihood of being unemployed and to their harsh working conditions; this is also related to their occupation and to their lower probability of career progression. Segmentation in the labour market and lower positions typically held by women contribute to their being more badly affected by the COVID-19 pandemic. In terms of policies, the authors suggest the introduction of protective measures by institutions through appropriate legislation, including paid sick leave, since many women may be obliged to work past retirement age to secure an adequate income in old age. EWL thus requires policies both by employers and at national level to improve work-life balance.

Chapter 11 assesses to what extent an "active ageing" perspective informs pension and welfare reforms including the provision of care for older people to extend working life in Croatia. The authors conclude that reforms are based on a narrow cost containment perspective, that many reforms have not been implemented, that not enough attention is paid to gender differences and that EWL is seen as a burden. They recommend that the benefits of EWL in terms of active ageing should be better promoted in Croatia and that gender-differentiated policies be introduced.

In summary, it is clear that EWL policies need to be considered in the context of the welfare state regime in which they are introduced and individual characteristics such as educational levels and health status but also may vary from one institutional context to another. As Madero-Cabib, Le Feuvre, & König (2021, p. 26) state "… concrete and practical implications of policies to encourage current or future generations of older workers to extend their working lives (OECD, 2017) will vary according to normative expectations (Radl, 2013) and preferences (Hofäcker, 2015) associated with different lifecourse regimes, and according to the socio-demographic characteristics of the older men and women targeted by such policies", need to be taken into account.

Concluding remarks

The heterogeneity of the countries analysed in terms of welfare systems, pension reforms, cultural factors and labour market status facilitates discussion of the extent to which observed country differences in the well-being dimensions of EWL are related to institutional and cultural factors in a gender perspective. Country case studies and comparative cross country analyses in this volume may be used to formulate specific social and employment policies aimed for national and EU policymakers that would benefit the health and economic well-being of older workers. Findings in this book highlight the fact that the workforce is not a homogenous group and should not be treated as such when national retirement policies are being developed and implemented. A more nuanced approach to retirement policy is required, one that takes into account the nature of work and other responsibilities such as informal caring.

Note

1 Countries examined by Dorn & Sousa-Poza (2010) were Canada, Cyprus, Denmark, France, Germany, Great Britain, Hungary, Italy, Japan, the Netherlands, New Zealand, Norway, Poland, Portugal, Slovenia, Spain, Sweden, Switzerland and the USA.

References

Aassve, A., Arpino, B. & Goisis, A. (2012). Grandparenting and mothers' labour force participation: A comparative analysis using the Generations and Gender Survey. *Demographic Research*, S11(3), 53–84.

Achdut, L., Turs-Sinai, A. & Troitsky, R. (2015). Transitions between states of labor-force participation among older Israelis. *European Journal of Ageing*, 12, 39–49.

Ahrenfeldt, L. J., Möller, S., Hvidt, N. C. & Lindahl-Jacobsen, R. (2018). Religiousness and lifestyle among Europeans in SHARE. *Public Health*, 165, 74–81.

Burr, V. & Colley, H. (2019). "I just felt as though I had to drop something": The implications of care for female working elder carers' working lives. *Ageing & Society*, 39(5), 877–898.

Carr, E., Fleischmann, M., Goldberg, M., Kuh, D., Murray, E., Stafford, M. & Head, J. (2018). Occupational and educational inequalities in exit from employment at older ages: Evidence from seven prospective cohorts. *Occupational and Environmental Medicine*, 75(5), 369–377.

D'Addio, A. (2015). *New OECD data and analysis revealing the wide gap in pension benefits between men and women*, OECD Gender Portal, Gender Equality. Available at http://www.oecd.org/gender/data/newoecddataanalysisrevealingthewidegapinpensionbenefitsbetweenmenandwomen.htm

Demou, E., Bhaskar, A., Xu, T., Mackay, D. F. & Hunt, K. (2017). Health, lifestyle and employment beyond state-pension age. *BMC Public Health*, 17(1), 971.

De Preter, H., Van Looy, D. & Mortelmans, D. (2013). Individual and institutional push and pull factors as predictors of retirement timing in Europe: A multilevel analysis. *Journal of Aging Studies*, 27(4), 299–307.

De Wind, A., Geuskens, G. A., Reeuwijk, K. G., Westerman, M. J., Ybema, J. F., Burdorf A., Bongers, P. M. & van der Beek, A. J. (2013). Pathways through which health influences early retirement: A qualitative study. *BMC Public Health*, 13(1), 292.

De Wind, A., Geuskens, G. A., Ybema, J. F., Blatter, B. M., Burdorf, A., Bongers, P. M. & van der Beek, A. J. (2014). Health, job characteristics, skills, and social and financial factors in relation to early retirement – Results from a longitudinal study in the Netherlands. *Scand J Work Environ Health*, 40(2), 186–194.

Dorn, D. & Sousa-Poza, A. (2010). "Voluntary" and "involuntary" early retirement: An international analysis. *Applied Economics*, 42(4–6), 427–438.

Edge, C., Cooper, A. & Coffey, M. (2017). Barriers and facilitators to extended working lives in Europe: A gender focus. *Public Health Review*, 38(2), 1–27.

Eurofound (2017). *Working conditions of workers of different ages, European Working Conditions Survey 2015*. Dublin: European Foundation for the Improvement of Working & Living Conditions. https://www.eurofound.europa.eu/surveys/european-workingconditions-surveys

Eurostat (2022). *Labour Market metadata, Duration of working life, (lfsi_dwl_a)* https://ec.europa.eu/eurostat/databrowser/view/lfsi_dwl_a/default/table?lang=en

Fontaine, X. & Haywood, L. (2018). On the comparison of group inequalities using subjective data. *Economics Letters*, 163, 17–21.

Gannon, B., Banks, J., Nazroo, J. & Munford, L. (2018). An econometric analysis of cognitive impairment and healthcare utilization in the ageing population. *Applied Economics*, 50, 5454–5463.

Ginn, J. & MacIntyre, K. (2013). UK pension reforms: Is gender still an issue?. *Social Policy and Society*, 12(1), 91–103.

Gros, D. (2019). Improvement in European labor force participation. Do structural reforms or educational expansion drive higher employment and participation rates?. *IZA World of Labor*, 449, 1–10.

Halmdienst, N. & Winter-Ebmer, R. (2014). Long-run relations between childhood shocks and health in late adulthood – Evidence from the survey of health, ageing, and retirement in Europe. *CESifo Economic Studies*, 60, 402–434.

Hofäcker, D. (2015). In line or at odds with active ageing policies? Exploring patterns of retirement preferences in Europe. *Ageing and Society*, 35(7), 1529–1556, 10.1017/S0144686X1400035X

Human Mortality Database (2022). Human mortality database. Available in http://www.mortality.org

Kanfer, R., Lyndgaard, S. F. & Tatel, C. E. (2020). For whom the pandemic tolls: A person-centric analysis of older workers. *Work, Aging and Retirement*, 6(4), 238–241.

Kim, Y., Baek, S. & Lee, S. S. (2018). Precarious elderly workers in post-industrial South Korea. *Journal of Contemporary Asia*, 48(3), 465–484.

Kenny, R. A., Whelan, B. J., Cronin, H., Kamiya, Y., Kearney, P., O'Regan, C. & Ziege, M. (2010). *TILDA: The design of the Irish longitudinal study on ageing*. Dublin: Trinity College Dublin.

Lain, D. (2012). Working past 65 in the UK and the USA: segregation into "Lopaq" occupations?. *Work, Employment & Society*, 26(1), 78–94.

Leijten, F. R. M., de Wind, A., van den Heuvel, S. G., Ybema, J. F., van der Beek, A. J., Robroek, S. J. W. & Burdorf, A. (2015). The influence of chronic health problems and work-related factors on loss of paid employment among older workers. *Journal of Epidemiology & Community Health*, 69(11), 1058–1065.

Lewis, J. (2006). Work/family reconciliation, equal opportunities and social policies: The interpretation of policy trajectories at the EU level and the meaning of gender equality. *Journal of European Public Policy*, 13(3), 420–437.

Ma, Y. & Nolan, A. (2017). Public healthcare entitlements and healthcare utilisation among the older population in Ireland. *Health Economics*, 26 (11), 1412–1428.

Madero-Cabib, I., Le Feuvre, N. & König, S. (2021). Gendered retirement pathways across lifecourse regimes. *Ageing and Society*, 1–30. doi:10.1017/S0144686X21001781

Madero-Cabib, I. & Biehl, A. (2021). Lifetime employment–coresidential trajectories and extended working life in Chile. *The Journal of the Economics of Ageing*, 19, 100309.

Marmot, M. (2010). *Fair society, healthy lives: Strategic review of health inequalities in England post 2010*. London: Marmot Review.

Mortelmans, D. & Vannieuwenhuyze, J. T. A. (2013). The age-dependent influence of self-reported health and job characteristics on retirement. *International Journal of Public Health*, 58(1), 13–22.

Moulaert T. & Biggs S. (2013). International and European policy on work and retirement: Reinventing critical perspectives on active aging and mature subjectivity. *Human Relations*, 66(1), 23–43. doi: 10.1177/0018726711435180

Murphy, C. M., Whelan, B. J. & Normand, C. (2015). Formal home-care utilisation by older adults in Ireland: Evidence from the Irish Longitudinal Study on Ageing (TILDA). *Health & Social Care in the Community*, 23(4), 408–418.

Ní Léime, A., Ogg, J., Street, D., Rasticova, M., Krekula, C., Madero Cabib, I. & Bediova, M. (eds.) (2020). Extended working life: International gender and health perspectives. Cham: Springer. https://link.springer.com/content/pdf/10.1007%2F978-3-030–40985-2.pdf

Ní Léime, Á., Street, D., Vickerstaff, S., Krekula, C. & Loretto, W. (2017). *Gender and extended working life: Cross-national perspectives*. Bristol: Policy Press.

Ní Léime, Á., & Street, D. (2017). Gender and age implications of extended working life policies in the US and Ireland. *Critical Social Policy*, 37(3), 464–483.

OECD (2006). *Live longer, work longer, ageing and employment policies*. Paris: OECD Publishing, 10.1787/9789264035881-en (accessed 5 February 2018).

OECD (2013). *Pensions at a glance*. OECD Publishing. Available from: 10.1787/pension_glance-2013-en (accessed 3February2018)

OECD (2015). *Pensions at a glance 2015. OECD pensions at a glance*. OECD Publishing. Available from: 10.1787/pension_glance-2015-en (accessed 2 February 2018).

OECD (2017). *Pensions at a glance 2017: OECD and G20 indicators*. Paris: OECD Publishing, 10.1787/pension_glance-2017-en (accessed 3 February 2018).

OECD (2021). *Pensions at a glance 2021: OECD and G20 indicators*. Paris: OECD Publishing, 10.1787/ca401ebd-en (accessed 9 March 2022).

Olesen, S. C., Butterworth, P. & Rodgers, B. (2012). Is poor mental health a risk factor for retirement? Findings from a longitudinal population survey. *Soc Psychiatry Psychiatr Epidemiol*, 47(5), 735–744.

Porcellato, L., Carmichael, F., Hulme, C., Ingham, B. & Prashar, A. (2010). Giving older workers a voice: Constraints on the employment of older people in the North West of England. *Work Employ Soc*, 24(1), 85–103.

Radl, J. (2013).Labour market exit and social stratification in Western Europe: The effects of social class and gender on the timing of retirement.*European Sociological Review*, 29(3), 654–668.

Rechel, B., Grundy, E., Robine, J. M., Cylus, J., Mackenbach, J. P., Knai, C. & McKee, M. (2013). Ageing in the European Union. *The Lancet*, 381, 1312–1322.

Reeuwijk K. G., de Wind A., Westerman M. J., Ybema J. F., van der Beek A. J. & Geuskens G. A. (2013). All those things together made me retire': Qualitative study on early retirement among Dutch employees. *BMC Public Health*, 13(1), 516.

Schröder, M. (2011). *Retrospective data collection in the survey of health, ageing and retirement in Europe. SHARELIFE Methodology*. Mannheim: MEA

SHARE (2019). *SHARE release guide 7.0.0*. [online]. http://www.share-project.org/fileadmin/pdf_documentation/SHARE_release_guide_7-0-0.pdf

Spijker, J. & MacInnes, J. (2013). Population ageing: The timebomb that isn't?. *British Medical Journal*, 347, f6598.

Swanberg, J. E., Scheindlin L., Betz G. & Zouhri A. (2020). A narrative review: Understanding how employment context influences the occupational health and well-being of older workers in low-wage jobs, In S. Czaja, J. Sharit & J. James (eds). *Current and Emerging Trends in Aging and Work*, Cham: Springer, 297–317.

Szinovacz, M. E. & Deviney, S. (2000). Marital characteristics and retirement decisions. *Research on Aging*, 22(5), 470–498.

Van der Horst M., Lain D., Vickerstaff S., Clark C. & Baumberg-Geiger B. (2017). Gender roles and employment pathways of older women and men in England. *Sage Open*, 7(4), 1–17.

2 Extended Working Life in Austria and the EU28 – How Do Gender, Health and Life Satisfaction Relate to Longer Working Life? What Else Matters?

Michaela Gstrein

Introduction

In the face of population ageing, tight state budgets and relatively early retirement in at least some European countries, extending the working lives of both men and women to secure both workforce availability and sustainable pension levels became one of the main EU policy targets quite some time ago (European Commission, 2012, p. 9). However, longer working lives have various gender and health impacts that need consideration, and the possible effects of gender- and health-related issues on exit or work extension decisions need investigation. Moreover, the definition of extended working life differs markedly across countries, with culture-specific work and retirement orientations as well as countries offering earlier or later retirement options. As such, extended working life strongly relates to nation-specific institutional factors, norms, attitudes and status of labour markets with different implications for well-being in a gender perspective (Addabbo et al., 2019).

Gender is one of the important factors impacting labour market exit or extended working life decisions, since older working women at higher working age typically have different jobs and lower income than men, work are more likely to work part-time and have different roles in their private life (Hasselhorn and Apt, 2015, p. 22). Generally, in many countries women tend to leave work at younger ages than men (OECD, 2019, p. 180). Health often plays a vital role too, with better (self-perceived) health related to longer labour market engagement (Haas et al., 2019).

Various drivers and barriers impact on extended working life, many of them related to gender, health and life satisfaction. I will use the European Quality of Life Survey (EQLS) and compare findings from the three most recent survey waves (2007/11/16; EQLS 2016). The groups in focus are the older working population, i.e. the 50–64 age category and those aged 65 and older (no upper age limit in this survey). While many exit the labour market early or when they reach official retirement age – which might be different for women and men at e.g. 60/65 or cohort-related or similar at age 66 or 67, etc. – some remain active into later life. Thus, the 50–64 age group is especially interesting to look at, since this seems in many countries the time when retirement becomes a potential option to prepare for and consider, with factors such as labour market situation, job availability, partner decisions, gendered retirement ages,

DOI: 10.4324/9781003145325-2

education/skills, low/high (family/own) income, overall family situation, (unpaid) care needs or health issues impacting on such decisions.

The chapter starts with background information on extended working life decisions. Following this, it looks into statistical evidence for Europe and the overall situation in 2018/19. As a country with a generally low labour force participation in older age groups but visible increases in female labour force participation among the 55–64 age group, Austria is cited as an example of successfully extending working lives in the last decade. In EU comparison, the labour force participation among the 55–64 age group in Austria is actually quite low, with about 54 per cent not working in 2019/20 – somewhat more among women and somewhat less among men. However, this proportion is about 10 per cent higher than ten years ago (International Labour Organisation, 2021), suggesting an effect of changing retirement legislation. The chapter concludes with a data analysis based on the EQLS, an EU-wide cross-sectional survey on living and working conditions, to investigate some potentially important drivers and barriers to extended working life in Europe.

Background

This section looks at some underlying concepts and findings from applied research. Which factors were found to impact on extended working life decisions or (early) retirement? In their analysis of the employment participation of older workers, Hasselhorn & Apt (2015) point out that retirement is generally a gradual process and determined by the interaction of multiple domains. Besides different labour market activity, retirement options and traditional retirement patterns, "complexity in retirement also derives from the fact that distinct social groups may undergo different processes and, hence, display varied retirement behaviour. For example, women typically have different kinds of jobs and often lower income than men of the same age, they work substantially more often part-time, have different roles in private life, and in most countries leave work at a younger age than men. In consequence, decisions about retirement may be assumed to involve a varied set of criteria and follow different decision-making processes among women and men, which also needs to be reflected in research" (Hasselhorn & Apt, 2015, p. 22) (Figure 2.1).

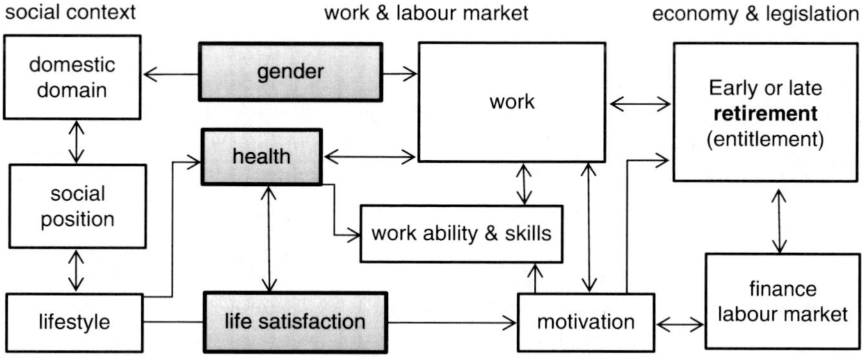

Figure 2.1 Factors impacting on extended working life decisions.

Source: *Author's own chart based on* Hasselhorn and Apt 2015: *24, Figure 2.*

The flow chart summarises various important factors that influence extended working life or retirement decisions. To reflect this chapter's specific focus on gender, health and life satisfaction, two additional boxes were added and the already existing health box has been highlighted. However, while the chart seems to indicate that earlier or later everyone reaches pension entitlement age, and this might well be true for the male working population, 6.2 per cent of the female population in Europe aged 65 to 74 years have no pension entitlement at all (European Parliament, 2016). Extending one's working life might or might not be a solution to that specific problem.

On the other hand, some EU countries (e.g. Denmark, the Netherlands and Sweden) have systems where people of a certain age receive a universal pension benefit regardless of their working careers, with no difference in these pension claims for men and women (Mayrhuber & Mairhuber, 2020a, p. 2). As a result, drivers and barriers to extended working life – especially since these are the countries with the highest expected working life (with more than 40 years already) – might be quite different from those in other countries. Nevertheless, when looking not at averages but at individuals and their decisions and considering that guarantee pension may only be one part of the overall (expected) pension, all factors presented in the above chart may of course matter to individuals. This may be especially true when gender gaps in several pension parts (making up the full sum of benefits received) are high. In 2016, based on figures from the Swedish Ministry of Health and Social Affairs, gender gaps amounted to 34 per cent in the national earnings-related pension, 27 per cent in the guaranteed pension, 17 per cent in housing allowances and 27 per cent in occupational and private pensions (Strahlberg, 2020).

In EU countries with (largely) employment-based pension systems, the Swedish model represents many relevant and decisive factors. With often occupational and private pensions not fully developed, people rely mainly on the state pension system for old age security. However, coverage effects for women and men differ markedly, not unrelated to the traditional and still generally persistent strongly gendered division of paid and unpaid work. Many women of the older generations were homemakers have no own pension entitlement. In Austria, this is the case for 18.4 per cent of women in the 65+ age group. Even when accounting for survivors' pensions and other regular old age income, more than one-tenth of women (11.4% as compared to only 0.6% of men) in Austria remain uncovered (Mairhuber & Mayrhuber, 2020b, p. 14f). High female coverage gaps, defined as the share of women without pension entitlements, are also prevalent in Malta (34%), Spain (27%), Belgium (17%), Ireland (16%) and Greece (13%) (Mayrhuber & Mairhuber, 2020a, p. 2). Extended working lives may improve the situation, especially after longer periods of non-activity or extensive care-related career gaps, allowing for the accumulation of a sufficient number of social security contribution months to become eligible for pension benefits. However, adequate job opportunities and wages would be needed to fill the gap unless some compensatory measures would entitle these women to be included and to receive pension benefits.

Extended working life can thus also be framed in terms of structural framework conditions and labour market access, in terms of impact on job opportunities, income and labour market exit or extended working life decisions as well as pensions coverage and retirement income. With lower income and shorter working careers, female pensions remain persistently lower than that of men. For example, social security data for Austria (Firzinger & Etlinger, 2020, p. 146) shows that average monthly old-age state pensions in Austria in 2019 amounted to €1,064 for women and €1,723 for men. The large gender pension gap is mostly the result of women's lower working incomes but also rather long (child care-related) absences from the labour market. While some compensatory measures are in place to make up for long child-related career breaks, the overall gender pension gap of around 38–40 per cent in the last decade is one of the highest in Europe (Eurostat, 2021b). That it dropped to unprecedented levels (36.6% in 2019 and 35.5% in 2020) looks positive but may only be temporary and related to increased early retirement (with lower benefits) related to the out-phasing of early retirement possibilities. Ways to improve the situation in terms of female pension levels in the EU need thus to be investigated and may "be found in the labour market (e. g. higher incomes, longer periods of employment), pension system (e. g. revaluation) and the structural framework conditions (e. g. care infrastructure)" (Mairhuber and Mayrhuber, 2020c, p. 6).

Health may also be a main driver or barrier to extended working life. With people working longer and at a life stage that is characterised by declining health, "ensuring that older workers have access to secure jobs which allow for control over work time, skill use and fair rewards will be essential if policy goals to boost participation and productivity, as well as reduce the health and care costs of the elderly, are to be met" (Welsh et al., 2016). A comparison of 14 European countries (OECD Health at a Glance report 2016, p. 21ff) showed that the prevalence of one or more chronic diseases (e.g. cardiovascular diseases, diabetes, cancer, musculoskeletal diseases or mental health conditions) as well as behavioural risk factors (obesity, heavy smoking, heavy alcohol drinking) visibly reduce the likelihood of employment of 50–59 year olds in all observed countries. Women appear to be more affected than men. Not unexpectedly, chronic diseases and behavioural risk factors result in lower productivity, fewer hours worked and lower wages, with those affected more likely to become disabled, unemployed or to take up early retirement schemes (OECD/EU, 2016, p. 25ff).

Perceived poor own (or partner's) health may also be a barrier to extended working life and a driver for (early) labour market exit. This applies especially to women who often take on unpaid care for partners or relatives in bad health (e.g. Biffl and Isaac, 2007; Eurofound, 2012, 2013).

Some statistical evidence

In 2018, the average effective age of labour market exit in the EU28 – still including the United Kingdom – was 64 for men and 62.3 for women, showing that women retired on average 1.7 years earlier than men (OECD, 2019, p. 180). The lowest average effective exit age was found in Luxemburg for men (60.5) and the Slovak Republic for women (59.9). Portugal displayed the highest figures for men with average effective exit age of 68.5 and Estonia for women (65.7). For Austria, a central European country with a traditional breadwinner-second earner model and a rather generous state pension system, the average effective labour market exit age in 2018 was 63.5 years for men and 60.8 years for women. On average, people in Austria thus retired earlier than on EU average, women again around 2.7 years earlier than men – with the difference partly explained by gender unequal retirement ages (to be phased out in the coming years to reach 65 for all) (Figure 2.2).

With life expectancy increasing over time, people tend to live longer and healthier lives, which allows them to enjoy an extended retirement phase. Accordingly, expected life years after labour market exit in the EU increased for both men and women. While in 1970 the remaining life expectancy at the age of average labour market exit was 14.5 for women and 10.5 for men, the respective figures in 2018 were 23.1 years for women and 18.2 years for men. France had the highest expected duration, with 26.9 years for women and 22.7 years for men. The lowest remaining number of years after labour market exit was found for women and men in Latvia (19.7 years for women and 13.9. for men). In Austria, women can expect to live 25 years or more once they leave the labour market, while the expected life years after labour market exit for men in 2018 were 19.3 years (OECD, 2019, p. 180f) (Figure 2.3).

In addition, working lives have shifted due to longer education and thus an often later start of working careers. However, with increased statutory retirement ages and several pension amount-related incentives to work longer, one would expect somewhat later but longer working lives. To measure this, Eurostat's indicator duration of working life (Eurostat, 2021a) estimates the number of years a person at the current age of 15 years is expected to be in the labour force throughout her or his life. Interesting to see that in the year 2020, the expected duration of working life in Europe (including employment but also unemployment) was found to be lower than before for the first time in 20 years, on average somewhat reduced from 35.9 in 2019 to 35.7 in 2020 and still longer for men (38.0 years) than for women (33.2 years). While this might be a temporary outcome of fewer opportunities during the COVID-19 crisis, the situation needs to be evaluated. Note also that recent increases in the duration of working life were mainly due to higher female labour market engagement: over the last 20 years, working life duration increased more for women (+4.5 years) than for men (+2.2 years) so that the marked gender difference of 7.1 years in Europe in 2000 was gradually reduced to 4.8 years in 2020.

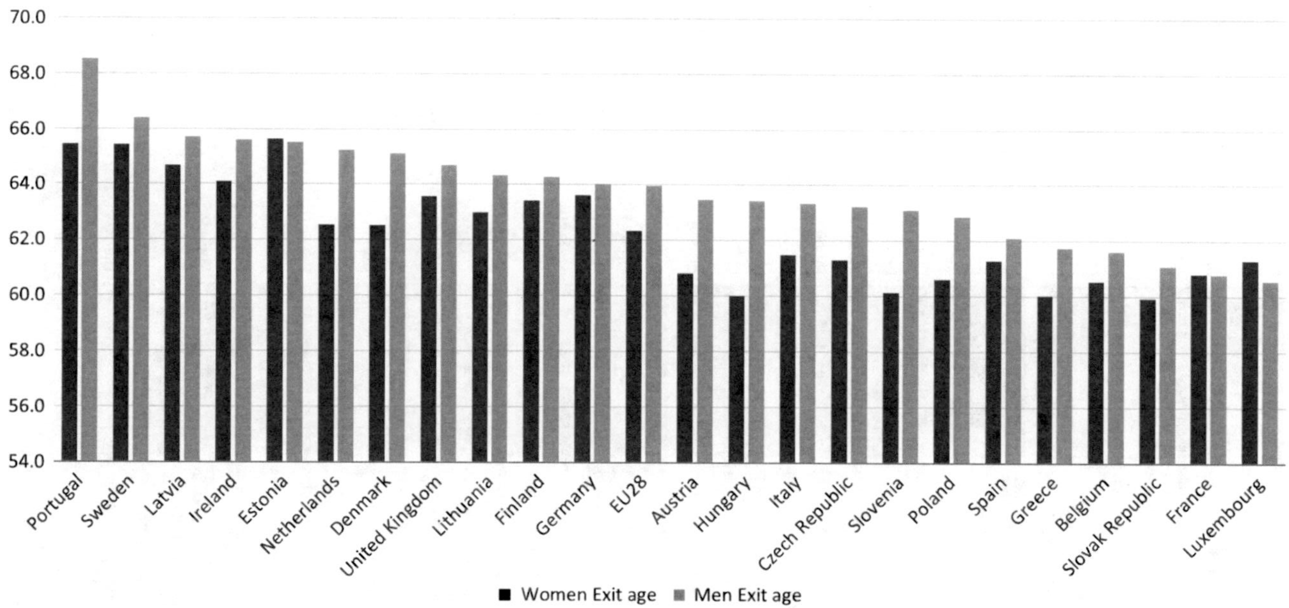

Figure 2.2 Average effective age at labour market exit by gender, EU 2018.

Source: *Own figure based on* OECD (2019: *181*), *Pensions at a Glance 2019, Fig. 6.11. Remaining life expectancy at labour market exit, by gender in 2018, Version 1 – Last updated: 25-Nov-2019.* EU 28 average, *EU countries (not included since not OECD: Bulgaria, Romania, Croatia, Malta, Cyprus).*

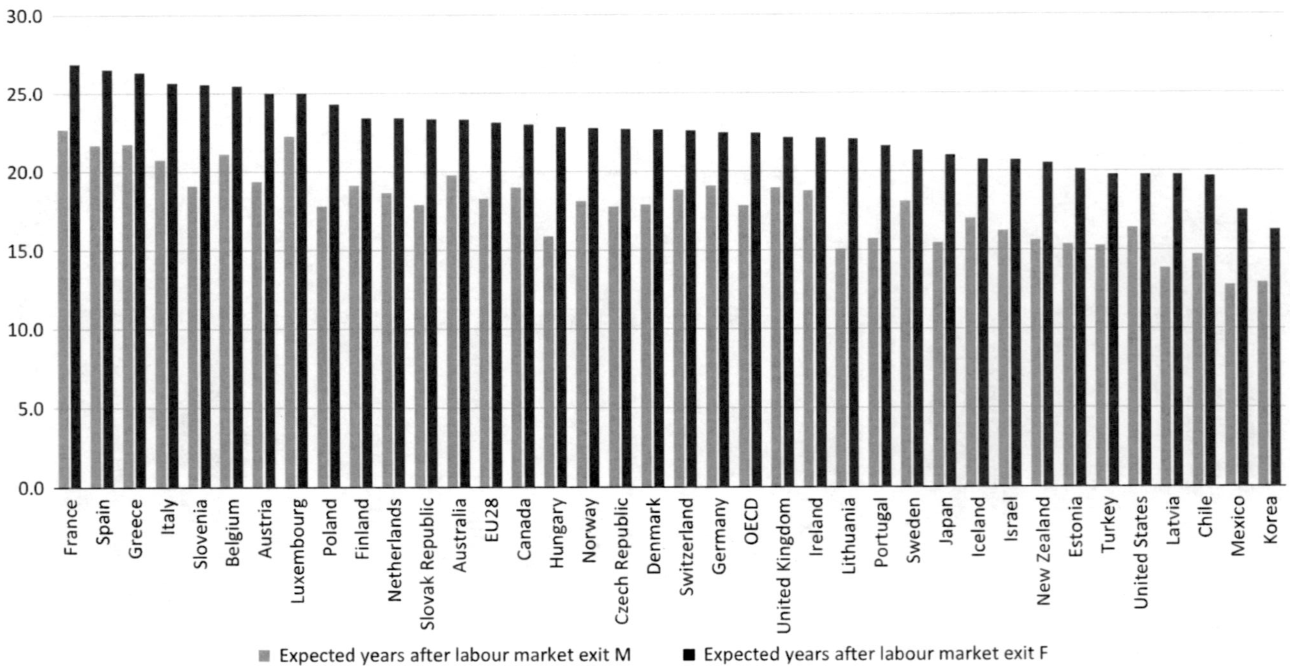

Figure 2.3 Factors impacting on extended working life decisions.

Source: Hasselhorn and Apt 2015: *24, Figure 2. Author's own additions (shaded).*

Expected durations of working life also vary across countries. In 2020 (latest available data), Sweden (42.0 years), the Netherlands (41.0) and Denmark (40.0) had the longest expected duration of working life while Italy (31.2 years), Croatia and Greece (both 32.8 years) displayed the shortest. With an estimated 37.5 years, Austria is one of the countries with a longer expected duration of working life. Men are currently expected to work around 39.5 years and women 35.3 years. With a difference of 4.2 years, the gender gap in expected duration of working life is below the EU average (Eurostat, 2021a).

From this point of view, there is room for extended working lives in many EU countries, a discussion which policy has taken up in many countries, not least in the current income and old-age poverty discussion but also in view of a needed sustainable funding of the pension system (Schuh et al, 2015; OECD, 2019, p. 25). Recent pension reforms in Europe have focused on limiting early retirement options, raising the (statutory and effective) retirement age, enhancing work incentives, changing contribution rates or expanding contribution options as well as adjusting the pension benefits to demographic changes and supporting the building up of private pensions. On the other hand, another focus was on expanding the coverage of (mandatory) pensions and developing auto-enrolment schemes as well as increasing or expanding the coverage for the first layer of old-age social protection to reduce old-age poverty (OECD, 2019, p. 25f).

The discussion also extends to public support for pension payments, since many countries have schemes that compensate for temporary absences from the labour markets (e.g. during unemployment, child breaks, elder care) or for some forms of early labour market exits (e.g. due to invalidity, long working careers). The focus has been on distributional effects of such compensating state support, and whether the observed outcome matches the current policy intention, in terms of social inclusion, agreed on compensation and final pension coverage and levels. Schuh et al. (2015, p. 2f) showed for the Austrian situation in 2015 that pension payments need not automatically increase with extended working careers since state compensation for very long working lives and/or physically highly demanding work may pre-empt such effect. In such cases, working longer would not result in higher pensions since maximum possible pension benefits would already be reached via such schemes. In addition, large compensation payments seem to go to those with already comfortable pension amounts (e.g. men with long working careers) while other groups (e.g. women with lower life income and thus lower overall pension contributions) end up with rather small pensions.

Related to the generally much lower pensions of women, it is often argued that their overall pension capital (when adding up the amount received over their longer duration of pension life) is not as low as it might appear but just spread over a longer time of receiving it (Schuh et al., 2015, p. 2). However, Mairhuber and Mayrhuber (2020c, p. 5) recently showed for the newly awarded old-age pensions in 2017 that even when considering their entire lives, women receive overall less of a pension: "Women draw a pension for an average of five years longer, because they retire earlier and have a longer life expectancy. Even if we look at this entire period, they still receive a lifetime pension total which is

36.2 per cent lower." The calculation was based on all newly awarded old-age pensions in 2017. In this year, women's newly awarded pensions (on a gross monthly median basis) were 51.4 per cent lower than those of men. For 2018, the gap remained similarly high (49.2 %). Note also that the calculation of the gender pension gap includes only those who receive a pension, which not all persons – especially women – do.

In this context, gender gaps in labour market activity, income and pension outcome are also under investigation, with studies focusing on the generally less favourable situation of women who tend to face employment and income inequalities and generally have shorter working careers, more breaks, less income and thus lower pensions and old age security (Mayrhuber and Mairhuber, 2020a).

Data analysis (the European Quality of Life Survey)

Based on above drivers and barriers to extended working life (e.g. Hasselhorn and Apt, 2015), this chapter tests the impact of various personal factors on work in later life and tries to quantify some main drivers and barriers to extended working life for the older age groups in Europe. It should be mentioned that the focus is not on social framework conditions – which admittedly are different in different EU countries – but on personal characteristics of potential workers in the older age group. This is why the dataset is not split by country but looked at as an integrated European sample. The main aim is to determine and quantify the overall effect of gender and health on work (likelihood to work) in older age groups.

The analysis relies on cross-sectional data from the EQLS run by the Dublin-based European Foundation for the Improvement of Living and Working Conditions (Eurofound). The survey is undertaken approximately every four years (2003, 2007, 2011 and 2016) and covers a range of indicators such as employment, income, education, housing, family, health and work-life balance. It also looks at subjective topics such as people's levels of happiness, how satisfied they are with their lives and how they perceive the quality of their societies.

Based on the latest available EQLS dataset (EQLS, 2016), the analysis of factors impacting on extended working life decisions in 2016 is listed in the following table. The analysis focused on the probability of working in later life (measured as being employed), with gender, health, education, family status, size of the household of the respondent and her/his income as main input factors. The basic model is the following:

> Probability of working (being employed) = f (gender, health, education, family status, life satisfaction, size of HH, income)

Table 2.1 shows the outcome of a logistic regression for probability of working (dependent variable = being employed) for the overall 2016 sample (first column)

Table 2.1 Factors impacting on extended working life (EQLS, wave 4, 2016), logistic regression

Dependent variable: being employed	*wave 4* n = 36 608 B (S.E.)	*wave 4, age 50–64 yrs* n = 9823 B (S.E.)	*wave 4, age 65+ yrs* n = 9389 B (S.E.)
Respondent sex/gender (0 m, 1 f)	−0.329*** (0.025)	−0.492*** (0.046)	−0.241* (0.106)
Q48: How is your health? (scale 1–5, increase = worse)	−0.352*** (0.015)	−0.390*** (0.028)	−0.377*** (0.063)
Education (primary or less = reference)			
Secondary or vocational education	0.735*** (0.030)	0.558*** (0.052)	0.460*** (0.125)
Higher education	1.048*** (0.034)	0.969*** (0.066)	0.670*** (0.134)
Household composition (reference = single)			
Lives with (step)child(ren)	1.052*** (0.079)	0.611** (0.221)	−18.767 (40.193)
Lives with partner	−0.761*** (0.029)	−0.396*** (0.051)	−0.493*** (0.117)
Separated	0.256*** (0.071)	0.455*** (0.122)	0.244 (0.283)
Widowed	−1.991*** (0.056)	−0.688*** (0.088)	−1.205*** (0.164)
Life satisfaction (higher = better)	0.039*** (0.006)	0.065*** (0.011)	0.019 (0.026)
Household size	0.075*** (0.01)	0.023 (0.021)	−0.082 (0.065)
Lowest income quartile	−0.744*** (0.04)	−0.891*** (0.075)	−0.664*** (0.184)
2nd income quartile	−0.185*** (0.038)	−0.276*** (0.071)	−0.626*** (0.167)
3rd income quartile	0.468*** (0.038)	0.274*** (0.07)	0.024 (0.152)
Highest income quartile	0.709*** (0.039)	0.574*** (0.071)	0.169 (0.155)
Constant	0.510*** (0.083)	1.200*** (0.159)	−1.283*** (0.382)

Source: *Author's own calculations*, EQLS, 2016 *(wave 4) data for EU28 countries; Explanation of abbreviations: B impact of each factor, (S.E.) standard error.*

* $p < 0.05$, ** $p < 0.01$, *** $p < 0.001$. regression measures effect of items on dependent variable "being employed".

and the relevant older labour market exit-prone age groups, i.e. those in the 50–64 years age group and those over 65 years.

Table 2.1 presents the results of regression analysis for the 2016 EQLS data set. Generally, gender (being female), reduced health, living with a partner, being widowed and having very or rather low income (lowest and second income quartile) have a negative impact on being employed in later life. Secondary or higher education, living with children, being separated, larger household size, higher income as well as life satisfaction have a positive impact. The largest effects are related to high education, living with children and widowhood.

Taking a closer look at the 2016 data split into different age categories, extended working life – measured as (still) being employed – shows a significant gender effect. For women, the probability of being employed as compared to men is lower in the overall sample as well as in both older age groups, with the strongest negative effect in the 50–64 years age group where labour market exit decisions are usually taken. For both older age groups, as well as for the overall sample of respondents (first column), lower self-reported health has a negative impact on the probability to work. The effect is again most pronounced for the 50–64 years group, perhaps indicating that health considerations of older workers should not be disregarded. Taking health considerations into account and offering, on the one hand, more adapted jobs as well as (public) support in private care-related issues might increase people's willingness to continue their working careers. Education and the type of job one holds also play a role. Not unexpectedly, higher than primary education has a positive effect on work, with higher (tertiary) education impacting stronger than secondary education. However, the effect of education becomes smaller in the later data sets, indicating that other factors might become more important. Family status and household size matter, in that they impact on available funds and finances needed. While living with a partner has a negative effect on the probability of work or extended working life, the presence of children or stepchildren – with higher financial need – is a driver of (extended) employment. Being separated increases the probability of employment until 65, while being widowed has a persistent negative effect. One explanation might be found in the existence of survivor benefits that reduce financial pressure, while social issues e.g. in the form of more (unpaid) engagement in the extended family might also play a role. Household size was found to impact negatively on the labour force engagement of the younger age groups. This effect is not observed in the older age groups, indicating that larger households for the younger cohort may result in more unpaid duties at home, or include family members supporting the household, reducing the pressure to find work related to financial needs. (Overall) life satisfaction is a driver of (extended) employment for the overall group of respondents as well as for the 50–64 age group. However, the effect is small and vanishes for the 65 and older age group, where it becomes insignificant. While people with lower income exhibit lower probabilities of working in all age groups including at older ages, being able to get or receiving higher income increases the probability of work. However, the effect becomes insignificant in the 65 and older age group, which might indicate that once pension payments become available, continuing employment becomes less attractive or impossible (if employers have maximum age limits for their workers). Interestingly, being in a lower income quartile keeps its negative effect also after 65 years, which might indicate that keeping one's job or taking on another job at older ages might not be an option for all.

Another interesting perspective to look at are developments over time. Are there any major changes detectable in the drivers and barriers to extended working life for older age groups over the last decade? The following table shows the outcome of logistic regression over time, looking at the second, third and fourth (above-discussed) waves of the EQLS data. It looks at respondents' answers for the years 2007, 2011 and 2016 and compares the outcome in terms of the effect certain variables have on extended working life, i.e. the probability of a person (still) being in employment. To account for the availability of variables used, the equation had to be amended (i.e. reduced) in terms of input indicators and now is:

> Probability of working (being employed) = f (gender, health, education, family status, life satisfaction, size of HH)

The outcome of the regression for both older age groups over time is mapped in the following table 2.2, indicating key impact factors (drivers and barriers) for employment in later life. When looking at the data of the different EQLS surveys, one should also keep in mind the general economic climate at the time of the data gathering: while the year 2007 was characterised by the end of the economic boom in Europe, 2011 turned out to be the year of the hight of the economic crisis in many EU countries. In 2016, however, economic recovery was apparent again and generally facilitated employment.

Table 2.2 illustrates the regression analysis results over time based on regression analysis on the second, third and fourth wave of the EQLS data for both older age groups. For the 50–64 age group, the age where labour market exit decisions are generally taken, gender keeps its negative impact over time while the effect of reduced health becomes a little less prominent over time, especially in 2016. As compared to primary education, upper secondary and higher education remain strong and positive drivers of employment and thus extended working life. Higher education proves to be the strongest driver of employment in this age group. Life satisfaction has a small but positive effect, which seems to be reinforced in the 2016 group of respondents where it doubles in size. Living with a partner has a negative effect on employment. However, the effect is much smaller in the third wave of the data. Having children around increases the probability of employment in all years while household size is mostly

Table 2.2 Factors impacting on extended working life (EQLS, 2007/11/16), logistic regression

	2007/w2, 50–64 n = 9873	*2011/w3, 50–64 n = 11068*	*2016/w4, 50–64 n = 9823*
	B (S.E.)	B (S.E.)	B (S.E.)
Respondent sex/gender (0 = m, 1 = f)	−0.596*** (0.046)	−0.428*** (0.042)	−0.533*** (0.044)
How is your health? (increase = worth)	−0.504*** (0.027)	−0.520*** (0.025)	−0.44*** (0.027)
Secondary or vocational education	0.584*** (0.051)	0.720*** (0.047)	0.667*** (0.051)
Higher education	1.189*** (0.068)	1.285*** (0.059)	1.225*** (0.063)
Life satisfaction (higher = better)	0.049*** (0.011)	0.047*** (0.01)	0.096*** (0.01)
Lives with partner	−0.263*** (0.049)	−0.174*** (0.045)	−0.135* (0.047)
Lives with partner and (step)child(ren)	0.597*** (0.103)	0.542*** (0.09)	0.472*** (0.101)
Household size	0.021 (0.021)	0.050** (0.018)	0.005 (0.021)
Constant	1.256*** (0.154)	0.817*** (0.137)	0.928*** (0.144)
	2007/w2, 65+ n = 7515	**2011/w3, 65+ n = 10280**	**2016/w4, 65+ n = 9389**
	B (S.E.)	B (S.E.)	B (S.E.)
Respondent sex/gender (0 = m, 1 = f)	−0.637*** (0.160)	−0.492*** (0.143)	−0.417*** (0.105)
How is your health? (increase = worth)	−0.577*** (0.086)	−0.617*** (0.081)	−0.427*** (0.062)
Secondary or vocational education	0.282 (0.169)	0.577*** (0.173)	0.577*** (0.124)
Higher education	0.686*** (0.192)	1.366*** (0.166)	0.953*** (0.129)
Life satisfaction (higher = better)	−0.041 (0.036)	0.083* (0.037)	0.036 (0.026)
Lives with partner	0.017 (0.154)	0.008 (0.138)	−0.017 (0.107)
Lives with partner and (step)child(ren)	1.213 (0.665)	0.743 (0.819)	2.528* (1.071)
Household size	0.234*** (0.067)	0.158* (0.064)	0.055 (0.059)
Constant	−1.574** (0.493)	−2.919*** (0.493)	−2.104*** (0.350)

Source: *Author's own calculations, EQLS 2007/11/16 (waves 2, 3 and 4) data for EU28 countries; Explanation of abbreviations: B impact of each factor, (S.E.) standard error.*
* $p < 0.05$, ** $p < 0.01$, *** $p < 0.001$.

insignificant. Overall, education and living with a partner and children have the most pronounced positive, while health and gender (being female) have the strongest negative effects.

For those in the 65 years and older age group, gender has a similar negative effect, even if this is more pronounced in 2007 than in 2016. Reduced health has an especially strong negative effect in 2007 but seems to become less of a barrier in 2016. Education has a significant positive effect in all years, with the exception of secondary education in 2007 – which might be related to the financial and economic crisis of these years since also higher education at that time had less impact. Life satisfaction is significant with a small positive impact in 2007 only, and living with partner or partner and children is relevant only in 2016, where it interestingly has a very strong positive impact for the 65 years and older age group. A larger household size has a positive effect on extended working life in 2007 and 2011 but not in 2016, where it becomes insignificant. Overall, the main drivers of longer working life match those of the 50–64 age group, even if education seems to matter less while living with others (partner, children) it recently seems to have become highly important for extending working life.

Concluding remarks

The above analysis indicates that decisions to extend working life in Europe are strongly influenced by health, education and life satisfaction but also by the household setting and overall household income. They seem to affect women and men in different ways, so that one might consider looking into structural framework conditions, the gendered labour market situation and pension system for ways to improve gender gaps and extend working life. This is true for all EU countries, even if the above analysis only looked at Europe as a whole, disregarding national differences.

While the economic situation, framework conditions and pension system regulations undoubtedly have a strong influence on labour market exit or extended working life decisions, it is interesting to see that in the above modelling for Europe overall, higher education has the most pronounced positive effect. Satisfaction with life also plays a role but this is difficult to measure; as do major life course events also play a role, but these are unfortunately not part of the survey.

It seems that during the economic crisis (see 2011 data set) bad health is a more frequent reason for labour market exit than in the other years. Exit via disability, long-term sickness or unemployment benefits might be seen as a route for exiting the labour market – of course depending on the level of benefits which will be different for each country.

Conversely, one possible reason why women, especially those in bad health, were slightly more likely to work than similar men at the height of the financial crisis in 2011 might be because of an economic need to compensate for their partner's job loss. In addition, given women's more discontinuous work profiles, their pension is generally going to be lower if they retire (early) than that of their (male) partners who as a rule tend to have (had) more continuous work profiles.

However, with often reduced working hours and income for all workers or job loss during the COVID-19 pandemic, it is now time to get back to working lives with more sustainable incomes and secure pension outlooks. It will be interesting to see if and how the COVID-19 pandemic will or will not affect the timing of retirement as well as any gender differences – but this is a task for future research.

References

Addabbo, T., Gstrein, M. & Siemienska R. (2019). Data issues and indicators, In: A. N. Laime, J. Ogg, M. Rasticova, D. Street, C. Krekula, M. Bediova & I. Madero-Cabib (eds), *Extended Working Life Policies. International Gender and Health Perspectives*, Springer, in: https://library.oapen.org/bitstream/id/3c3ee309-40b4-44e5-adfc-ae5164fb4c40/2020_Book_ExtendedWorkingLifePolicies.pdf. Accessed 17 June 2021.

Biffl, G. & Isaac, J. (2007). The challenge of ensuring a healthy workforce in an ageing society. Austria and Australia in comparison. *Ageing Societies, Austrian Economic Quarterly* 3/2007, 144–57. Wifo, Wien. http://www.wifo.ac.at/jart/prj3/wifo/resources/person_dokument/person_dokument.jart?publikationsid=30079&mime_type=application/pdf. Accessed 7 June 2021.

Eurofound (2012). *Third European quality of life survey – Quality of life in Europe: Impacts of the crisis*. Luxembourg: Publications Office of the European Union, doi:10.2806/42471. Accessed 5 May 2021.

Eurofound (2013). *Third European quality of life survey – Quality of society and public services*. Luxembourg: Publications Office of the European Union. doi:10.2806/37653. Accessed 3 May 2021

European Commission (2012). *White paper, an agenda for adequate, safe and sustainable pensions*, SWD (2012) 8 final, Brussels, 16.2.2012, COM(2012) 55 final. http://ec.europa.eu/transparency/regdoc/rep/1/2012/EN/1–2012-55-EN-F1-1.Pdf. Accessed 10 June 2021.

European Parliament (2016). *The gender pension gap: Differences between mothers and woman without children*. In: https://www.europarl.europa.eu/RegData/etudes/STUD/2016/571363/IPOL_STU(2016)571363_EN.pdf. Accessed 4 July 2021.

European Quality of Life Surveys (EQLS) (2016). Merged data set including all four waves (2003/07/11/16), download from UK data archive. Accessed 7 June 2021.

Eurostat (2021a). Duration of working life. *Eurostat statistics explained*, last update 6 July 2021. In: https://ec.europa.eu/eurostat/statistics-explained/index.php?title=Duration_of_working_life_-_statistics. Accessed 14 July 2021.

Eurostat (2021b). Gender pension gap by age group – EU-SILC survey [ilc_pnp13], Last update: 01–07-2021, in: https://appsso.eurostat.ec.europa.eu/

Firzinger, K. & Etlinger T. (2020). *Die österreichische Sozialversicherung im Jahr 2019*, in: Soziale Sicherheit 4/2020, 138–59, in: https://www.sozialversicherung.at/cdscontent/load?contentid=10008.735772&version=1590474046

Haas, B., Gstrein, M. & Bildsteiner, R. (2019). Gender, health and extending working life in Austria, In: A. N. Laime, J. Ogg, M. Rasticova, D. Street, C. Krekula, M. Bediova, I. Madero-Cabib (eds.), *Extended Working Life Policies. International Gender and Health Perspectives*, Springer, in https://library.oapen.org/bitstream/id/3c3ee309-40b4-44e5-adfc-ae5164fb4c40/2020_Book_ExtendedWorkingLifePolicies.pdf. Accessed 7 June 2021.

Hasselhorn, H. M. & Apt, W. (2015, Editors). *Understanding employment participation of older workers: Creating a knowledge base for future labour market challenges*, https://www.jp-demographic.eu/wp-content/uploads/2015/07/JPIUEP_Brochure.pdf. Accessed 12 July 2021.

International Labour Organisation (2021). *Database*, in: https://ilostat.ilo.org. Accessed 23 August 2021.

Mairhuber, I. & Mayrhuber, Ch. (2020b). *Trapez. Analyse. Geschlechtsspezifische Pensionsunterschiede in Österreich. Quantitative und qualitative Befunde*. BKA, Wien. In: https://www.forba.at/wp-content/uploads/2020/06/200624_TRAPEZ_Bericht_A4_BF.pdf. Accessed 2 July 2021.

Mairhuber, I. & Mayrhuber, Ch. (2020c). *Trapez. Analysis. Gender gaps in pensions in Austria: Quantitative and qualitative analysis*. BKA, Wien. In: https://www.trapez-frauen-pensionen.at/documents/TRAPEZ_Analyse_Bericht_2020-EN.pdf

Mayrhuber, Ch. & Mairhuber, I. (2020a). *The gender pension gap in Austria and Europe*. Austrian Society for European Politics, Policy Brief, 14'2020. Wien. In: https://www.oegfe.at/wp-content/uploads/2020/06/PB_142020_GGP.pdf. Accessed 28 June 2021.

Mayrhuber, Ch. (2017). Erwerbsunterbrechungen, Teilzeitarbeit und ihre Bedeutung für das Frauen-Lebenseinkommen, Oktober 2017, Österreichisches Institut für Wirtschaftsforschung, Im Auftrag des Arbeitsmarktservice Österreich, 2017/388-1/S/WIFO-Projektnummer: 6416, in: http://www.wifo.ac.at/wwa/pubid/61000

OECD (2019). *Pensions at a glance 2019*, OECD and G20 indicators. Paris: OECD publishing. 10.1787/b6d3dcfc-en. Accessed 10 July 2021.

OECD/EU (2016). *Health at a glance: Europe 2016: State of health in the EU cycle*. Paris: OECD Publishing. 10.1787/9789264265592-en. Accessed 10 July 2021.

Schuh, U., Berger, J., Graf, N. & Strohner, L. (2015). *Verteilungswirkung der Steuermittel in der gesetzlichen Pensionsversicherung*, Studie by Eco Austria – Institut für Wirtschaftsforschung, November 2015, in: https://www.jungeindustrie.at/media/filer_public/4d/57/4d578cb5–35d9-4d4a-9de9-8b42ae1aab12/ecoaustria_studie_verteilungpensionen_pub_po.pdf. Accessed 20 July 2021.

Strahlberg, A.-Ch. (2020). *The gender gap in pensions. Experiences from Sweden*. In: https://www.trapez-frauen-pensionen.at/documents/wk4-Stahlberg_the-gender-gap-in-pensions_experiences-from-sweden.pdf. Accessed 1 August 2021.

Welsh, J., Strazdins, L., Charlesworth, S., Kulik, C. & Butterworth, P. (2016). Health or harm? A cohort study of the importance of job quality in extended workforce participation by older adults. *BMC Public Health*, 16, 885, 10.1186/s12889-016-3478-y

3 The Discrepancy between Actual and Preferred Work and Working Hours. Proposing a Triple-A Approach to Understand Employment and Time Constraints in the "Rush Hour" and "Autumn" of Working Life

Barbara Haas, Michaela Kobler-Weiß, and Adila Sahbegovic

Introduction

Do women and men have the opportunity to fulfil their working time preferences in different national contexts? The answers will help explain the discrepancy between actual and desired labour force participation and the respective working hours. Underemployment is defined as working fewer hours than preferred or having no job at all. Overemployment, on the other hand, reflects either working too many hours or having a job even if one would prefer to work fewer hours or not being employed at all (anymore).

The novelty of this chapter is the synthesis of findings on the causes of underemployment and overemployment for the early and late stages of employment. The Triple-A approach reflects the interplay of availability, affordability and attractiveness of work and working time. The aim is to conceptualise how cross-national differences in employment and policy frameworks shape opportunities and needs, which also vary by gender, household and social stratification.

Focusing on the work and time preferences of the employed and inactive population, we find that underemployment is more common among those with lower levels of education, especially in countries with constraints in the form of low wages, high unemployment rates and a lack of part-time jobs. Overemployment, on the other hand, is more likely to be found among those with high levels of education, especially for women, regardless of the country context.

To explain a possible discrepancy between actual and preferred employment status and working hours in an extended working life, we need to examine what happens at earlier career stages (Bennett and Möhring, 2015). For example, a continuous career might increase the probability of early retirement, but only in countries with generous early retirement benefits. However, in countries with strong employment protection legislation, individuals with continuous careers

DOI: 10.4324/9781003145325-3

tend to stay in employment. To better understand the impact of cumulative advantages and disadvantages in working life, the chapter also focuses on the main working phase, the conditions of which have a strong impact on the later career phase.

The question is therefore: to what extent do actual and preferred working hours of men and women coincide in two specific life course phases in different countries? Career aspirations can collide with unpaid work, childcare obligations or leisure time, leading to time constraints in the main work phase, the so-called "rush hour of life". Reconciling work and family can be different from the late work phase, when issues of health and elder care can become pressing. We call this the 'autumn of working life' The aim is to gain a more holistic understanding of what influences labour market participation as well as respective time preferences at different life course stages.

The chapter is structured as follows: A brief literature review explaining work preferences is followed by an excursus on the specific situation during the COVID-19 health crisis and its impact on work. The next part explains the Triple-As of available, affordable and attractive working conditions. First, we address the characteristics of work and care at the micro and macro levels in the main occupational phase. We continue by showing to what extent men and women's work and working time preferences differ in the later career phase when the question of retirement arises. In the discussion section, we summarise the main findings and provide recommendations for how cross-national variations over the life course may be addressed in future studies.

Literature review and concepts

Explanations for preferences and mismatches

The ability and desire to integrate into the labour market differs greatly by socio-economic conditions in different countries (Muller et al., 2020). With regard to gender, some studies on workers' time preferences (Eurofound, 2017) show that there are no significant differences. The majority of employed men and women (about 58%) have a match between their preferred and actual working hours. However, others argue that this result could be misleading as it does not consider the fact that if working hours were reduced, earnings would decrease accordingly (Hiemer and Andresen, 2020). Moreover, the data used only to refer to the employed, while the unemployed or pensioners may also have a preference for participating in the labour market.

Whether actual and preferred working hours match depends on both the micro-level, which indicates the influence of the changing individual and household situation over the life course, and the macro-level, which reflects cultural and socio-political conditions.

At the micro-level, there are many factors that influence working time preferences, including one's health status (Jolivet and Lee, 2004; Steiber and Haas, 2021), willingness to work or (in)dependence on income earned

(Higgins et al. 2000). The desire to work more hours predominates among people with lower incomes (Schalembier et al., 2019).

Individual preferences are also strongly related to the household situation. Living alone, with or without a partner, children or parents (in-law) in need of care, shapes income and time preferences. While childcare tends to take place at the beginning of working life, care for older people tends to be taken up towards the end of working life. The majority of part-time workers have chosen this status to be able to combine work and care responsibilities (Pedulla, 2016; Treas and Widmer, 2000).

At the macro-level, we want to understand how individuals respond to national policy incentives and social norms regarding work and working hours. The availability of part-time jobs, public childcare facilities and leave options obviously have an impact (Jaumotte, 2003; Korpi, 2000, Ni Léime et al., 2020). Employees with a low level of education and/or low income make more use of public childcare facilities as these are cheaper than private childcare solutions (Steiber, et al., 2016). Country-specific differences in labour market participation of older workers are due to specific regulations such as early retirement options, earnings restrictions during retirement, partial retirement schemes or subsidies for employers to continue employing older workers (Börsch-Supan et al. 2021).

Based on a large panel data set of 15 European countries (Heger and Korfhage, 2020), there is evidence that elder care has a negative impact on employment rates and paid working hours for both men and women although gender differences still exist. Part-time employment is more common among women as reconciling paid work and care is a more pressing issue for them than for their male counterparts. As part-time employment is predominant in low-skilled occupations, these fields are often female-dominated and career breaks are not a major issue. By contrast, in full-time and highly skilled occupations, part-time arrangements are hardly ever available and long hours are more prevalent. Therefore, these occupations are traditionally male-dominated. When required to take on intensive caregiving duties, men thus tend to drop out of the labour force due to the lack of part-time opportunities. There is another reason for these gender differences. Because socially ascribed gender roles are still pervasive, women are often assumed to be the primary caregivers while men are seen as having a higher level of professional commitment. Thus, an employer (Heger and Korfhage, 2020) might view a reduction in working hours to fulfil caring responsibilities by a male employee less favourably.

Empirical studies on work/retirement preferences largely differ in their concepts, measurements and data sources and provide contradictory results. On the one hand, there is evidence of cross-national differences (Baumann and Madero-Cabib, 2021) and heterogeneity in terms of social class, family situation and gender (Ebbinghaus and Radl, 2015) while other findings suggest that the differences are rather insignificant (Struffolino and Zaccaria, 2020). However, these insights contrast with a study using multilevel modelling of European Social Survey data for 24 countries (Ebbinghaus and Radl, 2015), which shows considerable cross-national variation in the factors determining involuntary early retirement when retirees are asked ex-post.

To combine the micro- and macro-level findings over time, we see two strands of argumentation: on the one hand, female part-time employment is widely discussed as a more or less "voluntary" decision to combine paid work and care (European Commission, 2007; Wielers et al., 2014). On the other hand, however, it is shown that women are constrained in "choosing" the right level of paid work participation, which limits their upward mobility and pension options. Empirically, it remains open what impact the recent pandemic has had on labour market desires and decisions. In the following section, we briefly summarise the current state of knowledge.

Explaining mismatches through the Triple-A approach: Available, affordable and attractive employment and working hours

The following sections draw on the main findings of two different studies, one dealing with the main career phase (Steiber and Haas, 2018) and the other one with the late work phase (Steiber and Kohli, 2017) to illustrate how preferred and actual working hours do not always coincide. Both articles provide multivariate regression analyses of cross-sectional survey data from the European Social Survey (ESS, 2010–2012, Round 5) using consistent and thus comparable measures of mismatches. Based on these two articles and the analysis of the ESS data set we present a schematic representation of micro- and macro-level determinants of the discrepancy between actual and preferred work and working hours.

Concepts of mismatches

Actual and preferred work and hours of work reflect a self-report by individuals who have in mind that income would increase or decrease proportionally to the increase or decrease in time in paid work. Therefore, income plays a crucial role in understanding involuntary types of employment. The determinants of work and hour preferences might be completely different if there were full or partial wage compensation for a reduction in hours.

Underemployment means that individuals would rather be employed or work more hours. Overemployed individuals would like to leave the labour market or at least reduce paid working hours. In the late working phase, the question is when to retire and if so whether, voluntarily.

In the ESS dataset, respondents are asked about their current employment status, their usual number of hours worked per week (including paid or unpaid overtime) and their preferred working hours.

For the late career phase, retired respondents are retrospectively asked about their involuntary exit (underemployment). Involuntary work (a form of overemployment), on the other hand, implies that workers would like to retire but

Table 3.1 Actual and preferred work in the main and late career phase

	Preferring to work fewer hours or not to work at all (pension)	*Preferring to work more hours*
Actually, working long hours	overemployed	match
Actually, working few hours or not working at all (in pension)	match	Underemployed

need to remain employed for various reasons, some of which are explained later in this chapter.

In our Triple-A approach, we assume that the availability, affordability and attractiveness of a particular position in the labour market are useful concepts for understanding mismatches across different phases of work. Whether a full-time position (long working hours in Table 3.1), a part-time position (few working hours in Table 3.1) or no position at all is available, affordable and attractive depends on a variety of reasons located at the micro, meso- and macro-levels. Individual characteristics at the micro-level (e.g. gender, household and family situation, educational and occupational status) play a role as do employers and the structure of the labour market (meso-level). All these factors are embedded in state regulations at the macro-level (i.e. laws, taxes, transfers or institutions). For heuristic reasons, we can distinguish these determinants at the three abstract levels, while in reality they are of course strongly intertwined. We focus only on the micro- and macro-levels in this chapter, as the meso-level is beyond the scope of this chapter.

Main career phase

Micro-level: Attractiveness depends on the availability of a good quality job, affordability and caring responsibilities

Education or occupational status are proxies for social class differences. Research shows that both men and women with high levels of education are more likely to be employed and to work continuously longer than their peers with lower levels of education (England et al., 2012; Evertsson et al., 2009; Nieuwenhuis et al., 2012). However, contradictory factors are at play here: women are more likely to be partnered or married to men with the same level of education (Blossfeld and Timm, 2003; Schwartz and Mare, 2005). Highly educated women may then be able to afford to drop out of the labour market or work part-time, but are also more likely to outsource elder care as they can afford to do so (Spijker and Zueras, 2020). Less-educated women, by contrast, have stronger incentives to earn money because of their potentially low-earning partners (Haas et al., 2006; England et al., 2012; Killingsworth and Heckman, 1986).

In addition to economic reasons, labour supply decisions can also be influenced by the quality of work as well as attitudes towards paid work and gender roles. For example, highly educated women tend to have access to more satisfying and fulfilling jobs that offer intrinsic rewards (Gesthuizen and Verbakel, 2011, Steiber et al., 2016). Some occupations and professional positions allow or even require full-time employment, especially output-oriented highly skilled project work (Van Echtelt et al., 2006). Skilled workers are therefore at risk of overemployment.

People with lower levels of education tend to be paid less and face greater labour market insecurity. As they are more likely to have a partner whose low-wage employment is also insecure, they often face greater economic pressure to contribute to the household income (Erlinghagen, 2008; Konietzka and Kreyenfeld, 2010).

Furthermore, living alone or with a partner plays a crucial role, especially with children. (Single) parents are confronted with different types of discrepancies between actual and preferred work. The ESS data show that parents of pre-school-age children are not able to work the desired number of hours. Surprisingly, underemployment occurs both in male breadwinner models (with a full-time working father and a non-working mother) and in modified breadwinner models, meaning that the mother works part-time (Steiber and Haas, 2018). In summary, gender, education level, household and family situation clearly shape the gap.

Macro-level: Huge cross-country differences in the availability and affordability of employment and reduced working hours influence attractiveness

As we have seen at the micro-level, affordability plays a key role. Given the large cross-country differences in wage rates, the need for household members to work full-time is less pronounced in Western, Central and Northern Europe than in Eastern and Southern European countries. A limited choice for part-time work exists when total household disposable income is comparatively low and touches the poverty line, defined as an income below half the median household income (OECD, 2015).

The working time mismatch varies strongly not only by social inequality and wage level, but also by unemployment rate (De Moortel et al., 2017). Preferences for longer or shorter working hours are shaped by deteriorating economic conditions. If there is a fear of becoming unemployed, it becomes more difficult to find a new job that matches the preferred number of hours worked. Moreover, part-time jobs are rare and of comparatively lower quality in southern European countries such as Spain. This explains to some extent why we see a relatively high proportion of involuntary part-time workers in these countries (Lewis and Plomien, 2009). There is a vicious circle: the less affluent and the less equal a society is, the less satisfied people are with fewer hours worked (Horemans et al., 2016; Stier and Lewin-Epstein, 2003). Similarly, when part-time jobs are available and affordable, they are more likely to be accepted and even gain in popularity (Wielers et al., 2014). The large cross-national differences in the institutionalisation of part-time work have a strong influence on the quality of reduced working hours. We find high-quality part-time jobs in countries with more protective labour policies such as Sweden and the Netherlands. In these contexts, part-time workers do not have to fear occupational downgrading, but enjoy the same benefits as full-time workers, which significantly improves their perceived quality of working life (Roeters and Craig, 2014). A longitudinal study on employment transitions shows that Dutch women are less likely to leave the labour market due to part-time opportunities. However, part-time is rarely a stepping stone to full-time employment. Moreover, since women in general, and not only those with care responsibilities, are expected to work reduced hours, the female part-time norm perpetuates gender inequalities in the labour market as well as in unpaid work (Yerkes, 2009; Yerkes and Jana, 2019).

In Figure 3.1, we summarise the determinants of the discrepancy between actual and preferred work and working hours at the micro and macro levels described above.

Late career phase

Micro-level: Attractiveness of work versus retirement depends on the availability of a quality job, affordability and health

At the end of working life, the question arises again whether people can work their desired quota of hours or have to leave the labour market. In this section, we summarise the main findings for both male and female retirees (Steiber and Kohli, 2017). The analysis of different employment levels (from high to low controllers, non-manual routine, self-employed, manual supervisors to skilled managers) shows that both men and women in high-status occupations tend to prefer later retirement than their counterparts in low-status occupations whose work is less intrinsically rewarding. Surprisingly, and contrary to theoretical assumption, women in high-status occupations have a higher risk of involuntary retirement than either men or low-skilled women. Moreover, women in part-time employment are more likely to be affected by involuntary work compared to women in full-time employment.

Part-time work also shows another interesting gender difference. While men reduce paid work in order to extend their working lives, women are more likely to continue a part-time career. When men or women experience interrupted work histories, both tend to retire earlier than desired.

Unemployment or job loss late in a career are considered “exogenous shocks” (Steiber and Kohli, 2017: 369) that affect men and women regardless of other characteristics and are very likely to lead to involuntary retirement. This undesirable exit path also applies to women who leave their jobs for “personal or family reasons” (this item of the ESS seems to reflect care responsibilities for

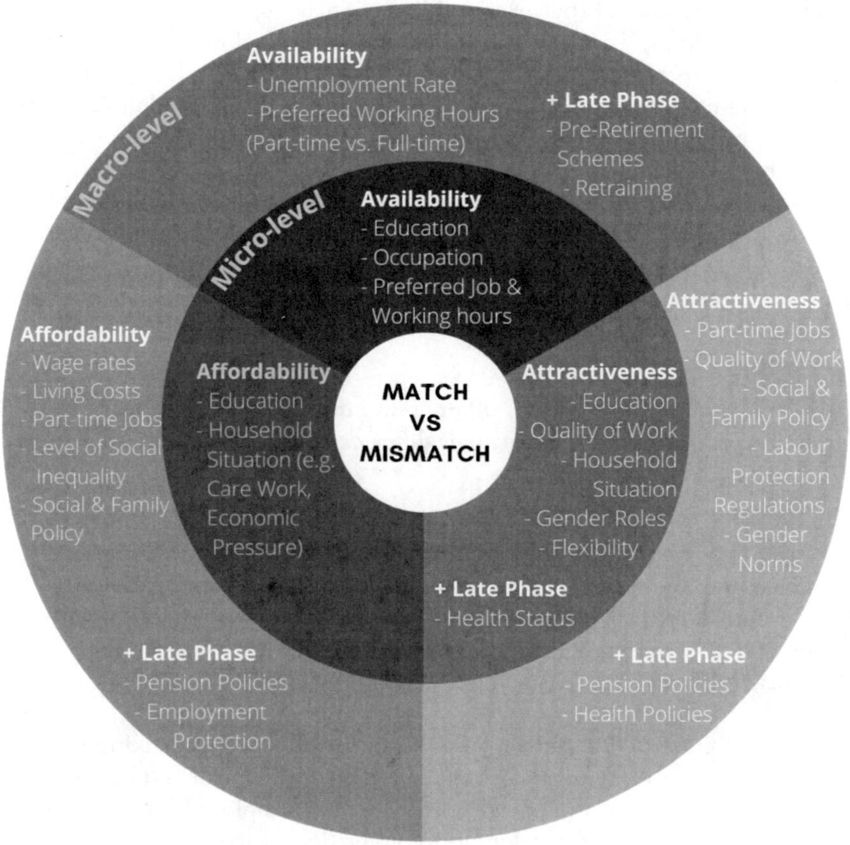

Figure 3.1 The Triple-A approach for work preferences.

Source: Own categorisation of the authors.

partners, parents or grandchildren, but in the absence of more precise information, caregiving cannot be tested more explicitly).

As wages increase with age (seniority principle), older workers are sometimes seen as a financial burden for employers. The lack of retraining opportunities for older workers is a relevant part of the explanation for involuntary early retirement (Steiber and Kohli, 2017). In addition, poor health may lead to voluntary or involuntary withdrawal from the labour market (Ebbinghaus and Hofäcker, 2013; Ebbinghaus and Radl, 2015; Steiber and Kohli, 2017). In contrast to these trends, the data show that the risk of involuntary retirement seems to have decreased in the younger cohorts of male and female pensioners.

Involuntary work, on the other hand, has increased significantly for both men and women, but for different reasons. Women with discontinuous careers due to caring responsibilities and women who are single, divorced, widowed or living with a low-income partner are often unable to retire at the preferred retirement age. They have to extend their working lives to make up for the missing social security contributions. For men who are involuntarily employed, care work plays a different role. As compared to childless men, fathers are more likely to prolong their working life involuntarily, which "(…) may be related to adult children's continuing need for financial support, the costs of late parenthood or fathers' desire to have more time for grand-parenting" (Steiber and Kohli, 2017: 374).

In summary, men and, to a lesser extent, women in highly skilled occupations in particular show a good match between actual and preferred hours of work and the age of retirement. Decent working conditions contribute to prolonging paid working life due to better health and subjective age perception (Steiber and Haas, 2021).

Macro-level: Do the availability, affordability and the attractiveness of desired working hours or retirement differ across countries and in terms of gender?

In this section, we focus on findings obtained by assessing the actual retirement age retrospectively, as done by Steiber and Kohli (2017) and by Ebbinghaus and Radl (2015). These studies are comparable as they both use the ESS as a data source. While the latter study analyses preferences for *early retirement* and the corresponding macro-level constraints, Steiber and Kohli (2017) deal with all kinds of matches and mismatches between work (hours) and retirement.

Due to the current trend in most EU countries to extend working lives by raising the statutory retirement age and reducing social benefits (Ni Léime et al., 2020), people may have a financial need to remain employed longer than desired. The phenomenon of involuntary prolongation of working life thus gains relevance, but the lack of available and affordable (early) retirement options is only one explanation for overemployment in the autumn of life.

Descriptively, there are large country differences. The share of older-aged men working involuntarily varies from 3% in Denmark to 36% in Greece. Greek women (about 44%) would like to retire earlier than they actually can, while involuntary work is not so widespread among Danish women (4.5%) (Steiber and Kohli, 2017). Focusing on individual-level determinants of (mis) matches in retirement trajectories, the authors measure country-fixed effects to control for comparable stable differences across 23 countries. They run separate regression models for men and women, as pension systems are gender-specific and in some countries the statutory retirement age for women is lower than for their male counterparts (e.g. see Haas et al., 2020).

The analysis shows that involuntary work is less common than involuntary retirement. Moreover, early retirement does not vary significantly by gender, but by country. In many European countries, a significant share of early retirement is due to a lack of employment opportunities for older workers, especially low-skilled workers, and the difficulty of finding a job after being laid off. Indeed, a higher national unemployment rate increases the risk of involuntary retirement. Besides labour market structures, employment regulations also play a role. Contradictory effects are shown by Ebbinghaus and Radl (2015): on the one hand, strong regulation, i.e. restrictions on flexible hiring and firing, makes it costly to dismiss older workers. On the other hand, high employment protection can also have the opposite effect, as unemployed older workers face difficulties in finding a new job, especially due to seniority wages.

In sum, higher levels of involuntary retirement suggest that it is not only preferences that determine retirement decisions, but that it is also influenced by conditions, such as availability and affordability, that shape the choice of a particular paths.

Discussion: Assumptions on generational regimes

In line with previous research (Bartoll, 2020; De Moortel, 2017), women, but also men in a lower social position (using education or occupational status as a proxy), are a vulnerable group in the labour market both in mid-life and in later life.

In terms of cross-national and gender differences, there seems to be more gender-specific evidence for the mid-life than for the later career stage. A significant proportion of middle-aged women in post-socialist countries and Southern Europe would like to increase labour force participation and working hours, but are rather constrained in doing so for various reasons such as a lack of both part-time and full-time employment opportunities, traditional gender roles or lacking institutional support (Steiber and Haas, 2012).

Although the macro context seems to substantially shape the pathways to (in)voluntary early retirement, cross-national differences do not follow existing welfare regime typologies, e.g. in early retirement patterns (Ebbinghaus and Radl, 2015). Moreover, following the findings of Steiber and Kohli, (2017), the incidence of the earliest possible exit from the labour market cannot be seen (only) as a result of attractive early retirement schemes. In many countries, the factors pushing older workers out of the labour market (job loss, health problems or care responsibilities) turn out to be stronger than the pull factors in terms of affordable early exit from the labour market. Older workers were found to be more likely to be underemployed (involuntary retirement) if their occupational status was comparatively low. The higher their social class position, the more likely it is that people will be able to realise their desired employment or retirement status. Under certain circumstances, such as the chance of retraining, a job change, better working conditions or a part-time job, the involuntarily retired would have remained in employment (Steiber and Kohli, 2017).

Early retirement is not always a genuine decision but rather a constrained choice. Health status and the corresponding policy framework, i.e. health, labour market, employment, retirement, social and family policies, have a significant influence. Previous research has shown that low-income workers, especially women are more dependent on government employment protection schemes to combat discrimination (Burn et al. 2020). In addition, public (elder) care facilities and the availability of affordable old-age care facilities are relevant for reducing the gender gap in the labour market as well as the disparities between men and women in retirement. To capture contextual differences in future studies, the classification of countries based on social and family policies (Saraceno and Keck, 2010) would be a good starting point to explain (mis) matches: first, the tendency to underemployment is more pronounced in countries that exhibit "familialism by default" (ibid). This generational regime shows a lack of available formal care facilities for children, offers limited public financial support and few services for the care of older people.

Second, the "supported familialism", on the other hand, allows for a better matching between preferences and behavioural choices "(…) when policies, usually through financial transfers – including taxation and paid leaves – support (specific) family members in keeping up their financial and care responsibilities" (ibid: 676).

Finally, Saraceno and Keck (2010) assume that the match between preferred and desired work (hours) and retirement is most pronounced in a regime referred to as "de-familialisation", because "(…) the individualisation of social rights (e.g. with regard to minimum income provision, or entitlement to higher education or to receiving care) reduces family responsibilities and dependencies" (ibid: 676).

Working time (preferences) before and during the COVID-19 crisis

The importance of social and labour market policies was clearly demonstrated by the strong need to protect workers during the COVID-19 pandemic (Ghilarducci and Farmand, 2020). Vulnerability becomes more evident in times of crisis (Lallement, 2011). For example, the years after 2008 have put significant pressure on women to increase their paid working hours (European Union, 2014; Rubery and Rafferty, 2013). Unemployment of one partner leads other household members to tend to increase their labour market participation, also known as the "added worker effect" (Buddelmeyer et al., 2008).

Analyses have shown different effects of this economic shock on the working time patterns of men and women. One reason that seems to explain this difference is sectoral composition. History has shown that economic downturns usually have a significant impact on some sectors, such as manufacturing, while others, such as health care or education, are comparatively less vulnerable. While men are usually overrepresented in sectors characterised by cyclical exposure, comparatively stable sectors tend to be dominated by women (Alon, 2020: 6). In the case of the pandemic, however, this pattern has been somewhat reversed. This means that women, who are overrepresented in high-risk sectors, are hit harder by the crisis than their male counterparts. The majority of male-dominated occupations are considered "critical", meaning that they are "[…] *essential in fighting the pandemic* […]" and that they "[…] *ensure economic continuity in times of crisis* […]" (Alon, 2020; Eurofound, 2020a and 2020b).

Besides gender, age is another important variable when it comes to the impact of the pandemic on employment status. Compared to their younger colleagues, older workers who lost their jobs during the pandemic are likely to be disadvantaged in the labour market. As they often lack digital literacy and adequate support and training tailored to their specific needs, it is even more difficult for them to find a job in a labour market that has changed radically over the years. Compared to young or mid-career workers, older workers are less involved in learning and training activities. This makes necessary retraining even more difficult when it comes to applying for a job in a different industry. Finally, the fact that older people are among the most vulnerable groups in terms of health during the pandemic could further expose them to stereotypes and perceptions of weakness (Centre for Ageing Better, 2020).

A three-round e-survey conducted by Eurofound (2021) between April 2020 and March 2021 sought to capture the impact of the COVID-19 health crisis on living and working conditions in EU Member States. When looking at the proportion of respondents who became unemployed, there is a small gender difference, with women being slightly more at risk of losing their jobs. Combining the variables of gender and age, the most vulnerable group appears to be young women aged 18–34, of whom 11% reported job loss, while among men and women aged 50 and older, 8% lost their jobs. Another impact of the COVID-19 pandemic is a reduction in working hours, which seems to have a comparatively large impact on women aged 50 and over in the medium term. In the first round of the survey in April 2020, there was little difference in the proportion of respondents with decreasing working hours between the age and gender groups. However, this difference has widened over time. In July 2020, the decline in working hours was most pronounced among women aged 50 and over (40%), compared to 33% of middle-aged women and 34% of young women (Eurofound, 2021).

Overall, these findings suggest that the COVID-19 health crisis could significantly change work cultures and preferences in different countries in the future (Chung et al., 2020; Arntz et al., 2020). The changes could affect men and women differently and age group differences are also likely. There are several gaps in our knowledge about the pandemic and its impact on employment status and work preferences. It would therefore be important to conduct further research on this topic, especially with regard to the situation after COVID-19 and possible long-term effects on the work preferences of different gender and age groups.

Limitations

The quantitative results of existing studies (Steiber and Haas, 2018; Steiber and Kohli, 2017) allow us to consider differences between individuals in different countries. While we can describe the importance of micro and macro factors, we are limited in explaining their interrelationships in detail. The figure above is a first step in conceptualising assumptions, but there are many gaps, especially in understanding the meso-level of late-career employers and labour market structures.

To get a more nuanced understanding of inequalities, we need to go beyond these rather limited categorisations of social class differences by using proxies such as education or occupational status. There is also a need for more recent cross-national data on working time preferences with large sample sizes. The assumptions regarding generational regimes mentioned above (Saraceno and Keck, 2010) could allow us to examine the interrelationships between factors at the micro and macro levels. In addition, qualitative or mixed-methods studies would provide more detailed data on the relevance of preferences over behaviour, especially during the recent pandemic. Ideally, panel data would allow for the detection of causes and effects that change over time.

Conclusion

The starting point for this work was to critically examine whether working or non-working men and women in different countries are able to work their preferred number of hours. Empirical evidence from the ESS data allows for a comparison between the mismatch in the peak and late stages of the career. The result of our analysis leads to the theoretical Triple-A model that is represented in Figure 3.1.

Both types of mismatches, overemployment and underemployment, indicate an insufficient allocation of time and money. This seems to be more pronounced in the eastern and southern parts of Europe than in the continental and Nordic countries. To understand the cross-national differences in the availability and affordability of jobs that allow people to work the desired number of hours, we need to examine the respective national institutions: care infrastructure, leave schemes and retirement arrangements in relation to the statutory retirement age, as well as public policies to manage the transition out of the labour force.

Labour force participation figures and preferences for longer or shorter working hours only partly reflect genuine individual "choices". More importantly, the misalignments are key indicators of constraints and structural failures of the state. We need to better understand how health and personal circumstances, as well as social gender norms, work culture and policy, influence each other. Policies should enable a better combination of paid work and care through affordable and attractive child and elder care facilities, as well as safe, quality part-time jobs that allow for a smooth transition into employment or retirement.

An important task for future research will be to further test the proposed links between affordable, available and attractive paid work integration and the respective working hours. Under what circumstances are individuals able to fulfil their preferences for paid work when income is taken into account? The discrepancy between actual and preferred work suggests that there are significant differences within and across societies. Closing the gap is a challenging task for (trans)national policies in a globalised economy where digitalisation and automation trends can influence the ability to fulfil desired working hours and corresponding income.

References

Alon, T. M., Doepke, M., Olmstead-Rumsey, J. & Tertilt, M. (2020). *The impact of COVID-19 on gender equality (Working Paper No. 26947)*. Cambridge, MA: National Bureau of Economic Research. 10.3386/w26947

Arntz, M., Yahmed, S. B. & Berlingieri, F. (2020). Working from home and Covid-19: The chances and risks for gender gaps. *ZEW expert brief*, 20–09.

Arts, & Gelissen (2002). Three worlds of welfare capitalism or more? A state-of-the-art report. *Journal of European Social Policy*, 12/2, 137–158.

Baumann, I. & Madero-Cabib, I. (2021). Retirement trajectories in countries with flexible retirement policies but different welfare regimes. *Journal of Aging & Social Policy*, 33(2), 138–160. doi:10.1080/08959420.2019.1685358

Bartoll, X. & Ramos, R. (2020). Working hour mismatch, job quality, and mental well-being across the EU28: A multilevel approach. *Int Arch Occup Environ Health*, 93, 733–745. 10.1007/s00420-020-01529-2

Bennett, J. & Möhring, K. (2015). Cumulative (dis)advantage? The impact of labour market policies on late career employment from a life course perspective. *Journal of Social Policy*, 44(2), 213–233. doi:10.1017/S0047279414000816

Blossfeld, H. P. & Timm, A. (Eds.) (2003). *Who marries whom? Educational systems as marriage markets in modern societies: A comparison of thirteen countries*. Dordrecht: Kluwer.

Börsch-Supan, A., Hanemann, F., Beach, B., Halimi, D., Harding, S., van der Waal, M., Watanabe, D. & Staudinger, U. M. (2021). Older adults' integration in the labour market: A global view. *Ageing and Society*, 41, 917–935. doi:10.1017/S0144686X1 9001454

Buddelmeyer, H., Mourre, G. & Ward, M. (2008). Why do Europeans work part-time? A cross-country panel analysis. *European Central Bank*, 872. Frankfurt am Main.

Burn, I., Button, P., Figinski, T. F. & McLaughlin, J. S. (2020). Why retirement, social security, and age discrimination policies need to consider the intersectional experiences of older women. *Public Policy & Aging Report*, 30(3), 101–106.

Centre for Ageing Better (2020). *A mid-life employment crisis: How COVID-19 will affect the job prospects of older workers*. doi: http://hdl.voced.edu.au/10707/567061

Chung, H., Seo, H., Forbes, S. & Birkett, H. (2020). *Working from home during the COVID-19 lockdown: Changing preferences and the future of work*. University of Kent.

De Moortel, D., Thévenon, O., De Witte, H. & Vanroelen, Ch. (2017). Working hours mismatch, macroeconomic changes, and mental well-being in Europ. *Journal of Health and Social Behavior*, 58(2), 217–231. Doi: 10.1177/0022146517706532

Ebbinghaus, B. & Hofäcker, D. (2013). Reversing early retirement in advanced welfare economies: A paradigm shift to overcome push and pull factors. *Comparative Population Studies*, 38(4), 807–840.

Ebbinghaus, B. & Radl, J. (2015). Pushed out prematurely? comparing objectively forced exits and subjective assessments of involuntary retirement across europe. *Research in Social Stratification and Mobility*, 41, 115–130. doi:10.1016/j.rssm.2015.04.001

England, P., Gornick, J. & Shafer, E. F. (2012). Women's employment, education and the gender gap in 17 countries. *Monthly Labor Review*, 135(4), 3–12.

Erlinghagen, M. (2008). Self-perceived job insecurity and social context: A multi-level analysis of 17 European countries. *European Sociological Review*, 24(2), 183–197.

Eurofound (2017). *Working time patterns for sustainable work*. Luxembourg: Publications Office of the European Union.

Eurofound (2020a). *Living, working and COVID-19*. COVID-19 series. Luxembourg: Publications Office of the European Union.

Eurofound (2020b). *Critical occupations in essential services, June 2020*. https://www.eurofound.europa.eu/observatories/eurwork/industrial-relations-dictionary/critical-occupations-in-essential-services (accessed 20 May 2021).

Eurofound (2021). *Living, working and COVID-19 dataset*. https://www.eurofound.europa.eu/data/covid-19/working-teleworking (accessed 29 May 2021).

European Commission (2007). *Report from the Commission to the Council, the European Parliament, the European Economic and Social Committee and the Committee of the Regions on Equality between Women and Men*, No. 49 final.

European Union (2014). *The gender impact of the crisis and the gap in total hours worked*. Employment and Social Developments in Europe 2013, Chapter 3, 173–230.

European Union (2014). *Use of childcare in the EU Member States and progress towards the Barcelona targets*. Short Statistical Report No. 1, available at: http://ec.europa.eu/justice/gender-quality/files/documents/140502_gender_equality_workforce_ssr1_en.pdf (accessed 3 May 2014).

Evertsson, M., England, P., Mooi-Reci, I., Hermsen, J., De Bruijn, J. & Cotter, D. (2009). Is gender inequality greater at lower or higher educational levels? Common patterns in the Netherlands, Sweden, and the United States. *Social Politics*, 16(2), 210–241.

Gesthuizen, M. & Verbakel, E. (2011). Job preferences in Europe. *European Societies*, 13, 663–686.

Ghilarducci, T. & Farmand, A. (2020). Older workers on the COVID-19-frontlines without paid sick leave. *Journal of Aging & Social Policy*, 32(4-5), 471–476. doi:10.1080/08959420.2020.1765685

Haas, B., Steiber, N., Hartel, M. & Wallace, C. (2006). Household employment patterns in an enlarged European Union. *Work, Employment & Society*, 20(4), 751–771.

Haas, B., Gstrein, M. & Bildsteiner, R. (2020). Austria, chapter 8: Gender, health and extending working life in Austria, In Léime, Á. N., Ogg, J., Rasticova, M., Street, D., Krekula, C., Bédiová, M. and Madero-Cabib, I.(eds.), *Extended Working Life Policies: International Gender and Health Perspectives*, Springer, 141–152.

Heger, D. & Korfhage, T. (2020). Short- and medium-term effects of informal eldercare on labor market outcomes. *Feminist Economics*, 26(4), 205–227. doi:10.1080/13545701.2020.1786594

Hiemer, J. & Andresen, M. (2020). When less time is preferred: An analysis of the conceptualization and measurement of overemployment. *Time & Society*, 29(1), 74–102.

Higgins, C., Duxbury, L. & Johnson, K. L. (2000). Part-time work for women: Does it really help balance work and family?*Human Resource Management*, 39(1), 17–32.

Horemans, J., Marx, I. & Nolan B. (2016). Hanging in, but only just: Part-time employment and in-work poverty throughout the crisis. *IZA Journal of European Labor Studies*, 5(5), 1–19.

Jaumotte, F. (2003). *Labour Force Participation of women: Empirical evidence on the role of policy and other determinants in OECD countries*. OECD Economic Studies Report, No. 37. Paris: Organisation for Economic Cooperation and Development.

Jolivet, A. & Lee, S. (2004). *Employment conditions in an ageing world: Meeting the working time challenge*. Conditions of Work and Employment Series No. 9. In: ILO Working Papers. Geneva: International Labour Organization.

Killingsworth, M. R. & Heckman, J. J. (1986). Female labor supply: A survey. In O. Ashenfelter & R. Layard (Eds.), *Handbook of Labor Economics*. New York: Elsevier Science, vol. 1, 103–204.

Konietzka, D. & Kreyenfeld, M. (2010). The growing educational divide in mothers' employment: An investigation based on the German micro-censuses 1976–2004. *Work, Employment & Society*, 24(2), 260–278.

Korpi, W. (2000). Faces of inequality: Gender, class, and patterns of inequalities in different types of welfare states. *Social Politics*, 7(2), 127–191.

Lallement, M. (2011). Europe and the economic crisis: Forms of labour market adjustment and varieties of capitalism. *Work, Employment and Society*, 25(4), 627–641.

Léime, Á. N., Ogg, J., Rasticova, M., Street, D., Krekula, C., Bédiová, M. & Madero-Cabib, I. (2020). *Extended Working Life Policies: International Gender and Health Perspectives*. Springer, online.

Lewis, J. & Plomien, A. (2009). "Flexicurity" as a policy strategy: The implication for gender equality. *Economy and Society*, 38(3), 433–459. doi:10.1080/03085140903020622

Muller, J. S., et al. (2020). The long-term costs of family trajectories: Women's later-life employment and earnings across Europe. *Demography*, 57(3), 1007–1034.

Nieuwenhuis, R., Need, A. & van der Kolk, H. (2012). Institutional and demographic explanations of women's employment in 18 OECD countries 1975–1999. *Journal of Marriage and Family*, 74, 614–630. doi:10.1111/j.1741-3737.2012.00965.x

OECD (2015). *In it together: Why less inequality benefits all*. Paris: OECD Publishing. 10.1787/9789264235120-en (accessed 04 January 2021).

Pedulla, D. S. (2016). Penalized or protected? Gender and the consequences of non-standard and mismatched employment histories, *American Sociological Review*, 81(2), 262–289.

Roeters, A. & Craig, L. (2014). Part-time work, women's work-life conflict, and jobs satisfaction: A cross-national comparison of Australia, the Netherlands, Germany, Sweden, and the United Kingdom. *International Journal of Comparative Sociology*, 53(3), 185–203.

Rubery, J. & Rafferty, A. (2013). Women and recession revisited. *Work, Employment and Society*, 27(3), 414–432.

Saraceno, C. & Keck, W. (2010). Can we identify intergenerational policy regimes in Europe?. *European Societies*, 12(5), 675–696.

Schalembier, B., Bleys, B., Van Ootegem, L. & Verhofstadt, E. (2019). How relative income affects work hours preferences. *Applied Economics*, 51(51), 5545–5558, 10.1080/00036846.2019.1613512

Schwartz, C. & Mare, R. (2005). Trends in educational assortative marriage from 1940 to 2003. *Demography*, 42(4), 621–646.

Spijker, J. & Zueras, P. (2020). Old-age care provision in Spain in the context of a new system of long-term care and a lingering economic crisis. *Journal of Population Ageing*, 13(1), 41–62.

Steiber, N., Berghammer, C. & Haas, B. (2016). Contextualizing the education effect on women's employment: A cross-national comparative analysis. *Journal of Marriage and Family*, 78(1), 246–261.

Steiber, N. & Haas, B. (2012). Advances in explaining women's employment patterns. *Socio-Economic Review*, 10(2), 343–367.

Steiber, N. & Haas, B. (2021). Working conditions and retirement preferences: The role of health and subjective age as mediating variables in the association of poor job quality with early retirement. In Burnay et al. (eds), *Older Workers and Labour Market Exclusion Processes*, Springer editor.

Steiber, N. & Haas, B. (2018). Too much or too little work? Couples' actual and preferred employment patterns and work hours mismatches in Europe. *Zeitschrift für Familienforschung (Journal of Family Research)*, 30(3), 269–292. doi:10.3224/zff.v30i3.03.

Steiber, N. & Kohli, M. (2017). You can't always get what you want: Actual and preferred ages of retirement in Europe. *Ageing & Society*, 37(2), 352–385. 10.1017/S0144686X15001130.

Stier, H. & Lewin-Epstein, N. (2003). Time to work: A comparative analysis of preferences for working hours. *Work Occup*, 30(3), 302–326.

Struffolino, E. & Zaccaria, D. (2020). Did you realize your preferences for early retirement? Insights on the agency-within-structure mechanism across welfare regimes. *Polis*, 351(4), 33. doi:10.1424/96439

Treas, J. & Widmer, E. D. (2000). Married women's employment over the life course: Attitudes in cross-national perspective. *Social Forces*, 78(4), 1409–1436.

Van Echtelt, P. E., Glebbeek, A. C. & Lindenberg, S. M. (2006). The new lumpiness of work: Explaining the mismatch between actual and preferred working hours. *Work, Employment and Society*, 20(3), 493–512.

Wielers, R., Münderlein, M. & Koster, F. (2014). Part-time work and work hour preferences. An international comparison, *European Sociological Review*, 30(1), 76–89.

Yerkes, M. A. & Jana, J. (2019). Creating capabilities: Childcare policies in comparative perspective. *Journal of European Social Policy*, 29(4), 529–544. doi:10.1177/0958928718808421

Yerkes, M. (2009). Part-time work in the Dutch welfare state: The ideal combination of work and care? *Policy & Politics*, 37(4), 535–552.

4 The Working Conditions of Older Workers in Comparative Perspective

Thierry Rossier, Nicky Le Feuvre, Jacques-Antoine Gauthier, and Boris Wernli

Introduction

The aim of this chapter is to understand the gender and health implications of extending working life policies and practices in countries characterised by contrasting gender regimes, pension systems and labour market structures (Ní Léime et al., 2020).[1] We begin by recognising the methodological and conceptual challenges associated with using survey data to study the working conditions of older men and women in the European context (Fagan and Burchell, 2002). Then by adopting an innovative research design, we attempt to avoid some of these biases, by using data from the sixth wave of the European Working Conditions Survey (EWCS) to identify and map the main factors that differentiate the working conditions of the 50+ age group across countries, without resorting to causal explanations. In order to achieve this objective, the chapter is structured in two parts.

Firstly, we use the OECD Employment Database[2] for 2015 and the Labour Force Survey (LFS)[3] to map the gendered employment patterns of the over 50s in a range of European countries, selected for their contrasting gender and welfare regimes. This analysis enables us to establish the varying contours of the population of "older workers" that is covered by the different waves of the EWCS.

Secondly, we use data from the sixth wave of the EWCS[4] to carry out Multiple Correspondence Analysis (MCA), aimed at identifying the factors that differentiate the employment experiences of older (50+) workers in the European context. Our largely descriptive MCA results enable us to identify two main *lines of differentiation* of the working conditions of this age group, represented by a horizontal and a vertical axis on a standard MCA *grid*. The most significant line of differentiation (represented by the horizontal axis of the MCA grid) is determined by the distribution of physically demanding working conditions and by the (in)ability to balance work and family life. A second, weaker, line of differentiation (represented by the vertical axis of the MCA grid) is determined by the distribution of (non-manual) working conditions, employment status (salaried versus self-employed) and working time patterns (full versus part-time).

DOI: 10.4324/9781003145325-4

In our conclusions, we stress the need to interpret the results of this MCA against the backdrop of gendered employment patterns across the life course (Hegewisch and Gornick, 2011; Worts et al., 2016) and in relation to country-specific welfare regimes and pension systems (Hofäcker et al., 2016).

The challenges of using comparative survey data to study working conditions

The first challenge relates to the "self-declaratory" nature of the data collected in the course of studies like the EWCS. This implies that individuals are likely to have varying levels of awareness about the nature of their working conditions, especially relative to those of other groups or occupations, and also to have different perceptions of the implications of their working conditions for their health and well-being. It is a well-documented fact that workers in countries and/or organisations that have implemented systematic health and safety regulations are more likely to recognise the potentially detrimental effect of certain working conditions on their health than their counterparts in countries with less well-developed regulations and controls (Fagan and Burchell, 2002).

Secondly, according to the level of horizontal and vertical segregation of the labour market, by gender and by age, older men and women are more or less likely to experience similar or contrasting working conditions, according to the societal context. Furthermore, they are more or less likely to consider particular aspects of their working conditions as "normal" or problematic, depending on the strength of gender stereotypes that prevail in their societal or organisational environment. Since these perceptions and expectations are likely to vary across national contexts, it is particularly difficult to draw firm conclusions about the prevalence of particular working conditions among particular groups of workers from this kind of survey data.

In third place, particularly where older workers are concerned, there is the risk of data on working conditions being misinterpreted, due to what has been termed a "healthy worker effect" (McMichael, 1976) on the size and composition of the older workforce in different national settings. In a nutshell, in countries where older workers who are experiencing health problems have the opportunity to leave the labour market, either through early retirement or through disability schemes, the share of older workers covered by surveys like the EWCS, which only collect data on those in employment, can be quite small. This selection bias is not easy to control for in an international survey. In some countries, it could be that, by definition, those older workers being surveyed represent a (more or less selective) sub-sample of all older citizens, restricted to those men and women who benefit from good health and whose working conditions are conducive to them maintaining their commitment to the labour market into old age. In other countries, where alternative routes out of the labour market are less readily available, the EWCS survey will cover a much larger share of the older population, and will probably include those workers with underlying health problems and/or with challenging working conditions, who simply don't have the same opportunities to withdraw from employment that are offered to their counterparts in another national contexts (Wahrendorf et al., 2017a, 2017b).

Finally, the gender composition of the EWCS survey population obviously depends to a large extent on the "gender regime" (Connell, 1987), "gender arrangements" (Pfau-Effinger, 1998) or "life-course regimes" (Möhring, 2016) that prevail in each national context, at a particular point in time. Thus, the EWCS survey may only cover a small share of the 50+ female adult population in countries where (married) women of this generation are likely to have left the labour market relatively early, on marriage or at the birth of a first child, never to return. In contrast, the survey could include almost all female members of a given cohort in countries where women's labour market participation rates are relatively high, irrespective of their conjugal arrangements and (grand-)parental responsibilities (Madero-Cabib and Fasang, 2016). Thus, a high percentage of Italian or Irish women declaring challenging physical working conditions at 50+ could actually mask the fact that the vast majority of older women in these two countries are no longer in employment beyond age 50, whereas the vast majority of their Czech or Swedish counterparts are still in employment well into their late-50s.

These methodological biases explain to a large extent why the successive EWCS surveys have always concluded that the 50+ age group are relatively protected from the most challenging working conditions (EUROFOUND, 2017). From a gender perspective, these conclusions are rather tautological, since they simply confirm that remaining in employment beyond the age of 50 is a socially selective practice in some European countries.

Framing extending working lives in comparative perspective

One of the main challenges associated with analysing the working conditions of older workers from a cross-national comparative perspective lies in the fact that the share of men and women still in the labour market as they age varies considerably from one country to another (OECD, 2009, 2019). Previous research has identified two main policy responses to population ageing: "employment exit" policies, which encourage the early retirement of older workers, and "employment maintenance" policies, which provide opportunities for extending working lives (Blossfeld et al., 2006). Conditions fostering the adoption of an "employment exit" logic are strong insider-outsider distinctions within highly regulated labour markets, whereas "employment maintenance" policies are more likely to be adopted in weakly regulated labour markets, characterised by high job and occupational mobility.

Furthermore, the sociodemographic characteristics of those remaining in employment until – or beyond – the legal retirement age also vary according to the societal context (Madero-Cabib et al., 2021). In some cases, those with higher levels of education and continuous employment careers are able to retire early on relatively comfortable pensions (Oesch, 2008). In this case, "older workers" appear as a socially disadvantaged group, whose members are unable to avail themselves of "employment exit" opportunities, usually due to insufficient pension rights accumulated over the adult life-course. In other county contexts, the category of "older workers" may be mostly composed of men and women who don't have any serious health issues and who enjoy relatively comfortable working conditions, making it possible for them to extend their working lives until full retirement age, without negative implications for their health or well-being (Riekhoff and Järnefelt, 2017). In this case, it is rather those individuals who are unable to maintain their link to the labour market until full retirement age that appear to be the most disadvantaged, since they run the highest risk of poverty and ill-health in later life (Jansen, 2018).

As outlined earlier, this cross-national variation in the socioeconomic profile of "older workers" makes it extremely difficult to interpret international survey data on the working conditions of older workers. However, the innovative data analysis techniques used in this chapter enable us to build on existing research that points to the differential impact of policies aimed at extending working lives on the health and well-being of different categories of older workers, in specific national contexts (Ní Léime and Ogg, 2019), but also in different employment sectors within a given national context (Wiss, 2015, 2020).

Mapping the employment patterns of older workers in comparative perspective

The difficulty in analysing the gendered distribution of working conditions and its influence on retirement decisions lies in the fact that, in most Western countries, a larger share of women than men are located out of the labour market at any point in their adult life course. The gendered nature of employment histories has been recognised for some time in relation to the child-rearing phase of the life course (Möhring, 2016), but less so in relation to the ageing workforce. In this chapter, we use data from the EWCS to map the working conditions of the over 50s in 30 different countries, but we also focus on a smaller range of countries (Czech Republic, Ireland, Italy, Sweden, Switzerland and the United Kingdom), characterised by contrasting welfare and gender regimes (Daly, 2020).

The notion of a "gender regime" (Connell, 1987), defined as the normative environment that shapes gendered aspirations, expectations and representations in a given historical and societal context, is useful for framing cross-national comparisons. It suggests that in different societal contexts, particular gender arrangements are preferred over others, and that people are actively encouraged to conform to "gender norms" (Widmer and Spini, 2017) through a variety of material and symbolic mechanisms (e.g. taxation systems, (un)availability of childcare facilities, shop opening hours, working time arrangements, cultural representations of motherhood) that tend to reinforce dominant value systems and stereotypes. Conformity to these arrangements is associated with a series of material and symbolic rewards. Aspirations for an alternative lifestyle may be difficult to enact or may come at great material, symbolic or emotional cost to the individuals concerned (Le Feuvre et al., 2015).

Previous research has acknowledged the diversity of these normative gender arrangements, which are usually defined with the help of typologies, each designed to highlight a particular aspect of the "gendering" process. Different authors have used a variety of concepts to demonstrate the forceful character of national-level "gender contracts" and "gender regimes" (Connell, 1987), "gender arrangements" (Pfau-Effinger, 1998) or "life-course regimes" (Möhring, 2016), which are usually characterised according to the importance and legitimacy given to women's labour market participation, particularly in the presence of young children and other care commitments. Western gender regimes typically range from an individualistic "dual earner/dual carer" model, promoted in some Nordic countries, to a couple-based "male breadwinner/female carer" model, characteristic of Western European countries with a historically strong manufacturing base (e.g. Germany, Austria, Switzerland). The Nordic gender regime is based on a universal, "adult worker" model of social integration, with limited reciprocal influence of the life chances of men and women, even when they live together and share parenthood. Here, individual autonomy is guaranteed by the widespread provision of publicly funded services to support individuals in managing the work-life interface, and with the explicit aim of reducing social inequalities. By contrast, the "male breadwinner/female carer" model of gender relations, based on highly differentiated social roles for men and women (Krüger and Levy, 2001), depends more on the (married) couple as a basic unit of social integration and implies a greater degree of interdependence and mutual influence of the life paths of those individuals who enter into intimate relationships, adopt common living arrangements and share parental responsibilities, in line with the notion of "linked lives" (Elder, 1998). Such is the case for the "modified male breadwinner" model (Crompton, 1999) that has emerged in some European countries, based on women's large-scale integration into employment on a part-time and/or discontinuous basis across the life course, leading to particular risks of vulnerability for women in later life (Daly, 2020). Fourth, the so-called Mediterranean or Southern European gender regime extends the perimeter of mutual dependence beyond the conjugal unit to impose reciprocal duties for care and subsistence within the extended family network, with only limited support from the State (Ferrera, 1996). In fifth place, the Eastern European countries that were under Soviet rule until the end of the 1980s are characterised by the combination of employment and care for women, but lack the kind of State support offered to families under the Nordic gender regime. Here, full-time, continuous employment remains the socially accepted norm for men and women alike and the work-family interface is managed through extended maternity leave and/or early retirement arrangements (Dudová and Pospíšilová, 2022). Finally, the so-called Liberal model of social protection, prevalent in the United States and the United Kingdom, combines the individualistic rationale of the Nordic model with an assurance-based provision of social services, thereby leading to greater diversity in the ability of individuals to reduce their dependence on their spouse and close family members for support and also to higher levels of social inequality (Daly, 2020).

These normative gender regimes have consequences for the conditions under which individuals experience "critical" moments in the life course such as the transition to retirement (Möhring and Weiland, 2021; Madero-Cabib and Fasang, 2016). Recent research has stressed that, within a given national context, different sectors or occupations may selectively integrate and adapt elements of these societal-level "gender regimes" into their recruitment, remuneration or promotion practices, thus creating internal variation in the normative expectations placed on male and female workers, at different stages in their life course (Le Feuvre et al., 2015).

A growing body of research has attempted to apply the "gender regime" framework to the analysis of the later stages of working life, the transition to retirement (Madero-Cabib et al., 2021) and the likely effects of policies aimed at extending the duration of working lives across a range of societal contexts (Ní Léime et al., 2020). This framework proves to be useful for explaining some of the variations observed in the OECD data concerning the employment patterns of older workers across countries. Thus, Table 4.1 shows that in OECD countries, just under half of all adults (47.6%) are still in employment up until the age of 64 years, while almost 25 per cent are still working beyond the age of 65 years. However, this pattern varies by country and by gender. For example, in Italy (57.7%) and Ireland (64.5%), less than two-thirds of women

Table 4.1 Employment rates, by sex and age groups (50+), 2015 (%)

Country	*Gender*	*50–54*	*55–59*	*60–64*	*65–69*	*Total*
Czech Republic	Men	90.5	84.2	47.8	13.8	**65.1**
	Women	87.2	72.8	22.0	8.1	**48.1**
	Total	88.9	78.4	34.3	10.7	**56.4**
Ireland	Men	78.6	72.4	56.1	25.2	**61.7**
	Women	64.5	55.9	35.5	13.7	**49.6**
	Total	71.5	64.1	45.8	19.4	**55.6**
Italy	Men	81.9	73.3	43.5	13.0	**52.2**
	Women	57.7	49.1	25.6	4.6	**34.7**
	Total	69.6	60.9	34.2	8.6	**43.1**
Sweden	Men	87.5	84.5	69.2	26.2	**68.8**
	Women	83.2	80.7	63.6	17.6	**64.4**
	Total	85.4	82.6	66.4	21.9	**66.6**
Switzerland	Men	90.7	85.3	66.3	27.1	**70.7**
	Women	81.0	76.1	49.6	16.3	**59.2**
	Total	86.0	80.8	57.9	21.2	**64.9**
United Kingdom	Men	85.6	77.2	58.5	25.9	**64.9**
	Women	78.1	68.8	40.2	16.6	**54.6**
	Total	81.8	73.0	49.1	21.1	**59.6**
OECD countries	*Men*	*83.2*	*76.0*	*56.4*	*31.4*	**64.3**
	Women	*67.3*	*59.6*	*39.4*	*19.1*	**48.0**
	Total	*75.1*	*67.6*	*47.6*	*24.9*	**55.9**

Source: OECD online database.

aged at ages 50–54 are in the labour market, compared to a female employment rate equal to or above 80 per cent in the other OECD countries. In the Czech Republic, there is a sharp drop in employment rates (from 78.4% to 34.3%) after the age of 60 and early labour market exit is particularly common for Czech women. This is similar to the Italian case, where the share of women in employment falls from almost 50 per cent at ages 55–60 to just 25 per cent at ages 60–64.

These patterns of labour market participation in later life stand in sharp contrast to the Nordic case, where, for example, 69.2 per cent of Swedish men and 63.6 per cent of their female counterparts are still in employment at ages 60–64 years. In the United Kingdom (49%) and Ireland (46%) a similar share of 60–64 years-olds are in employment, but the gender gap is much larger than in the Swedish case. This is also the case in Switzerland, where 58 per cent of 60 to 64-year-olds are in employment, but just under 50 per cent of Swiss women, as compared to two-thirds of Swiss men. In the 65–69 age group, Italy and the Czech Republic stand out as having very low employment rates (barely above 10%), about 21 per cent of 65 to 69-year olds are in employment elsewhere, with very similar employment patterns for older men and women across the remaining countries (approximately 25% of men and just over 15% of women).

If we turn now to an analysis of working-time patterns (Table 4.2), we observe contrasting rates of part-time work, by gender, but also across the 50+ age

Table 4.2 Share of part-time work, by sex and age groups (50+), 2015 (%)

Country	*Gender*	*50–54*	*55–59*	*60–64*	*65–69*	*Total*
Czech Republic	Men	1.3	1.7	6.1	–	2.5
	Women	4.0	5.2	21.4	–	7.4
	Total	2.6	3.4	11.2	–	4.7
Ireland	Men	10.1	12.2	16.0	23.8	12.3
	Women	41.8	40.4	49.7	66.6	35.4
	Total	25.2	25.1	30.2	39.4	23.3
Italy	Men	6.5	7.1	11.7	22.7	8.5
	Women	32.2	30.2	35.3	41.3	32.8
	Total	17.4	16.7	20.9	27.9	18.7
Sweden	Men	4.3	6.2	12.7	46.2	10.6
	Women	12.1	12.7	18.1	59.6	18.0
	Total	8.1	9.4	15.3	51.6	14.1
Switzerland	Men	6.0	9.6	16.0	60.8	10.9
	Women	49.1	50.4	57.8	84.3	45.0
	Total	25.8	28.8	34.3	70.4	26.8
United Kingdom	Men	6.6	10.2	19.8	43.3	11.9
	Women	33.1	38.0	52.1	73.5	37.7
	Total	19.5	23.6	33.5	55.4	24.0
OECD Countries	*Men*	*5.4*	*6.8*	*13.1*	*42.5*	*9.4*
	Women	*23.6*	*24.9*	*32.8*	*63.4*	*25.9*
	Total	*13.8*	*15.1*	*21.7*	*50.6*	*16.8*

Source: OECD online database. Part-time work=less than 30 hours per week in main job.

groups. In general, the rate of part-time employment is extremely low for men in all countries up until the age of 65 years. After this point, the situation changes somewhat. In Ireland and Italy, the proportion of men working part-time at ages 65–69 is double the rate in the 50–54 age group. In Switzerland, this rate is ten times higher for older (65+) male workers (60.8%) than for their younger counterparts (6.0% at ages 50–54). In Sweden and the United Kingdom, almost half (43%) of the men still working beyond the age of 65 are doing so on a part-time basis.

For women, the share of part-time employment also varies across countries and by age. Ireland and Switzerland are characterised by high levels of part-time work, even for women aged 50–54. These figures increase progressively across the age groups, to reach two-thirds of women aged 65 and over in Ireland and almost 85 per cent of the same age group in Switzerland. In contrast, Sweden and the Czech Republic have a very low rate of female part-time employment across younger age groups, but this rate increases dramatically for Swedish women working beyond the age of 65 years, to almost 60 per cent part-time, whereas there are almost no women from this age group still in employment in the Czech context. In Italy, about a third of working women are in part-time jobs across all the older age groups and there is only a very slight increase in this rate (to 41.3%) beyond the age of 65 years. In the United Kingdom, rates of part-time work for women are similar to those for Italy up until age 60, when they increase in two stages: up to 52.1 per cent of the 60–64 years-olds, and up to 73.5 per cent for the over 65s.

In all countries, except the Czech Republic, education levels influence the rate of full-time employment for older women (Table 4.3). In general, there is a

Table 4.3 Share of full-time (vs part-time) workers at age 50+, by sex and education, 2015 (%)

Country	*Gender*	*Primary & Secondary*[5]	*Higher Education*
Czech Republic	Men	93.8	89.2
	Women	86.1	87.0
Ireland	Men	83.8	89.9
	Women	49.8	67.0
Italy	Men	91.6	90.6
	Women	70.2	83.9
Sweden	Men	83.6	80.7
	Women	55.5	69.2
Switzerland	Men	78.8	74.1
	Women	23.9	31.0
United Kingdom	Men	81.7	79.9
	Women	48.4	59.1
Total 30 countries (EU without Germany + Norway, Iceland & Switzerland)	*Men*	*88.0*	*87.4*
	Women	*67.5*	*76.0*

Source: European Union Labour Force Survey 2015.

+10 per cent difference in the proportion of women with higher education credentials working full-time, as compared to their less well-qualified compatriots. This gap reaches almost 17 per cent in Ireland. For men, education has a much more limited influence on working time patterns, with better-qualified men being slightly more likely to work part-time than their less well-qualified counterparts, except in Ireland, where the correlation is reversed, and similar to the pattern for women.

Concerning unemployment rates (Table 4.4), we observe that older workers of both sexes are less likely to be unemployed than workers at younger ages. However, the risk of unemployment is relatively high for older workers in Ireland and Italy, compared to those in the other countries studied here. Unemployment rates are particularly low for the over-65-year olds of both sexes, suggesting that retirement acts as an effective alternative to employment for this age group in most countries. In the Czech Republic, men and women aged 55–59 are the most vulnerable to unemployment and this is also the case for men in Switzerland.

Having mapped the employment patterns of older workers in these contrasting national contexts, we now turn our attention to the working conditions of older workers, in order to establish the main lines of differentiation that appear from the MCA carried out on data from the 2015 sixth wave of the

Table 4.4 Unemployment rate, by sex and age group (50+), 2015 (%)

Country	*Gender*	*50–54*	*55–59*	*60–64*	*65–69*	*All ages*
Czech Republic	Men	3.6	4.5	3.3	1.2	**4.2**
	Women	4.9	5.8	2.0	1.1	**6.1**
	Total	4.2	5.1	2.8	1.2	**5.0**
Ireland	Men	9.1	8.5	8.5	1.9	**10.9**
	Women	8.4	7.2	7.6	4.1	**9.6**
	Total	8.8	7.9	8.2	2.7	**10.3**
Italy	Men	7.5	6.7	5.8	2.3	**11.3**
	Women	7.1	4.8	3.1	3.8	**12.7**
	Total	7.3	5.9	4.8	2.7	**11.9**
Sweden	Men	5.1	5.5	6.7	2.3	**7.5**
	Women	4.4	4.4	4.9	3.1	**7.2**
	Total	4.8	5.0	5.8	2.6	**7.4**
Switzerland	Men	3.7	4.8	3.8	2.1	**4.7**
	Women	4.1	3.7	3.2	2.5	**4.9**
	Total	3.9	4.3	3.6	2.3	**4.8**
United Kingdom	Men	3.8	3.9	3.4	2.3	**5.7**
	Women	3.2	3.3	2.9	2.1	**5.3**
	Total	3.5	3.6	3.2	2.2	**5.5**
OECD countries	Men	5.2	5.4	5.2	3.3	**6.7**
	Women	4.9	4.6	4.0	2.6	**6.9**
	Total	5.1	5.1	4.7	3.0	**6.8**

Source: OECD online database.

EWCS.[6] In the following section of the chapter, we focus on individuals aged 50 or more (n = 34,649 individuals), from 30 different European countries.

Methodology: MCA techniques and data

In this section, we use MCA to model differences in the working conditions of older workers and to identify the structural and individual characteristics that are associated with different types of working conditions. MCA is a descriptive statistical technique that is particularly useful for modelling inequalities. It enables us to reduce the complexity of the available data by revealing the most significant forms of differentiation between individuals or variables in relation to a particular topic (Lebaron, Castro and Andrés, 2018). Thus, MCA is a useful method for identifying the influence of various individual characteristics (gender, age, ethnicity, educational credentials, social class, etc.) on the distribution of respondents along the principle *lines of differentiation* previously identified.

The MCA technique produces a geometric representation of multiple cross-tabulations between a set of so-called *active* variables, which are those that contribute to the most significant lines of differentiation that form an MCA *grid*. The analysis begins by calculating Chi-square distances between different variables in order to identify the strongest oppositions. This calculation results in the first *axis* of the MCA grid. The second (and successive) axes indicate weaker forms of differentiation. Each axis contributes to constructing a multi-dimensional grid, where each variable and survey respondent can then be located. The closer individuals are located to each other on the grid, the more characteristics they have in common. Conversely, the closer variables are located to each other on the grid, the larger the group of respondents who share these characteristics.

The *contribution* of a given variable indicates its importance for the construction of the axis. Variables that have an above-average influence on the construction of an axis are usually emphasised in the interpretation of the resulting grid.[7] Once the main axes of the grid have been calculated, *supplementary* variables that do not contribute directly to constructing the axis can be projected onto the grid. Within the resulting *proximity clouds*, a distance between coordinates equal to or above 0.5 is usually considered as noteworthy, and a distance of 1.0 as significant (although not necessarily in the statistical sense of the term). It is standard practice in MCA to retain the axes that account for about 80 per cent of the rates of variance (Hjellbrekke, 2018; Le Roux & Rouanet, 2010)[8] and the variables we have included in this study account for 78.4 per cent of the inertia.

Using data from the 2015 EWCS, we explored a number of alternatives before selecting 34 *active variables* corresponding to working conditions, declared satisfaction at work, as well as employment status and working time patterns.[9] As *supplementary variables* (see Appendix 4.4), we use the country of residence, education, age group, occupation (using the ISCO 1-digit classification) and income level (according to income deciles in the country of residence).[10]

Our analysis reveals two main *axes of differentiation* that are presented and illustrated below. A first (horizontal) axis accounts for 58.3 per cent of the variance and a second (vertical) axis accounts for 20.1 per cent of this variance. This means that the first axis has three times the weight of the second in the formation of the grid and is therefore twice as important in explaining the distribution of respondents and variables within the grid.

The first (horizontal) axis of differentiation is based on the distribution of physical working conditions and satisfaction with the work-life interface and the second (vertical) axis is based on the distribution of non-manual working conditions, employment status (salaried/self-employed), working time patterns and support networks. This graphic representation of the distribution of working conditions according to a series of variables obviously needs to be interpreted in the light of the gendered employment patterns of older workers identified in the OECD and LFS data presented earlier.

The main differentiating factors: The distribution of (physically) demanding working conditions and the (in)ability to articulate work and family life

The horizontal axis enables us to observe the distribution of the survey population according to the frequency with which they declare experiencing a certain number of working conditions and the effects these have on their health and general well-being. The following 14 variables make an above-average contribution (2.9% or more)[11] to the definition of this horizontal axis (Figure 4.1)[12]: being subjected to painful or tiring positions (8.0%), high (7.0%) or low (5.8%) temperatures, vibrations (5.6%), noise (6.3%), stress (3.9%), repetitive movements (2.9%), carrying heavy loads (7.3%), effects of work on health (8.0%), ability to do household chores after work (6.7%), support and encouragement of immediate superior (3.1%), ability to do the current job until the age of 60[13] (3.2%), level of satisfaction with working conditions (5.0%) and subjective evaluation of work-life balance (4.0%). In addition, 31 categories of variables make an above-average contribution (=1.1% or more)[14] to this horizontal axis.

On the left-hand side of this horizontal axis, we find respondents who stated that they are **never** subjected to the following working conditions: tiring positions (3.6%),[15] carrying heavy loads (2.3%), high (1.7%) or low (1.3%) temperatures, repetitive movements (1.8%), noise (1.7%), stress (1.3%) and vibrations (1.1%). In addition, we find respondents who declare that they are **never** too tired after work to do their household chores (2.5%) and who believe their work doesn't negatively affect their health (1.8%).

On the right-hand side of this horizontal axis, we find respondents who declare that they are **sometimes** or **always** subjected to the following working conditions: high (5.3%) or low (4.5%) temperatures, carrying heavy loads (5.0%), vibrations (4.5%), tiring positions (4.4%), noise (4.6%), stress (2.6%), emotionally disturbing situations with clients (1.5%), repetitive movements

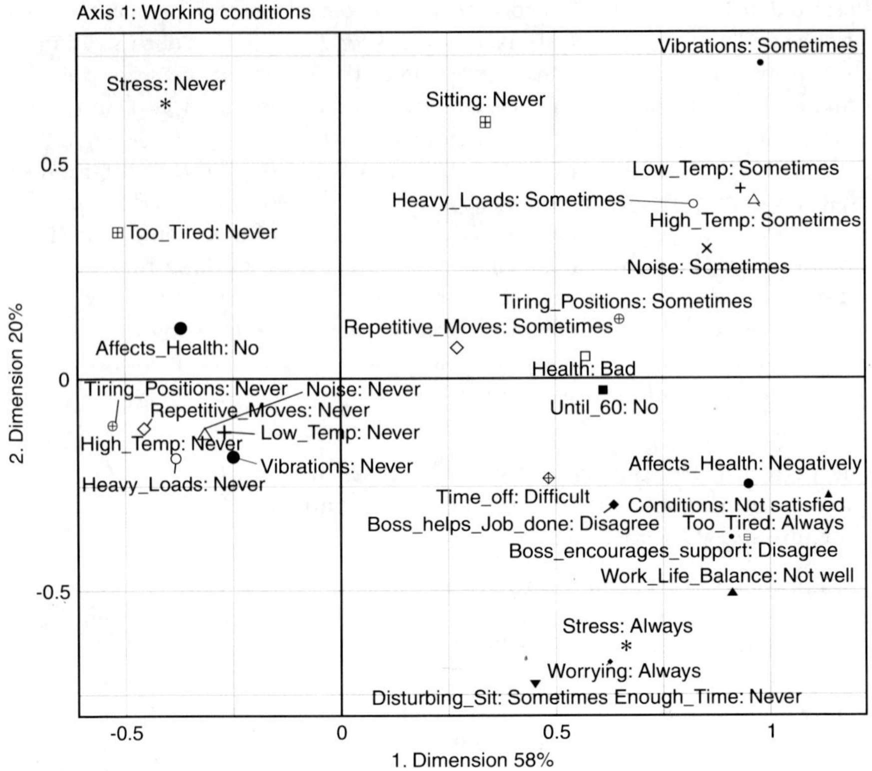

Figure 4.1 Distribution of variables with an above average contribution to the definition of the first (horizontal) axis of differentiation.

(1.1%); but also that their work **never** involves sitting (1.1%). Unsurprisingly, this side of the axis is also associated with respondents who declare that their work has a negative effect on their health (5.7%) and think that their health is bad in general (1.8%), who are **always** too tired after work to do their household chores (4.2%), who are not satisfied with their working conditions (4.3%), who find it difficult to negotiate time off work to deal with personal matters (1.8%), who feel that their work isn't compatible with their family or social commitments (3.3%), who are always worrying about their work, even when they are at home (1.4%) and who feel unable to do their current job until the age of 60 (2.2%). More generally, they do not feel they encounter the support of their immediate superior (2%), particularly in getting the job done (1.4%) and actually do not think that they have enough time to get the job done (1.3%).

This horizontal axis therefore summarises the opposition between individuals who experience challenging physical working conditions, and who find it difficult to reconcile their work with other aspects of their lives, as opposed to those who experience few physically demanding tasks at work, and who are able to achieve a satisfactory work-life balance.

In Figure 4.2, we plot the demographic characteristics of the EWCS respondents onto the first axis of our MCA grid. In order to determine the influence of (supplementary) structural variables on the distribution of respondents along this horizontal axis, we calculated the distances associated with the variables age, sex by level of education, occupation and income deciles (Figure 4.2) and country of residence (Figure 4.3).[16]

First, we observe that men with lower levels of education are more likely to experience at least some of the physically challenging working conditions listed above, whereas more educated men and all categories of women are less likely to be subjected to such conditions. Quite logically, we therefore find an opposition between clerical support workers, professionals, technicians and associate professionals and managers on the left-hand side of the grid, and craft and related trades workers, skilled agricultural, forestry and fishery workers, plant and machine operators, and, to a lesser extent, other low-skilled blue-collar occupations, on the right-hand side of the grid.

We see that neither age category nor income levels produce notable distances between the variables that contribute to the definition of this horizontal axis.

When we consider the influence of the country of origin of the respondents on their distribution along this horizontal axis, we observe a polarisation between the Nordic and some continental countries (Denmark, Norway and Sweden, along with the Netherlands, Ireland, Italy, Switzerland and the United Kingdom, for example), where the older respondents are less likely to declare that they experience these difficult manual working conditions and, on the other hand, Southern European countries, such as Croatia, Greece, France, Spain and Romania, where older (50+) workers are more likely to experience these challenging working conditions. Thus, less educated men working in certain types of manual occupations and residing in a particular range of countries are more likely to be confronted with a range of physically demanding working conditions, while finding it difficult to reconcile their work and other aspects of their lives. These results obviously have to be interpreted in the light of the gendered employment patterns outlined earlier and with insights from the "gender & welfare regimes" literature in mind (Daly, 2020).

The secondary differentiating factors: The distribution of non-manual working conditions, employment status and working time patterns

The following 11 variables make an above-average contribution (2.9% or more) to the definition of the vertical axis (Figure 4.2): working time arrangements (3.1%), working with computers (13.1%), exposition to vibrations (4.6%), level of stress at work (8.9%), emotionally disturbing situations at work (8.4%), working sitting down (8.8%), angry customers (8.2%), dealing with people outside the workplace (7.6%), too tired after work to do household jobs (3.0%), worrying about work when not working (6.6%) and to have enough time to get the job done (1.6%).

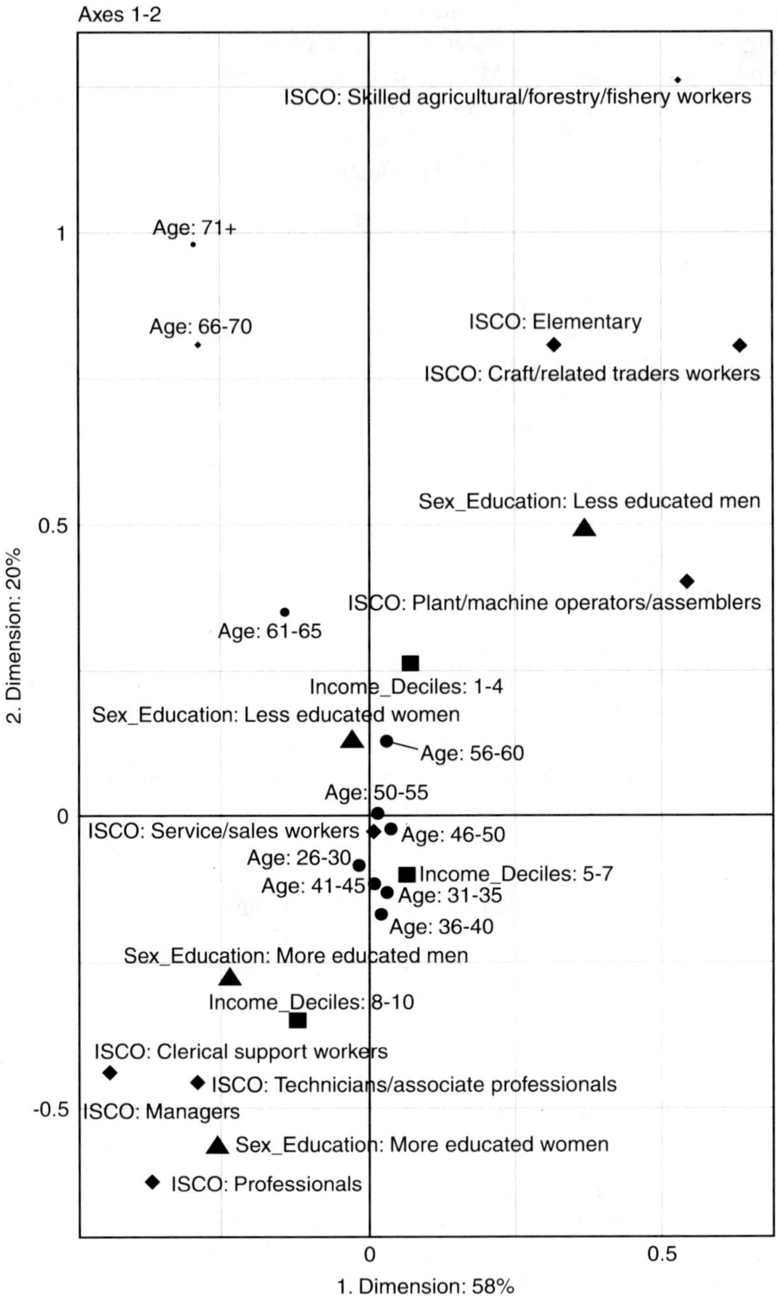

Figure 4.2 Distribution of age, gender, education, occupation and income variables along the horizontal and vertical axes of the MCA grid.

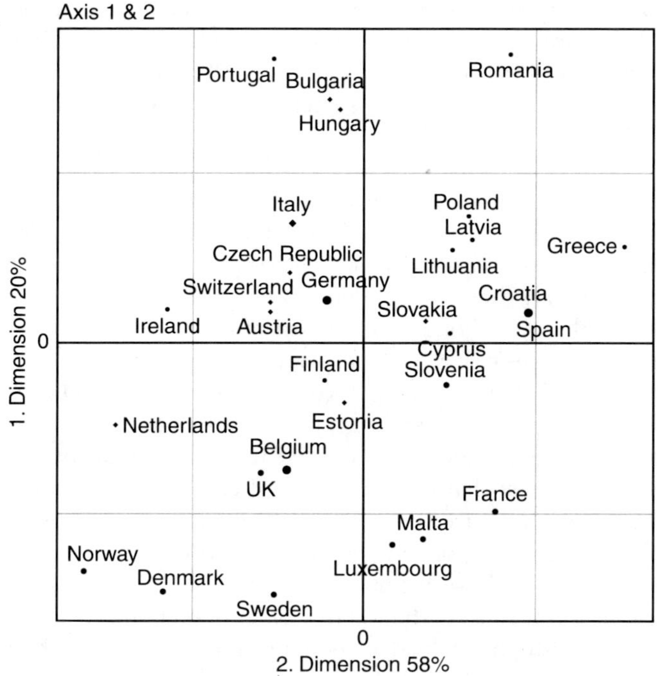

Figure 4.3 Distribution of country of residence across the horizontal and vertical axes of the MCA grid.

Twenty-seven categories of variables make an above-average contribution (=1.1% or more) to this vertical axis.

At the lower extreme of the vertical axis, we find respondents who declare that their working time arrangements are flexible within limits (1.7%). These are respondents who declare that they are **always** stressed (3.5%) and that they are sometimes (1.5%) or always (2.4%) worrying about work when they are at home, that they sometimes feel under-qualified for the job (1.6%) and that they never have enough time to get the job done (1.6%). These respondents declare **sometimes** using computers (5.8%) and working sitting down (3.7%). In the absence of physically demanding conditions, they nevertheless have to deal with: emotionally disturbing situations (5.7%), angry customers (5.3%) and people outside the workplace (2.6%). Overall, they declare an absence of work-life balance (1.5%).

On the upper end of this vertical axis, we find an over representation of self-employed respondents (1.5%), with the ability to determine their own working time arrangements (1.4%) and who actually work on a very short part-time basis (i.e. 1–20 hours per week) (1.4%). These are respondents who declare **never** having to deal with angry customers or clients (2.9%), emotionally disturbing situations (2.7%) or people outside the workplace (5.0%). Here we find very low levels of stress (4.9%), individuals who are never too tired after work to do household jobs (1.6%) and who never worry about work outside of work (2.7%), on the part of respondents who **never** use computers (7.3%) or work sitting down (5.1%). Their working activities involve **sometimes** carrying heavy loads (1.8%), exposition to higher (1.4%) or lower (1.5%) temperatures and vibrations (3.7%).

The vertical axis thus plots an opposition between, on the lower part of the grid, full-time, non-manual employees in physically comfortable, but emotionally demanding jobs that are nevertheless carried out in quite supportive employment contexts, on the one hand, and those respondents in part-time, self-employed positions with no stress at all, located on the upper part of the grid.

All the supplementary variables that we selected have an impact on this vertical axis (Figures 4.2 and 4.3). Firstly, the two poles of the axis are associated with different age groups. The top part of the axis is associated with oldest age groups (61+), while the lower parts of the grid are associated with pre-retirement age groups. This would seem to suggest that working on a self-employed, short part-time basis, in jobs that are relatively stress-free, is a condition for the satisfactory extension of the working lives of respondents who are subject to the types of challenges associated most frequently with manual occupations.

Previous results from the EWCS survey showed that older workers are generally less likely to be confronted with physically demanding working conditions than their younger counterparts (EUROFOUND, 2017). In the light of the LFS and OECD data presented previously, our results would also seem to suggest that those older workers who were confronted with the most physically challenging working conditions in their later years are likely to have left the labour market (via early retirement or disability routes) before reaching full retirement age. In other words, the EWCS survey reflects a "healthy worker effect" that is well-documented in research on the transition to retirement (McMichael, 1976). In contrast, working full-time with relatively limited possibilities to determine one's own working time patterns appears to be possible for older workers in non-manual jobs, on the condition that support is available from bosses and/or colleagues (Figure 4.4).

Secondly, higher levels of education are located at the lower pole of the axis, whereas primary and secondary education levels are more prevalent at the upper end of the vertical axis. More precisely, well-qualified women are located at the bottom of this vertical axis, where working conditions are difficult, while men with secondary-level qualifications are located at the top of the graph, associated with less challenging working conditions. Unsurprisingly, this is reflected in the distribution of occupations and income deciles, with people working in relatively well-paid non-manual jobs as managers, professionals, technicians and associate professionals or clerical support staff clustered towards the lower end of the axis, whereas low-paid skilled agricultural, forestry and fishery workers, as well as craft and related trade workers, elementary occupations and, to a lesser extent, plant and machine operators, are positioned in the upper level of the graph.

Figure 4.4 Distribution of variables with an above average contribution to the definition of the second (vertical) axis of differentiation.

Finally, the distribution of countries along this vertical axis is slightly different to that observed in the previous case. The Nordic and some of the more affluent European countries (Denmark, Sweden, Norway, France, Luxembourg) are located towards the lower pole of the axis. In contrast, Portugal, Romania, Bulgaria and Hungary are located in the upper half of the axis. This distribution of countries would seem to reflect both the overall structure of the labour market (e.g. share of tertiary *versus* primary or secondary sector jobs), as well as the gender composition and working time patterns of the older workforce.[17]

Conclusions

In the light of the contrasting employment patterns of older male and female workers outlined in the first part of the chapter, our MCA analysis confirms that the working conditions of older workers vary according to their personal characteristics (gender, education, employment status) and their societal context. The Nordic countries stand out as contexts where the share of older workers confronted with physically challenging working conditions is relatively low, but also as countries where the share of well-qualified older workers in stressful and emotionally demanding jobs is particularly high. However, these are also the countries where the proportion of men and women working (massively full-time) in the 60–64 age group is highest (over 65%, as compared to less than 25% in the Czech Republic and Italy, for example). The relatively high employment rates of older men and women in the Nordic countries would seem to suggest that the EWCS data is relatively representative of the whole of the older population in these countries. In this context, older workers are effectively protected against the most physically demanding working conditions, although they do have to deal with the emotionally challenging conditions associated with many (highly feminised) non-manual occupations. They appear to be able to deal with these working conditions on a full-time basis up until relatively advanced ages, without any negative consequences for their self-defined health or ability to reconcile work and other life spheres. The key to this extended working life pattern for men and women alike would seem to reside in a highly supportive working environment. One could hypothesise that recent pension and other policy reforms in favour of extending working lives in the Nordic context (Krekula, 2020) have been accompanied with organisational adaptations to accommodate the needs of an ageing workforce.

In the other countries studied here, it would appear that physically or emotionally challenging working conditions are more frequently associated with early labour market exit strategies (Madero-Cabib et al., 2021). In the Czech Republic, Italy and Ireland, the sharp decrease in employment rates for men and women aged 60+ would seem to suggest that the relatively low levels of challenging physical or emotional working conditions declared in the EWCS actually reflect the "healthy worker effect" described in the first section of this chapter (McMichael, 1976). In this case, individuals subject to unfavourable working conditions are more likely to opt for labour market exit strategies than those who are not subject to such challenges (Wahrendorf et al., 2017a). One could hypothesise that older workers in this group of countries would run the highest risk of negative health implications were the opportunities for early labour market exit to be reduced or removed.

Switzerland and United Kingdom would seem to present intermediary cases. In these countries, the employment rates of men and women at 60+ years are relatively high. The proportion of older workers declaring difficult physical working conditions is relatively low in both countries, although the share of those facing stressful and emotionally challenging full-time jobs is significantly higher in the United Kingdom than in Switzerland. In this case, it would seem that reduced working hours provide older women with an alternative to early labour market exit. In these countries, working part-time into older age represents something of a continuation of female employment patterns at younger ages. This may represent a strategy to protect their health and enable them achieve a better level of work-life balance in later life. However, the shift to part-time jobs is clearly less of an option for men in these countries, at least before they reach the age of 65. It is probably in these two countries (and also in Ireland) that we could expect the health and work-life balance implications of extending working lives to be the most gender differentiated (Ní Léime and Ogg, 2019).

To sum up, although the largely descriptive MCA techniques used here to map out the working conditions of older (50+) workers in the European context are devoid of statistical inference, we believe that they nevertheless provide a useful indication of the main sources of inequality between older workers in different national and occupational contexts. In this chapter, we have insisted on the potential biases inherent in the EWCS data, which fail to account for the share of (older) workers actually subject to any type of working conditions in a given societal context. This bias is particularly regrettable for understanding the implications of policies aimed at extending working lives for the health and well-being of older women in different national contexts. However, we have demonstrated that, when they are used in conjunction with LFS data, information about the distribution of (un)favourable working conditions, across countries and among different groups of older workers, can help us to identify the most discriminating aspects of working conditions, which can then be the focus of more in-depth, qualitative analysis, such as the occupational case studies we have carried out under the DAISIE project (Airey et al., 2020; Le Feuvre and Rougier, 2022; Ní Léime and O'Neill, 2021).

Notes

1 The chapter is based on the Dynamics of Accumulated Inequalities for Seniors in Employment (DAISIE) project that was carried out under the NORFACE – DIAL programme (project n° 462.16.110), with additional support from the LIVES Centre at the University of Lausanne. The authors thank the Swiss National Science Foundation and the other NORFACE funding institutions for their support.
2 http://www.oecd.org/employment/onlineoecdemploymentdatabase.htm
3 https://ec.europa.eu/eurostat/web/microdata/european-union-labour-force-survey (n° = 1,731,416 individuals, from 30 countries).
4 https://www.eurofound.europa.eu/surveys/european-working-conditions-surveys (n° = 34,649 individuals, from 30 countries).
5 The differences between primary and secondary educated respondents are marginal in the countries selected here.
6 https://www.eurofound.europa.eu/surveys/european-working-conditions-surveys
7 Several indicators of the inertia (*i.e.* the variance explained by an axis) are used to measure the importance of a given axis. Since these rates (e.g. eigenvalue, percentage variance, etc.) are usually low, they are recalculated as *modified rates* in order to better appreciate the importance of the axes. Here, we have adopted the solution proposed by Le Roux & Rouanet (2010), which neutralises the effects of missing values in the formation of an axis by considering them as *passive*.
8 We used the soc.ca package of the R software, developed by Anton Grau Larsen, with contributions from Christoph Ellersgaard and Stefan Andrade: https://cran.r-project.org/web/packages/soc.ca/soc.ca.pdf

9 A complete list of the variables retained here and their contributions to the grid formation can be found in the Appendices. As advised by MCA experts (see Lunding et al., 2021), we opted for a large number of variables, so that the *proximity clouds* are not distorted by a so-called horseshoe effect (Hjellbrekke, 2018). We are conscious that a number of variables referring to comparable working conditions could have been combined (see Soares Costa et al., 2013) in order to improve the visibility of the MCA grid. However, the variables we selected for their contribution to the axis were not easily convertible into scales, and were thus not conducive to Principal Component Analysis (PCA). The circular shape of our clouds confirms the pertinence of our decision not to combine variables at this stage of the analysis.

10 In the early stages of this study, we also looked at the employment status of the partner (full or part-time, not working, no partner) and the influence of having (or not) a supervisory role at work. These variables did not contribute to defining the axes of the MCA grid, and so we decided not to retain them for further analysis. We also tested the sex and education variables separately, but found that the weight of these variables was more important when they were combined (e.g. men with primary or secondary level educational credentials, women with higher education), so this is the solution adopted here.

11 Calculated as follows: 100 divided by the number of variables retained (34) = an average of 2.9%.

12 The figure in brackets refers to the relative contribution of the variable to the structure of the axis.

13 Or for five more years for respondents aged over 55 years.

14 Calculated as follows: 100 divided by the number of responses (92) = an average of 1.1%.

15 In this case, the figure in brackets refers to the relative contribution of a variable to the structure of the axis.

16 The coordinates of the supplementary variables (and the distances between them) can be found in the Appendices.

17 Due to the large number of respondents (34,469), we didn't have the computer power required to perform cluster analysis on our MCA results, although we recognise that this could have produced some interesting results.

References

Airey, L. & Jandrić, J. (2020). United Kingdom. In Ní Léime, A., Ogg, J., Rašticov, M., Street, D., Krekula, C., Bediova, M., & Madero-Cabib, I. (eds.), *Extending Working Life Policies: International Gender and Health Perspectives*, London: Springer, 469–479.

Arpino, B. (Ed.) (2021). *Care, retirement & wellbeing of older people across different welfare regimes*. Florence: N-IUSSP e-book. https://www.niussp.org/ebooks/6989/

Blossfeld, H. P., Buchholz, S. & Hofäcker, D. (eds.) (2006). *Globalization, uncertainty and late careers in society*. London: Routledge.

Connell, R. W. (1987). *Gender and power: Society, the person and sexual politics*. Stanford, CA: Stanford University Press.

Crompton, R. (Ed.) (1999). *Restructuring gender relations and employment: The decline of the male breadwinner*. Oxford: Oxford University Press.

Daly, M. (2020). *Gender inequality and welfare states in Europe*. Cheltenham: Edward Elgar.

Dudová, R. & Pospíšilová, K. (2022). Why women retire earlier: What is behind women's earlier labour market exit in the Czech Republic. *Czech Sociological Review* (in press).

Elder, G. H. (1998). The life course as developmental theory. *Child Development*, 69(1), 1–12. 10.2307/1132065

EUROFOUND (2017). *Working conditions of workers of different ages*, European working conditions survey 2015. Dublin: European Foundation for the Improvement of Working & Living Conditions. https://www.eurofound.europa.eu/surveys/european-working-conditions-surveys

Eurostat Labour Force Survey (EU LFS) (2015). https://ec.europa.eu/eurostat/web/microdata/european-union-labour-force-survey

Fagan, C. & Burchell, B. (2002). *Gender, jobs and working conditions in the European Union*. Dublin: European Foundation for the Improvement of Living and Working Conditions. http://www.eurofound.ie/publications/files/EF0249EN.pdf

Fasang, A. E. (2010). Retirement: Institutional pathways and individual trajectories in Britain and Germany. *Sociological Research Online*, 15, 1–16. 10.5153/sro.2110

Ferrera, M. (1996). The "Southern Model" of welfare in Social Europe. *Journal of European Social Policy*, 6, 17–37. 10.1177/095892879600600102

Hegewisch, A. & Gornick, Janet C. (2011). The impact of work-family policies on women's employment: A review of research from OECD countries. *Community, Work & Family*, 14, 119–138.

Hjellbrekke, J. (2018). *Multiple correspondence analysis for the social sciences*. Oxford: Routledge.

Hofäcker, D., Hess, M. & König, S. (2016). *Delaying retirement: Progress and challenges of active aging in Europe, the United States and Japan*. London: Palgrave Macmillan.

Jansen, A. (2018). Work-retirement cultures: A further piece of the puzzle to explain differences in the labour market participation of older people in Europe? *Ageing & Society*, 38, 1527–1555. doi:10.1017/S0144686X17000125

Krekula, C. (2020). *European extended working life policies: On pension systems, public finances and biopolitical disciplining*. Karlstad, Sweden: Karlstad University, NORFACE DIAL Working Paper 13/2020.

Krüger, H. & Levy, R. (2001). Linking life courses, work, and the family: Theorizing a not so visible nexus between women and men. *Canadian Journal of Sociology/Cahiers canadiens de sociologie*, 26(2). 10.2307/3341676

Le Feuvre, N., Kuehni, M., Rosende, M. & Schoeni, C. (2015). Gendered variations in the experience of ageing at work in Switzerland. *Equality, Diversity, Inclusion: An International Journal*, 34(2), 168–181. 10.1108/EDI-03-2014-0017

Le Feuvre, N., Davoine, E. & Cangía, F. (2022). When mobility meets gender in the transnational life course, In Spini, D. & Widmer, E. (Eds.) *Withstanding Vulnerability throughout Adult Life. Dynamics of Stressors, Resources, and Reserves*, Basingstoke: Palgrave Macmillan (in press).

Le Feuvre, N. & Rougier, N. (2022). Extending working life policies in the Swiss finance sector: When seeing is not necessarily believing. *Retraite & société*, special issue Careers, Work & End-of-Career Trajectories (in press).

Le Roux, B. & Rouanet, H. (2010). *Multiple correspondence analysis*. London: SAGE.

Lebaron, F., Castro, T. & Andrés F. (2018). Some contributions from Geometry to linear models' construction in Social Sciences. *Bulletin of Sociological Methodology*, 140, 90–109.

Levy, R. & Widmer, E. D. (Eds.) (2013). *Gendered life courses between standardization and individualization: A European approach applied to Switzerland*. Zürich: Verlag.

Lunding, J. A., Ellersgaard, C. H. & Larsen, A. G. (2021). The established and the delegated: The division of labour of domination among effective agents on the field of power in Denmark. *Sociology*, 55(1), 110–128.

Madero-Cabib, I., & Fasang, A. E. (2016). Gendered work-family life courses and financial well-being in retirement. *Advances in Life Course Research*, 27, 43–60. 10.1016/j.alcr.2015.11.003

Madero-Cabib, I., Corna, L. & Baumann, I. (2020). Aging in different welfare contexts: A comparative perspective on later-life employment and health. *The Journals of Gerontology: Series B*, 75(7), 1515–1526. 10.1093/geronb/gbz037

Madero-Cabib, I., Le Feuvre, N., & König, S. (2021). Gendered retirement pathways across life-course regimes. *Ageing and Society*. 10.1017/S0144686X21001781

McMichael A. J. (1976). Standardized mortality ratios and the "healthy worker effect": Scratching beneath the surface. *Journal of Occupational Medicine*, 18, 165–168.

Möhring, K. (2016). Life course regimes in Europe: Individual employment histories in comparative and historical perspective. *Journal of European Social Policy*, 26, 124–139.

Möhring, K. (2018). Is there a motherhood penalty in retirement income in Europe? The role of life-course and institutional characteristics. *Ageing & Society*, 38, 2560–2589.

Möhring, K. & Weiland, P. (2021). Couples' life courses and women's income in later life: A multichannel sequence analysis of linked lives in Germany. *European Sociological Review*. 10.1093/esr/jcab048

Ní Léime, Á. & O'Neill, M. (2021). The impact of the COVID-19 pandemic on the working lives and retirement timing of older nurses in Ireland. *International Journal of Environmental Research and Public Health*, 17(18), 1–18. 10.3390/ijerph181910060

Ní Léime, Á., Ogg, J., Street, D., Rasticova, M., Krekula, C., Cabib, I. M. & Bediova, M. (eds.) (2020). *Extended Working Life: International Gender and Health Perspectives*. Cham: Springer. https://link.springer.com/content/pdf/10.1007%2F978-3-030-40985-2.pdf

Ní Léime, Á. & Ogg, J. (2019). Gendered impacts of extended working life on the health and economic well-being of older workers. *Ageing and Society*, 39(10), 2163–2169. doi.10.1017/SO144686X18001800. https://www.cambridge.org/core/journals/ageing-and-society/issue/1BFA667C43504593059EBEF300EC5D19

Ní Léime, Á., Street, D., Vickerstaff, S., Krekula, C. & Loretto, W. (Eds.) (2017). *Gender, ageing and extended working life: Cross-national perspectives*. Bristol: Policy Press.

OECD online Employment Database. http://www.oecd.org/employment/online oecdemploymentdatabase.htm

OECD (2009). *Pensions at a glance*. Paris: OECD Publishing.

OECD (2010). Labour Market Statistics in 2010. https://stats.oecd.org/. [Accessed 25 November2021].

OECD (2011). *Pensions at a glance*. Paris: OECD Publishing. 10.1787/19991363.

OECD (2017). *Pensions at a glance*. Paris: OECD Publishing. 10.1787/pension_glance-2017-en

OECD (2018). *Good jobs for all in a changing world of work: The OECD jobs strategy*. Paris: OECD Publishing. 10.1787/9789264308817-en

OECD (2019). *Working better with age, ageing and employment policies*. Paris: OECD. 10.1787/c4d4f66a-en

Oesch, D. (2008). Stratifying welfare states: Class differences in pension coverage in Britain, Germany, Sweden and Switzerland. *Swiss Journal of Sociology*, 34(3), 533–554.

Pfau-Effinger, B. (1998). Gender cultures and the gender arrangement. A theoretical framework for cross-national gender research. *Innovation: The European Journal of Social Science Research*, 11, 147–166. 10.1080/13511610.1998.9968559

Radl, Jonas (2013). Labor market exit and social stratification in Western Europe: The effects of social class and gender on the timing of retirement. *European Sociological Review*, 29, 654–668.

R Core Team (2019). *R: A language and environment for statistical computing*. Vienna: R Foundation for Statistical Computing.

Riekhoff A. J. & Järnefelt N. (2017). Gender differences in retirement in a welfare state with high female labour market participation and competing exit pathways. *European Sociological Review*, 33, 791–807.

Soares Costa, P., Correia Santos, N., Cunha, P., Cotter, J. & Sousa, N. (2013). The use of multiple correspondence analysis to explore associations between categories of qualitative variables in healthy ageing. *Journal of Ageing Research*, Article ID 302163. DOI: 10.1155/2013/302163

Wahrendorf, M., Akinwale, B., Landy, R., Matthews, K. & Blane, D. (2017a). Who in Europe works beyond the state pension age and under which conditions? Results from SHARE. *Journal of population ageing*, 10, 269–285.

Wahrendorf, M., Zaninotto, P., Hoven, H., Head, J. & Carr, E. (2017b). Late life employment histories and their association with work and family formation during adulthood: A sequence analysis based on ELSA. *The Journals of Gerontology*: Series B, 73, 1263–1277.

Widmer, E. D. & Spini, D. (2017). Misleading norms and vulnerability in the life course: Definition and illustrations. *Research in Human Development*, 14(1), 52–67. 10.1080/15427609.2016.1268894

Wiss, T., Schmidthuber, L. & Bordone, V. (2020). Quality of working conditions, sector of employment and age at retirement. *Management Revue*, 31(2), 145–166. 10.5771/0935-9915-2020-2-145

Wiss, T. (2015). From welfare states to welfare sectors: Explaining sectoral differences in occupational pensions with economic and political power of employees. *Journal of European Social Policy*, 25(5), 489–504. 10.1177/0958928715611006

Worts, D., Corna, L., Sacker, A., McMunn, A. & McDonough, P. (2016). Understanding older adults' labour market trajectories: A comparative gendered life course perspective. *Longitudinal and Life Course Studies*, 7, 347–367. 10.14301/llcs.v7i4.389

Appendix

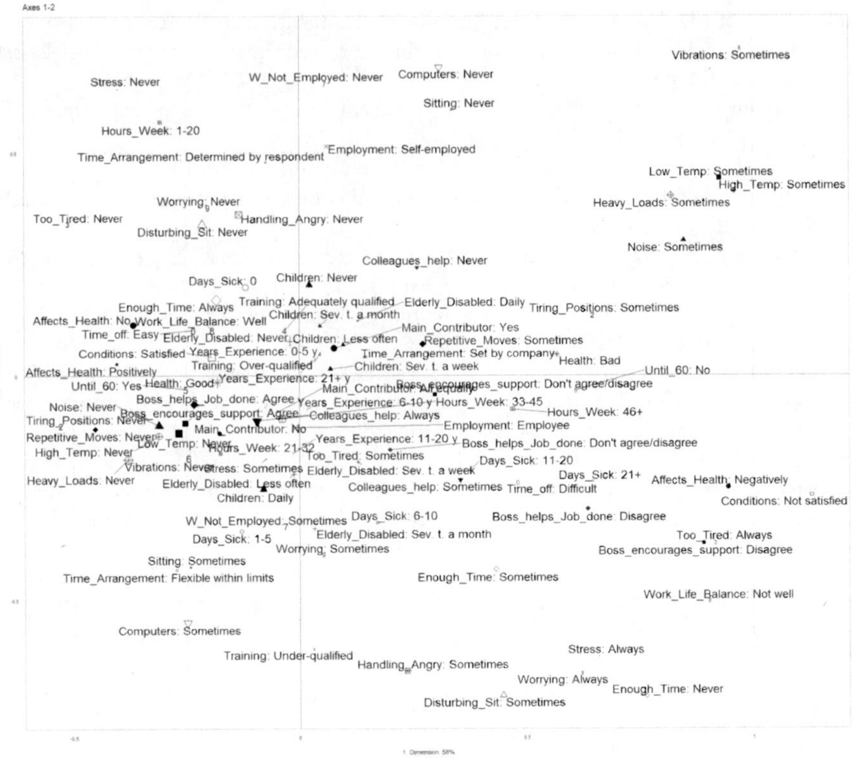

Figure A4.1 Specific multiple correspondence analysis, axes 1 and 2. Proximity clouds.

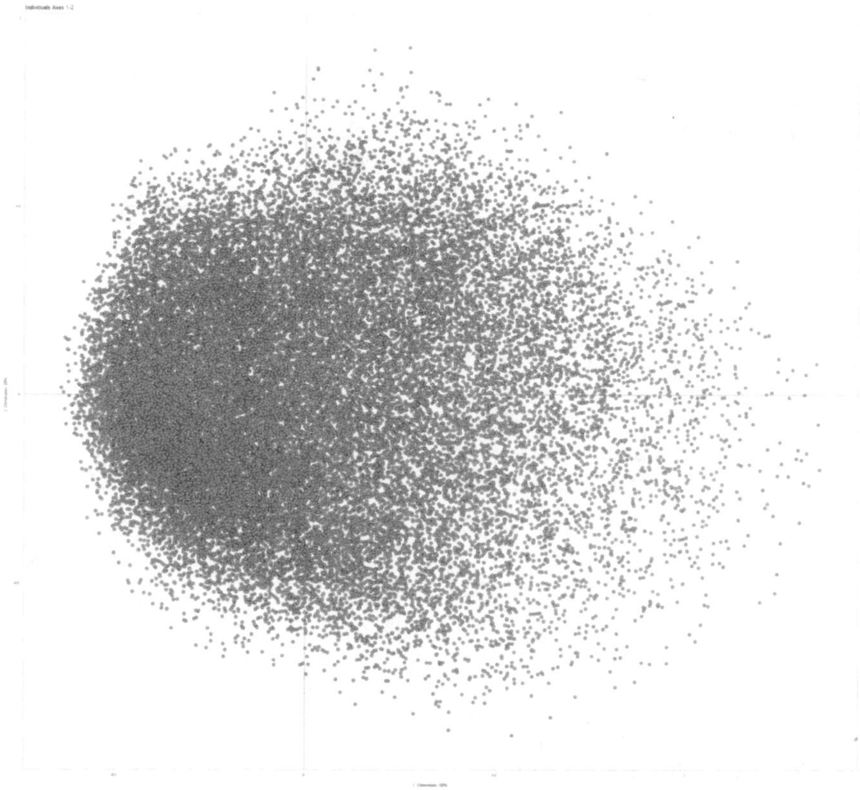

Figure A4.2 Specific multiple correspondence analysis, axes 1 and 2. Respondent cloud.

Table A4.1 Contribution of the active variables to the two axes of the MCA

Variable	*Modality*	*Dim.1*	*Dim.2*	*Freq.*
Work affects health	Positively	0.5	0.0	4229
	Negatively	5.7	0.6	9353
	Not at all	1.8	0.3	19962
	Total	**8.0**	**0.9**	**33544**
Immediate boss encourages and supports the respondent's development	Agree	0.8	0.2	18906
	Disagree	2.0	0.5	3609
	Neither agree nor disagree	0.3	0.0	4961
	Total	**3.1**	**0.7**	**27476**
Immediate boss is helpful in getting the job done	Agree	0.7	0.1	17821
	Disagree	1.4	0.4	5060
	Neither agree nor disagree	0.1	0.1	4578
	Total	**2.2**	**0.6**	**27459**

(*Continued*)

Table A4.1 (Continued)

Variable	*Modality*	*Dim.1*	*Dim.2*	*Freq.*
Caring for/educating children, grandchildren	Daily	0	0.7	11366
	Several times a week	0	0	4003
	Several times a month	0	0	2787
	Less often	0	0	3199
	Never	0	0.5	11228
	Total	**0**	**1.2**	**32583**
Colleagues help and support the respondent	Always	0.1	0.2	22541
	Sometimes	0.4	0.3	4646
	Never	0.1	0.2	2968
	Total	**0.6**	**0.7**	**30155**
Job involves computers	Never	1.0	7.3	15313
	Sometimes	0.8	5.8	19226
	Total	**1.8**	**13.1**	**34539**
Satisfaction with working conditions	Not satisfied	4.3	0.4	4964
	Satisfied	0.7	0.1	29449
	Total	**5.0**	**0.5**	**34413**
Number of days due to sick leave in the past 12 months	0	0.2	0.7	17390
	1-5	0.1	0.8	6806
	6-10	0.1	0.3	2734
	11-20	0.2	0.1	2015
	21+	0.6	0.1	2143
	Total	**1.2**	**2**	**31088**
Job involves emotionally disturbing situations	Never	0.7	2.7	23383
	Sometimes	1.5	5.7	11094
	Total	**2.2**	**8.4**	**34477**
Caring for elderly/disabled relatives	Daily	0	0	1573
	Several times a week	0	0.1	1871
	Several times a month	0	0.3	2501
	Less often	0	0.2	4345
	Never	0	0.1	23167
	Total	**0**	**0.7**	**33457**
Employment situation	Employee	0.0	0.4	28522
	Self-employed	0.0	1.5	5700
	Total	**0.0**	**1.9**	**34222**
The respondent has enough time to get the job done	Always	0.6	0.7	25673
	Sometimes	0.7	1	5379
	Never	1.3	1.6	3143
	Total	**2.6**	**3.3**	**34195**
Job involves handling angry clients, customers, patients, pupils, etc.	Never	0.3	2.9	22287
	Sometimes	0.5	5.3	12210
	Total	**0.8**	**8.2**	**34497**
General State of Health	Bad	1.8	0.0	8322
	Good	0.6	0.0	26278
	Total	**2.4**	**0.0**	**34600**
Job involves carrying or moving heavy loads	Never	2.3	0.8	23643
	Sometimes	5.0	1.8	10915
	Total	**7.3**	**2.6**	**34558**

(*Continued*)

Table A4.1 (Continued)

Variable	*Modality*	*Dim.1*	*Dim.2*	*Freq.*
Job involves exposition to high temperatures	Never	1.7	0.5	26092
	Sometimes	5.3	1.4	8413
	Total	**7.0**	**1.9**	**34505**
Hours of work per week	1–20	0.3	1.4	4411
	21–32	0.1	0.1	3686
	33–45	0.0	0.2	20021
	46+	0.8	0.0	5450
	Total	**1.2**	**1.7**	**33568**
Job involves exposition to low temperatures	Never	1.3	0.4	26812
	Sometimes	4.5	1.5	7691
	Total	**5.8**	**1.9**	**34503**
Person who contributes the most to the household income	All contribute equally	0.0	0.0	2331
	No	0.2	0.2	9525
	Yes	0.1	0.1	22551
	Total	**0.3**	**0.3**	**34407**
Job involves exposition to noise	Never	1.7	0.3	25285
	Sometimes	4.6	0.8	9243
	Total	**6.3**	**1.1**	**34528**
Job involves repetitive movements	Never	1.8	0.2	12972
	Sometimes	1.1	0.1	21537
	Total	**2.9**	**0.3**	**34509**
Job involves sitting	Never	1.1	5.1	14391
	Sometimes	0.8	3.7	20157
	Total	**1.9**	**8.8**	**34548**
The respondent experiences stress at work	Always	2.6	3.5	8848
	Sometimes	0.0	0.5	13421
	Never	1.3	4.9	11879
	Total	**3.9**	**8.9**	**34148**
Working time arrangements	Determined by respondent	0.0	1.4	6095
	Flexible within limits	0.4	1.7	8891
	Set by company	0.3	0.0	19408
	Total	**0.7**	**3.1**	**34394**
Time off during work to take care of personal or family matters	Difficult	1.8	0.6	11137
	Easy	0.9	0.2	22803
	Total	**2.7**	**0.8**	**33940**
Job involves tiring or painful positions	Never	3.6	0.2	19010
	Sometimes	4.4	0.3	15485
	Total	**8.0**	**0.5**	**34495**
Too tired after work to do household jobs	Always	4.2	1.0	7248
	Sometimes	0.0	0.4	12944
	Never	2.5	1.6	14088
	Total	**6.7**	**3.0**	**34280**
Training/skills in work	Adequately qualified	0.0	0.2	19928
	Over-qualified	0.0	0.0	9875
	Under-qualified	0.0	1.6	4418
	Total	**0.0**	**1.8**	**34221**
	No	2.2	0.0	8629

(*Continued*)

Table A4.1 (Continued)

Variable	*Modality*	*Dim.1*	*Dim.2*	*Freq.*
Ability to do current job until 60/in five years' time	Yes	1.0	0.0	22716
	Total	**3.2**	**0.0**	**31345**
Job involves exposition to vibrations	Never	1.1	0.9	27614
	Sometimes	4.5	3.7	6905
	Total	**5.6**	**4.6**	**34519**
Job involves dealing directly with people who are not employed at workplace	Never	0.0	5.0	11698
	Sometimes	0.0	2.6	22816
	Total	**0.0**	**7.6**	**34514**
Work life balance (working hours fit with family or social commitments)	Not well	3.3	1.5	5964
	Well	0.7	0.3	28472
	Total	**4.0**	**1.8**	**34436**
Worrying about work when not working	Always	1.4	2.4	5349
	Sometimes	0.0	1.5	9640
	Never	0.5	2.7	19317
	Total	**1.9**	**6.6**	**34306**
Years in company	0–5	0.0	0.1	13229
	6–10	0.0	0.0	7189
	11–20	0.0	0.2	7501
	21+	0.0	0.0	5855
	Total	**0.0**	**0.3**	**33774**

Notes: n = 34,649. Missing values are not displayed in the table since they are set as passive categories. Categories with above average contribution to the axis are in light grey, variables with above average contribution to the axis are in dark grey.

Table A4.2 Coordinates of the supplementary variables on the two axes of the MCA

Variable	*Modality*	*Axis 1*	*Axis 2*	*Freq*
Age	26–30	−0.01	−0.08	3 636
	31–35	0.03	−0.13	4 103
	36–40	0.02	−0.17	4 742
	41–45	0.01	−0.12	4 914
	46–50	0.03	−0.02	5 140
	50–55	0.02	0.00	4 885
	56–60	0.03	0.13	3 978
	61–65	−0.14	0.35	2 026
	66–70	−0.29	0.81	680
	71+	−0.29	0.98	545
Education level by sex	Primary/secondary men	0.37	0.49	10 420
	Primary/secondary women	−0.03	0.13	9 526
	Post-secondary men	−0.24	−0.27	6 467
	Post-secondary women	−0.26	−0.57	8 111
Occupation (ISCO 2008, 1 digit)	Clerical support workers	−0.44	−0.44	3 093
	Craft and related trades workers	0.63	0.81	4 108

(*Continued*)

Table A4.2 (Continued)

Variable	*Modality*	*Axis 1*	*Axis 2*	*Freq*
	Elementary occupations	0.32	0.81	3 573
	Managers	−0.29	−0.45	2 353
	Plant and machine operators, and assemblers	0.54	0.40	2 390
	Professionals	−0.37	−0.63	6 626
	Service and sales workers	0.01	−0.03	6 944
	Skilled agricultural, forestry and fishery workers	0.50	1.25	1 170
	Technicians and associate professionals	−0.29	−0.46	4 137
Deciles of income (calculated by country)	1–4	0.07	0.26	11 308
	5–7	0.07	−0.10	8 928
	8–10	−0.12	−0.35	8 727
Country	Belgium	−0.11	−0.18	2 399
	Bulgaria	−0.05	0.36	995
	Czech Republic	−0.11	0.10	938
	Denmark	−0.29	−0.37	899
	Germany	−0.05	0.06	1 919
	Estonia	−0.03	−0.09	931
	Greece	0.38	0.14	933
	Spain	0.24	0.04	3 101
	France	0.19	−0.25	1 414
	Ireland	−0.29	0.05	954
	Italy	−0.10	0.17	1 351
	Cyprus	0.12	0.01	823
	Latvia	0.16	0.15	918
	Lithuania	0.13	0.14	923
	Luxembourg	0.04	−0.30	947
	Hungary	−0.03	0.34	964
	Malta	0.09	−0.29	883
	Netherlands	−0.36	−0.12	916
	Austria	−0.14	0.05	919
	Poland	0.15	0.19	1 021
	Portugal	−0.13	0.42	979
	Romania	0.21	0.42	994
	Slovenia	0.12	−0.06	1 524
	Slovakia	0.09	0.03	925
	Finland	−0.06	−0.06	959
	Sweden	−0.13	−0.37	921
	United Kingdom	−0.15	−0.19	1 463
	Croatia	0.23	0.04	938
	Norway	−0.41	−0.33	870
	Switzerland	−0.14	0.06	928

Notes: Missing values (n = 125 for Education level by sex; n = 255 for Occupation; and 5686 for Income) are not displayed in the Table.

5 The Impact of Age and Perceived Age Discrimination on Job Satisfaction and Mental Health

Tindara Addabbo and Elena Sarti

Introduction

Policy shifts towards extended working lives in Europe, and the trend of demographic ageing is reflected by an increased share of the workforce that is older. According to the OECD (2020), at a macro-level older workers' inclusion and a multigenerational workforce are estimated to increase Gross Domestic Product by 19 per cent over the next three decades, and, at a micro-level, improve team performance by means of age and skill complementarities between younger and older workers.

However, there are barriers to the inclusion of older workers in the labour market; there is a higher probability that they will experience longer periods of unemployment and age discrimination at work, or worse working conditions (Phillipson, 2012). The barriers that older workers face in the labour market create inequalities in access to work, in satisfaction about job and job retention, with negative effects on health.

In this chapter we explore to what extent individual ageing can impact on job outcomes and well-being in a labour market environment that is exposed to the risk of age discrimination (Harris et al., 2018). We first investigate the extent of the perception of age discrimination by age across European countries in 2015. Then, by using the latest available data from the European Working Conditions Survey (EWCS), we analyse the determinants of job satisfaction and mental health by including personal characteristics (e.g. gender, age and education level), indicators of working conditions and of different types of discrimination.

Special attention is devoted to age, both as a specific individual characteristic that can impact on job satisfaction and mental health and in terms of the experience of age discrimination. We disaggregate the sample analysed into two different age groups (<50 and 50+) to investigate the impact of the same independent variables for people in employment on their job satisfaction and mental health.

The chapter is structured as follows. The section "Literature review" introduces the main literature in the field of age discrimination, mental health and job satisfaction. Sections "Data" and "Empirical method" present the data and method, respectively, while the section "Descriptive statistics" outlines

DOI: 10.4324/9781003145325-5

some descriptive statistics. The section "Job satisfaction analysis" reports the empirical model and the main findings of the regression analysis on job satisfaction, while in the section "Mental health analysis" we discuss the impact of individual characteristics, working conditions and discrimination on mental health by means of a Multiple Indicators Multiple Causes (MIMIC) model that treats mental health as a latent (i.e. not directly observable) variable. Finally, the section "Discussion and conclusion" provides some concluding remarks.

Literature review

Evidence of age discrimination has been identified both in gaining access to work (recruitment) and retention (Roscigno et al., 2007; Neumark et al., 2019). It has also been found in the workplace, in training and career opportunities (Chou & Choi, 2011; Posthuma & Campion, 2009). Lower access to training for older workers can bring about a negative effect on their productivity and wages (Lee et al., 2022; Lee et al., 2019) and increase the likelihood of retiring earlier (Berg et al., 2017; Zaniboni, 2015). The main literature in the field has shown a negative impact of discrimination, as measured by individual perception, on job satisfaction (Marchiondo et al., 2019; Taylor et al., 2013).

In this study we focus first on the impact of age and age discrimination on job satisfaction. There is considerable evidence of the interaction between job satisfaction and organisational outcomes such as higher commitment, performance, lower turnover and absenteeism (Dayal & Verma, 2021; Snape & Redman, 2003; Srivastava, 2013; Topino et al., 2021) and on the positive effect of job satisfaction on life satisfaction, happiness, individual well-being and health (Berger, 2013; Pearson, 2008; Cannas et al., 2019).

A crucial dimension of well-being that affects older workers and extended working life, among others, is health (Nilsson et al., 2011). In particular, as suggested by Stansfeld & Candy (2006), working life characteristics are related to mental health conditions. In the same vein, Cottini & Lucifora (2013) show the negative impact of poor working conditions with respect to job demands and job hazards on worker's mental health across European countries, and they have also detected heterogeneity by country. Marchiondo et al. (2019) have identified a negative long-lasting impact of perceived age discrimination on mental and physical health.

In line with these findings and to further explore the main literature in the field, we investigate the impact of different independent variables on both job satisfaction and mental health, with particular attention paid to what happens for younger (those aged less than 50 years old) and older (those aged 50+) age groups.

Data

In order to assess job satisfaction and mental health we make use of the EWCS, which has been conducted by the European Foundation for the Improvement of Living and Working Conditions (Eurofound) since 1991. Its aim is to measure working conditions across European countries, analyse the interaction between different aspects of working conditions, identify at-risk groups and assess working conditions over time. The Survey helps in identifying policy suggestions with particular reference to the quality of work and employment (Eurofound, 2017).

The EWCS sixth wave was carried out in 2015 in 35 European countries: the 27 European Member States plus the United Kingdom, Albania, the former Yugoslav Republic of Macedonia, Montenegro, Serbia and Turkey, as well as Norway and Switzerland. Our selected sample includes 35 countries. The final sample refers to 33,801 employees (excluded self-employed), aged from 15 to 86 (on average, 42 years old), and 52 per cent are women.

Since the EWCS allows us to recover data on different working dimensions and contains indicators on the perception of different forms of discrimination and variables allowing us to measure job satisfaction and mental health (Eurofound, 2017), we draw on this information to investigate the impact on job satisfaction and mental health in terms of the experience of age discrimination.

In doing so, we select specific variables from the Survey. In particular, we employ an indicator for the experience of age discrimination. This variable is collected by analysing the answers of those employees who stated that over the past 12 months they have been subjected to age discrimination at work. We also control for other types of discrimination such as gender, ethnicity, religion and disability. In addition, we include variables on work-life balance, wages, education level, type of contract, firm size, profession, industry and country.

Job satisfaction has been measured by analysing those answers to the EWCS question, "On the whole, are you very satisfied, satisfied, not very satisfied or not at all satisfied with working conditions in your main paid job?" This represents a categorical variable and its values go from 1 (very satisfied) to 4 (not at all satisfied). We have rescaled the variables, so that higher values indicate higher job satisfaction.

Furthermore, in line with the literature on job demand and job hazard models (Cottini & Lucifora, 2013), we have aggregated some specific indicators in order to build two composite indicators for job demand and job hazard.

More specifically, job demand includes different dummy variables on a job's organisational characteristics, such as complexity of tasks; repetitive hand or arm movement; shift work; handling angry clients, customers, patients, pupils etc.; not having enough time to get the job done; hiding feelings at work and whether the immediate boss does not encourage and support worker's development. Higher values indicate worse working conditions.

Job hazard, instead, includes dummy variables on a job's physical characteristics, such as exposure at work to vibrations from hand tools, machinery, etc.; noise so loud that you would have to raise your voice to talk to people; high temperatures which make you perspire even when not working; low temperatures whether indoors or outdoors; breathing in smoke, fumes (such as welding or exhaust fumes), powder or dust (such as wood dust or mineral dust), etc.; tobacco smoke from other people; handling or being in direct contact with materials which can be infectious such as waste, bodily fluids, laboratory materials, etc. Higher values indicate worse working conditions.[1]

Empirical method

In order to estimate the impact of individual characteristics, working conditions and experiences of discrimination on job satisfaction, we apply multivariate models with OLS (Ordinary Least Squares) regressions by age groups.

We briefly introduce the standard notation of the OLS regression:

$$Y_i = \beta_0 + \beta_1 X_1 + \beta_2 X_2 + \ldots + \beta_p X_p + \varepsilon_i \quad (5.1)$$

and in matrix notation

$$y = X\beta + \varepsilon \quad (5.2)$$

where y and ε are $(n \times 1)$ vectors of the response variables and the errors of the *n* observations respectively, while *X* is an $(n \times p)$ matrix of regressors.

As a further investigation, we include in our empirical strategy analysis of mental health. The model assumes that mental health can be interpreted as a latent factor (i.e. not directly observable), which manifests itself through a set of observed mental health indicators, whose validity has been simultaneously tested. The MIMIC model can be represented as follows:

$$y_i = \Lambda f_i + \varepsilon_i \text{ Measurement Equations} \quad (5.3)$$

$$f_i = Bx_i + \nu_i \text{ Causal Relationships} \quad (5.4)$$

with $V(\varepsilon_i) = \psi$ and $V(\nu_i) = \sigma^2 I_m$, and where $f_i(m \times 1)$ is a vector of latent factors of individual *i* (*m* = number of latent dimensions). $y_i(k \times 1)$ is a vector of observed indicators (*k* = number of indicators), $x_i(n \times 1)$ is a vector of latent exogenous variables (*n* = number of exogenous variables), and Λ and B are corresponding coefficient matrices (Joreskog, & Goldberger, 1975).

Equation 5.3 shows that the latent factor (i.e. mental health) manifests itself through some observed variables and for each one a weight (called factor loading) is estimated to see how much it counts in explaining the latent concept. In our model, the indicators chosen are those found in the EWCS Survey – question Q87, which refers to the World Health Organisation – Five Well-Being Index (WHO-5) (WHO Collaborating Center for Mental Health, 1998), a self-reported measure of mental well-being.

We make use of the Cronbach's alpha coefficient (which goes from 0 to 1) to measure the internal consistency of the WHO-5 indicators. The coefficient equals 0.8817 for the whole sample 15+, denoting a very good level of internal consistency of WHO-5 indicators.

Equation 5.4 instead, shows the influence of exogenous variables (such as those related to individual characteristics, working conditions, etc.) on the latent factor. The disturbance terms (ε_i and v_i) are assumed to have zero means and to be not correlated.

Descriptive statistics

We have disaggregated the sample by age groups and estimated the multivariate models on job satisfaction and mental health on the total sample and, then, split it by age group, identifying those aged 50+ as older workers (as in OECD, 2006; Steel & Tuori, 2019).

Before presenting the main findings of the empirical models, we show descriptive statistics by gender and age groups on both job satisfaction and mental health. Table A5.3 in the Appendix reports descriptive statistics on a set of variables by gender and age group. As expected, the sample of employees analysed shows marked gender differences in the degree of involvement in unpaid care and housework with the highest degree of involvement for women aged less than 50 (when care for young children is more likely to occur for women) followed by women aged older than 50. The degree of work-life balance is high, and the gap to the advantage of women is higher among those aged less than 50. Part-time employment is more frequent among women.

The highest experience of age discrimination is found among young people (15–24 years old) and women. In fact, 8 per cent of young women have been subjected to age discrimination in the previous 12 months. Perception of age discrimination decreases for those aged 25 to 49 years old, touching the minimum value in the age group 35–49 for both men and women and in the age group 65+ only for men (Table 5.1).

On average, in the sample of people in employment, there is a high level of job satisfaction, especially for those who do not perceive that they are discriminated against on the basis of their age at work (i.e. 88.4 out of 100) with similar percentages for men and women. However, as expected, job satisfaction significantly decreases when people experience age discrimination at work, especially if young women and for employees aged 50+ (Table 5.2).

Table 5.1 Experience of age discrimination by age and gender (%)

Age group	*M (%)*	*F (%)*	*Total (%)*
15–24	7.4	8.0	7.7
25–34	3.5	3.4	3.5
35–49	1.9	1.8	1.8
50–64	4.4	4.3	4.4
≥ 65	1.9	5.7	3.7
Total (≥15)	3.4	3.4	3.4
Observations	16,292	17,424	33,716

Table 5.2 Job satisfaction (% score out of 100) by age, sex and perceived age discrimination

Age group	*No age discrimination*			*Age discrimination*			*Total*		
	Total	M	F	*Total*	M	F	*Total*	M	F
15–49	88.3	88.2	88.4	83.6	84.3	82.9	88.2	88.1	88.2
50+	88.6	88.6	88.5	82.6	82.5	82.6	88.3	88.4	88.3
Total	88.4	88.3	88.4	83.2	83.6	82.8	88.2	88.2	88.2
Obs.	32,574	15,769	16,799	1,148	523	625	33,722	16,292	17,424

Source: Our analysis of EWCS data.

Table 5.3 Mental health score (%) by age and gender

Age group	M (%)	F (%)	*Total (%)*
15–24	71.1	68.7	70.0
25–34	69.3	68.4	68.9
35–49	68.2	66.3	67.2
50–64	68.5	66.1	67.3
≥ 65	76.2	69.6	73.1
Total (≥15)	68.9	66.9	68.0
Observations	16,221	17,347	33,568

Source: Our analysis of EWCS data.

The measure of mental health used is the subjective WHO-5 indicators of the World Health Organisation (WHO Collaborating Center for Mental Health, 1998; Bech et al., 2003), which is a short self-reported measure of mental well-being. The 5-item World Health Organisation Well-Being Index (WHO-5) is one of the most widely used for subjective psychological well-being.

More specifically, the five questions focus on the degree of feeling cheerful and in good spirits; calm and relaxed; active and vigorous; fresh and rested; and living a life filled with things that interest. Answers go from 5 (all of the time) to 0 (at no time). The final percentage score ranges from 0 to 100, as the raw score is multiplied by 4. A score of 0 represents the worst scenario, whereas a score of 100 represents the best possible quality of life (Regional Office for Europe WHO, 1998; Bech, 2004).

In line with the WHO-5, the indicators for mental health included in the EWCS are related to positive mood (relaxation and good spirits); vitality (being active and waking up fresh and rested) and general interest in things. The literature shows that the WHO-5 indicators are a good measure for detecting depression.

In our sample of people in employment, mental health expressed by means of WHO-5 indicator is lower for women for all age groups and reaches the highest level at the youngest (15–34) and at the oldest (65+) age (Table 5.3).

Women display lower levels of mental health than men and, as expected, at all age groups mental health is lower for those who perceive age discrimination, especially if female (Table 5.4).

Job satisfaction analysis

This section analyses the impact of different independent variables on job satisfaction, making use of OLS regression models by age groups (i.e. whole sample 15+, less than 50 and 50+) as specified in section "Empirical method".

When we control for potential confounding factors, we are not able to observe a statistically significant impact of gender on job satisfaction (Table 5.5). This result is in line with what has been found in the descriptive statistics (Table 5.2 on total job satisfaction by gender). Age decreases job satisfaction among those aged 50+, while age discrimination has a negative impact for both subgroups with a larger impact on employees in the 50+ group.

Table 5.4 Mental health and perceived age discrimination

Age group	*No age discrimination*			*Age discrimination*			*Total*		
	Total	M	F	*Total*	M	F	*Total*	M	F
15–49	68.4	69.2	67.5	59.5	61.4	57.5	68.1	68.9	67.2
50+	68.2	69.4	66.9	57.9	60.9	54.8	67.7	69.0	66.4
Total	68.3	69.2	67.3	58.9	61.2	56.5	68.0	69.0	67.0
Obs.	32,366	15,667	16,693	1,140	520	620	33,506	16,187	17,313

Source: Our analysis of EWCS data.

Table 5.5 Determinants of job satisfaction by age groups

Job satisfaction	*Total (15+)*	*Age group: <50*	*Age group: 50+*
Female	−0.002	−0.008	0.019
	(−0.015)	(−0.018)	(−0.028)
Age	−0.018***	−0.014	−0.174***
	(−0.004)	(−0.009)	(−0.033)
Age squared	0.000***	0.000	0.001***
	0.000	(−0.000)	(−0.000)
Secondary school diploma	0.011	0.016	0.007
	(−0.022)	(−0.027)	(−0.035)
University degree	−0.023	−0.027	−0.021
	(−0.026)	(−0.032)	(−0.043)
Work-life balance	0.328***	0.347***	0.267***
	(−0.020)	(−0.023)	(−0.036)
Log(wage)	0.079***	0.081***	0.068***
	(−0.012)	(−0.015)	(−0.021)
Part-time employment	−0.060***	−0.072***	−0.034
	(−0.019)	(−0.023)	(−0.031)
Temporary employment	−0.042**	−0.049**	−0.017
	(−0.020)	(−0.023)	(−0.040)
No contract	−0.056*	−0.062	−0.031
	(−0.033)	(−0.039)	(−0.061)
Job demand	−0.060***	−0.056***	−0.072***
	(−0.003)	(−0.004)	(−0.006)
Job hazard	−0.014***	−0.015***	−0.011
	(−0.005)	(−0.006)	(−0.009)
Manufacturing	−0.066	−0.147***	0.144*
	(−0.045)	(−0.054)	(−0.082)
Construction	−0.045	−0.124**	0.143
	(−0.050)	(−0.060)	(−0.088)
Trade	−0.107**	−0.201***	0.134
	(−0.046)	(−0.055)	(−0.082)
Finance	−0.019	−0.090	0.158
	(−0.061)	(−0.074)	(−0.103)
Information and communication	−0.058	−0.106	−0.020
	(−0.060)	(−0.069)	(−0.125)
Estate	−0.087	−0.199	0.158
	(−0.122)	(−0.159)	(−0.162)
Administration and education	−0.084*	−0.165***	0.105
	(−0.046)	(−0.056)	(−0.082)
Profession	−0.013	−0.086	0.132
	(−0.055)	(−0.065)	(−0.110)
Other	−0.072	−0.136**	0.074
	(−0.047)	(−0.057)	(−0.085)
Manager	0.141***	0.133***	0.168***
	(−0.034)	(−0.041)	(−0.056)
Professional	0.153***	0.157***	0.162***
	(−0.026)	(−0.032)	(−0.046)
Technician	0.141***	0.150***	0.130***
	(−0.025)	(−0.030)	(−0.044)

(*Continued*)

Table 5.5 (Continued)

Job satisfaction	*Total (15+)*	*Age group: <50*	*Age group: 50+*
Clerical support	0.096***	0.105***	0.083**
	(−0.025)	(−0.032)	(−0.041)
Service and sales	0.080***	0.092***	0.065
	(−0.023)	(−0.028)	(−0.040)
Subjected to age discrimination	−0.222***	−0.151***	−0.347***
	(−0.040)	(−0.052)	(−0.056)
Subjected to ethnicity discrimination	−0.199***	−0.248***	0.014
	(−0.062)	(−0.069)	(−0.132)
Subjected to gender discrimination	−0.194***	−0.232***	−0.099
	(−0.049)	(−0.056)	(−0.096)
Subjected to discrimination for religion	0.007	0.015	−0.035
	(−0.074)	(−0.086)	(−0.130)
Subjected to discrimination for disability	−0.050	−0.145*	0.100
	(−0.076)	(−0.081)	(−0.143)
Firm with at least 250 employees	−0.030**	−0.019	−0.049*
	(−0.015)	(−0.019)	(−0.026)
United Kingdom and Ireland	0.058*	0.075*	0.019
	(−0.034)	(−0.041)	(−0.061)
Continental	−0.027	−0.008	−0.063
	(−0.027)	(−0.032)	(−0.047)
Southern	0.007	0.001	0.042
	(−0.021)	(−0.025)	(−0.042)
Nordic	0.032	0.033	0.037
	(−0.029)	(−0.035)	(−0.049)
Baltic	−0.060***	−0.023	−0.127***
	(−0.021)	(−0.027)	(−0.032)
Constant	3.409***	3.368***	7.808***
	(−0.098)	(−0.167)	(−0.978)
Observations	24,445	17,005	7,440
R-squared	0.163	0.167	0.174

Source: Our analysis of EWCS data.

Notes
Robust standard errors in parentheses
* $p < 0.01$.
** $p < 0.05$.
*** $p < 0.1$.

On the other hand, considering the two age groups perceived discrimination for ethnicity, gender or disability negatively affects job satisfaction only for the younger age group. As expected, job demand and job hazard reduce job satisfaction (job hazard only for the youngest) and higher work-life balance positively affects it, especially among those less than 50 years old.

The impact of being a part-time worker and having a temporary contract on job satisfaction is negative for the youngest, while working in a big firm (with at least 250 employees) reduces job satisfaction for older people (50+). Finally, living in United Kingdom or Ireland increases job satisfaction for those aged less than 50, while living in the Baltic area reduces it for those aged 50+ compared to Central Eastern countries (i.e. the reference group).

Mental health analysis

Before evaluating the effect of sociodemographic and working conditions on mental health, we first assess the validity of the latent variable. As results for the measurement part of the model suggest, all WHO-5 indicators play a key role in explaining the latent concept of mental health (i.e. all variables are significant) and have a positive sign. To obtain a more complete understanding of the latent mental health variable, we also show in the same table the MIMIC model results for the under 50 and 50+ age groups. The indicator with the highest impact for all age groups is the one on feeling active and vigorous over the past two weeks, followed by the one on feeling cheerful and in good spirits (for the whole sample and the sample of employees younger than 50), and feeling calm and relaxed for the 50+ employees (Table 5.6).

To better understand the indicators chosen for mental health and those exogenous variables that influence this latent concept, the MIMIC model

Table 5.6 MIMIC model for mental health (measurement part) by age groups

	Total (15+)		*Age group: <50*		*Age group: 50+*	
	Coefficient	*Robust Std. Err.*	*Coefficient*	*Robust Std. Err.*	*Coefficient*	*Robust Std. Err.*
I have felt cheerful and in good spirits						
WHO-5	0.784***	0.007	0.786***	0.008	0.779***	0.015
cons	3.886	0.133	3.805	0.211	8.017	1.312
I have felt calm and relaxed						
WHO-5	0.780***	0.007	0.777***	0.009	0.789***	0.012
cons	3.251	0.130	3.130	0.208	7.544	1.329
I have felt active and vigorous						
WHO-5	0.825***	0.007	0.826***	0.008	0.822***	0.012
cons	3.348	0.138	3.256	0.221	7.723	1.382
I woke up feeling fresh and rested						
WHO-5	0.768***	0.007	0.767***	0.009	0.771***	0.013
cons	2.909	0.128	2.792	0.205	7.101	1.300
My daily life has been filled with things that interest me						
WHO-5	0.648***	0.010	0.642***	0.012	0.666***	0.017
cons	3.394	0.112	3.310	0.177	6.968	1.128

Source: Our analysis of EWCS data.

results are shown according to the earlier used age groups: less than and at least 50 years old.

Again, the Cronbach's alpha is very good (0.8803 for the subsample of people aged <50 years and 0.8849 for the 50+ group), indicating that the WHO-5 indicators are internally consistent.

Turning to the effect of personal characteristics and working conditions on mental health (structural part of the model – Table 5.7) results for people aged 15+ (i.e. the whole sample) suggest that being a woman decreases mental health and being older negatively affects it for those aged 50+ and for those aged 15+, but in a non-linear way. The MIMIC model catches the effect of the age-related exogenous variables (i.e. age and age squared) very well. In addition, the perception of age discrimination has a negative impact on mental health for all age groups, and especially for the group aged 50+.

As expected, an increase in wages has a positive effect on mental health, while job demand has a negative impact. Being a part-time worker has a negative effect on mental health for people less than 50 years old, as well as job hazard, working in a large firm with at least 250 employees and working as a manager.

We do find a positive effect of work-life balance on mental health and this is consistent with other studies in the field (see, for instance, Lunau et al., 2014). Discrimination by age is negative for mental health in all age groups. Variables on discrimination by gender and disability display a negative and statistically significant coefficient for people less than 50 years old.

Compared to the agriculture, forestry and fishing sector (i.e. the reference group) working in all other sectors negatively affects mental health for the youngest (except for the financial and insurance sector and the category grouping "other" services), while working sectors are not statistically significant for people aged 50+.

Finally, living in the United Kingdom or Ireland negatively affects mental health compared to living in Central Eastern countries (i.e. the reference group) at all ages, while for Continental and Nordic countries this is true only for people aged less than 50 years old.

Discussion and conclusion

In this chapter, we analyse the effect of ageing and the experience of age discrimination on job satisfaction and mental health for people in employment.

Descriptive analysis shows age discrimination is especially reported by young people (15–24 years old) and women. These results are consistent with the literature (Taylor and Smith, 2017; Chou & Choi, 2011; Gee et al., 2007).

In addition, the estimated multivariate model results are largely in accord with the literature on job satisfaction and mental health. Being subjected to age discrimination negatively affects job satisfaction and mental health at all ages, but especially for people aged 50+. Work-life balance and wage levels remain important positive factors for both and working conditions (i.e. explored

Table 5.7 MIMIC model for mental health (structural part) by age groups

	Total (15+)		*Age group: <50*		*Age group: 50+*	
WHO-5 (Mental health)	*Coefficient*	*Robust Std. Err.*	*Coefficient*	*Robust Std. Err.*	*Coefficient*	*Robust Std. Err.*
Female	−0.073***	0.012	−0.066***	0.015	−0.089***	0.023
Age	−0.327***	0.078	−0.127	0.120	−0.979***	0.256
Age squared	0.268***	0.075	0.052	0.117	0.997***	0.254
Secondary school diploma	0.007	0.018	0.009	0.023	−0.008	0.030
University degree	−0.025	0.020	−0.032	0.024	−0.032	0.033
Work-life balance	0.179***	0.012	0.185***	0.015	0.155***	0.023
Log(wage)	0.115***	0.017	0.123***	0.020	0.091***	0.030
Part-time employment	−0.036***	0.012	−0.039***	0.015	−0.027	0.023
Temporary employment	0.018*	0.010	0.025**	0.012	−0.007	0.017
No contract	−0.008	0.012	−0.017	0.015	0.017	0.021
Job demand	−0.207***	0.012	−0.208***	0.015	−0.200***	0.023
Job hazard	−0.031**	0.013	−0.031*	0.016	−0.034	0.024
Manufacturing	−0.084***	0.032	−0.119***	0.037	−0.000	0.061
Construction	−0.029	0.020	−0.050**	0.024	0.022	0.039
Trade	−0.053	0.035	−0.095**	0.042	0.045	0.063
Finance	−0.016	0.019	−0.027	0.022	0.012	0.035
Information and communication	−0.023	0.015	−0.033*	0.018	−0.003	0.023
Estate	−0.022*	0.013	−0.029*	0.016	−0.005	0.020
Administration and education	−0.066*	0.035	−0.089**	0.040	0.004	0.072
Profession	−0.020	0.017	−0.041*	0.021	0.030	0.026
Other	−0.029	0.033	−0.048	0.038	0.018	0.065
Manager	−0.029**	0.012	−0.037***	0.014	−0.004	0.023
Professional	0.019	0.015	0.010	0.018	0.045*	0.027
Technician	0.019	0.014	0.017	0.017	0.020	0.023
Clerical support	−0.001	0.014	−0.003	0.017	−0.001	0.024
Service and Sales	0.011	0.014	0.005	0.017	0.026	0.022

Subjected to age discrimination	−0.044***	0.011	−0.036**	0.014	−0.065***	0.019
Subjected to ethnicity discrimination	−0.009	0.012	−0.010	0.015	−0.001	0.023
Subjected to gender discrimination	−0.036***	0.011	−0.041***	0.012	−0.025	0.025
Subjected to discrimination for religion	−0.007	0.013	−0.017	0.015	0.016	0.024
Subjected to discrimination for disability	−0.020	0.014	−0.028*	0.015	−0.006	0.027
Firm with at least 250 employees	−0.025**	0.012	−0.026*	0.014	−0.019	0.022
United Kingdom and Ireland	−0.129***	0.019	−0.134***	0.022	−0.120***	0.037
Continental	−0.062***	0.020	−0.085***	0.024	−0.007	0.038
Southern	−0.000	0.015	−0.000	0.018	−0.014	0.028
Nordic	−0.025*	0.013	−0.049***	0.015	0.038	0.027
Baltic	0.001	0.004	0.006	0.004	−0.005	0.007
Estimation method = ml	Number of observations: 24,402		Number of observations: 16,979		Number of observations: 7,423	

Source: Our analysis of EWCS data.

through job demand and job hazard composite variables) have an important role in determining job satisfaction and mental health levels. In particular, job demand and job hazard (this one only for people less than 50 years old) reduce both job satisfaction and mental health (Cottini & Lucifora, 2013).

Turning to age, it negatively affects mental health, but in a non-linear way. More specifically, estimating the models by age groups allows us to identify the known statistically significant negative effect of ageing on mental health and job satisfaction only for the older group of employees. The impact of gender on job satisfaction is not statistically significant as in Sousa-Poza and Sousa-Poza (2000) and being a part-time worker or having a temporary contract decrease job satisfaction for people aged less than 50 years.

Our results suggest that investing in work-life balance policies and controlling job demand and job hazard can result in higher well-being in terms of both mental health and job satisfaction. Observing different types of perceived discrimination and controlling for other job and individual characteristics allow us to disentangle the impact of age and age discrimination on employees in different age groups. Particular attention should be paid to the prevention of age stereotyping and age discrimination with special regard, for employees age 50+, to discrimination related to age. Our findings suggest the need to foster policies aimed at encouraging the inclusion of older workers and supporting employers and managers in the development of age-management practices (Garavaglia et al., 2021; OECD, 2020). To help achieve this, positive intergenerational contact in the workplace should be promoted (Abrams et al., 2006; Henry et al., 2015; Iweins et al., 2013; Marchiondo et al., 2019).

Note

1 A detailed definition of each variable included in the empirical models is provided in Table A5.2 in the Appendix.

References

Abrams, D., Eller, A. & Bryant, J. (2006). An age apart: The effects of intergenerational contact and stereotype threat on performance and intergroup bias. *Psychology and Aging*, 21, 691–702.

Bech, P., Olsen, L. R., Kjoller, M., & Rasmussen, N. K. (2003). Measuring well-being rather than the absence of distress symptoms: A comparison of the SF-36 Mental Health subscale and the WHO-Five Well-Being Scale. *Int. J. Methods Psychiatr. Res.*, 12, 85–89.

Bech, P. (2004). Measuring the dimensions of psychological general well-being by the WHO-5. *QoL Newsletter*, 32, 15–16.

Berg, P. B., Hamman, M. K., Piszczek, M. M., & Ruhm, C. J. (2017). The relationship between employer-provided training and the retention of older workers: Evidence from Germany. *International Labour Review*, 156(3–4), 495–524.

Berger, E. M. (2013). Happy working mothers? Investigating the effect of maternal employment on life satisfaction. *Economica*, 80(317), 23–43.

Cannas, M., Sergi, B. S., Sironi, E., & Mentel, U. (2019). Job satisfaction and subjective well-being in Europe. *Economics and Sociology*, 12(4), 183–196.

Chou, R. J. A. & Choi, N. G. (2011). Prevalence and correlates of perceived workplace discrimination among older workers in the United States of America. *Ageing & Society*, 31(6), 1051–1070.

Cottini, E., & Lucifora, C. (2013). Mental health and working conditions in Europe. *Industrial and Labor Relations Review*, 66(4), 958–988.

Dayal, G. & Verma, P. (2021). Employee satisfaction and organization commitment: Factors affecting turnover intentions and organization performance. *Ilkogretim Online*, 20(5), 3315–3324.

Eurofound (2017). Sixth European Working Conditions Survey – Overview report (2017 update). *Publications Office of the European Union, Luxembourg*.

Garavaglia, E., Marcaletti, F. & Iñiguez-Berrozpe, T. (2021). Action research in age management: The quality of ageing at work model. *Work, Aging & Retirement*, 7(4), 339–351.

Gee, G. C., Pavalko, E. K. & Long, J. S. (2007). Age, cohort and perceived age discrimination: Using the life course to assess self-reported age discrimination. *Social Forces*, 86(1), 265–290.

Harris, K., Krygsman, S., Waschenko, J. & Laliberte Rudman, D. (2018). Ageism and the older worker: A scoping review. *The Gerontologist*, 58(2), e1–e14.

Henry, H., Zacher, H. & Desmette, D. (2015). Reducing age bias and turnover intentions by enhancing intergenerational contact quality in the workplace: The role of opportunities for generativity and development. *Work, Aging and Retirement*, 1(3), 243–253.

Iweins, C., Desmette, D., Yzerbyt, V. & Stinglhamber, F. (2013). Ageism at work: The impact of intergenerational contact and organizational multi-age perspective. *European Journal of Work and Organizational Psychology*, 22, 331–346.

Joreskog, K. G. & Goldberger, A. S. (1975). Estimation of a model with multiple indicators and multiple causes of a single latent variable. *Journal of the American Statistical Association*, 70(351), 631–639.

Lee, J. W., Kwak, D. W. & Song, E. (2022). Can older workers stay productive? The role of ICT skills and training. *Journal of Asian Economics*, 79.

Lee, J. W., Han, J. S. & Song E. (2019). The effects and challenges of vocational training in Korea. *International Journal of Training Research*, 17, 96–111.

Lunau, T., Bambra, C., Eikemo, T. A., van der Wel, K. A., & Dragano, N. (2014). A balancing act? Work–life balance, health and well-being in European welfare states. *European Journal of Public Health*, 24(3), 422–427.

Marchiondo, L. A., Gonzales, E. & Williams, L. J. (2019). Trajectories of perceived workplace age discrimination and long-term associations with mental, self-rated, and occupational health. *The Journals of Gerontology: Series B: Psychological Sciences and Social Sciences*, 74(4), 655–663.

Neumark, D., Burn, I. & Button, P. (2019). Is it harder for older workers to find jobs? New and improved evidence from a field experiment. *Journal of Political Economy*, 127(2), 922–970.

Nilsson, K., Rignell, H. A. & Rylander, L. (2011). Factors influencing the decision to extend working life or to retire. *Scandinavian Journal of Work Environment & Health*, 37, 473–480.

OECD (2020). *Promoting an age-inclusive workforce: Living, learning and earning longer*. Paris: OECD Publishing, 10.1787/59752153-en.

OECD (2006). *Live longer, work longer*. Paris, France: OECD Publishing.

Pearson, Q. M. (2008). Role overload, job satisfaction, leisure satisfaction, and psychological health among employed women. *Journal of Counseling & Development*, 86(1), 57–63.

Phillipson, C. (2012). The future of work and retirement. *Human Relations*, 66, 143–153.

Posthuma, R. A. & Campion, M. A. (2009). Age stereotypes in the workplace: Common stereotypes, moderators, and future research directions? *Journal of Management*, 35, 158–188.

Regional Office for Europe WHO (1998). *Use of well-being measures in primary health care* – The DepCare project. Health for All, Target 12.

Roscigno, V. J., Mong, S., Byron, R. & Tester, G. (2007). Age discrimination, social closure and employment. *Social Forces*, 86(1), 313–334.

Snape, E. & Redman, T. (2003). Too old or too young? The impact of perceived age discrimination. *Human Resource Management Journal*, 13(1), 78–89.

Sousa-Poza, A. & Sousa-Poza, A. A. (2000). Well-being at work: A cross national analysis of the levels and determinants of job satisfaction. *Journal of Socio-Economics*, 29, 517–538.

Srivastava, S. (2013). Job satisfaction and organizational commitment relationship: Effect of personality variables. *Vision*, 17(2), 159–167.

Stansfeld, S. & Candy, B. (2006). Psychosocial work environment and mental health – a meta-analytic review. *Scandinavian Journal of Work, Environment and Health*, 32(6), 443–462.

Steel, T. & Tuori, A. (2019). Older jobseekers' temporal identity work. *Nordic Journal of Working Life Studies*, 9(3), 25–43.

Taylor, P., Mcloughlin, C., Meyer, D. & Brooke, E. (2013). Everyday discrimination in the workplace, job satisfaction and psychological wellbeing: Age differences and moderating variables. *Ageing & Society*, 33(7), 1105–1138.

Taylor, P. & Smith, W. (2017). What's age got to do with it? Towards a new advocacy on ageing and work. *Per Capita*.

Topino, E., Di Fabio, A., Palazzeschi, L. & Gori, A. (2021). Personality traits, workers' age, and job satisfaction: The moderated effect of conscientiousness. *PloS One*, 16(7).

WHO Collaborating Center for Mental Health (1998). *WHO-5 well-being index*. Geneva: World Health Organization.

Zaniboni, S. (2015). The interaction between older workers' personal resources and perceived age discrimination affects the desired retirement age and the expected adjustment. *Work, Aging and Retirement*, 1(3), 266–273.

Appendix

Table A5.1 List of countries in the sample

Countries
Austria, Belgium, France, Germany, Luxembourg Switzerland, Ireland, United Kingdom, Cyprus, Italy, Spain, Greece, Portugal, Malta, Norway, Sweden, Finland, Denmark, the Netherlands, Estonia, Latvia, Lithuania, Bulgaria, Croatia, Czech Republic, Poland, Hungary, Romania, Slovakia, Slovenia, Montenegro, FYROM, Serbia, Albania, Turkey.

Table A5.2 Variables' definition

Variable	*Definition*
Job satisfaction	It corresponds to question Q88 in the EWCS questionnaire about satisfaction with working conditions in the main paid job. It goes from 1 (very satisfied) to 4 (not at all satisfied) and has been rescaled (higher values indicate higher job satisfaction).
Mental health*	It corresponds to questions Q87A-Q87B-Q87C-Q87E in the EWCS questionnaire. Values go from 1 (all of the time) to 6 (at no time). Each question corresponds to a WHO-5 item. The composite variable (normalisation of the sum of each value and then multiplied by 100) has been rescaled (higher values indicate higher mental health score).
Female	Dummy variable equals to 1 if female and 0 otherwise.
Age	Person's age
Age squared	Age^2
Lower Education Level (reference group)	Dummy variable equals to 1 if the person has an early childhood education, a primary school certificate or a lower secondary education level, and 0 otherwise.
Secondary school diploma	Dummy variable equals to 1 if the person has an upper secondary education or a post-secondary non-tertiary education, and 0 otherwise.
University degree	Dummy variable equals to 1 if the person has a short-cycle tertiary education, a bachelor, a master or a doctorate or equivalent, and 0 otherwise.
Work-life balance	Variable corresponding to question Q44 in the EWCS questionnaire stating "In general, how do your working hours fit in with your family or social commitments outside work?" Dummy variable equals 1 if working hours fit in well or very well with family or social commitments outside work, and 0 otherwise.
Unpaid	Variable obtained by summing up and normalise the replies to questions Q95c (involvement in caring for and/or educating children, grandchildren), Q95d (involvement in cooking and housework), Q95e (involvement on caring for elderly/disabled relatives). The variable ranges from 0 to 100 and it is increasing in the degree of involvement on the whole in the three unpaid work activities.
Log(wage)	Logarithm of net hourly wage in national currency converted to Euro.
Part-time employment	Dummy variable equals to 1 if part-time worker, and 0 otherwise.
Temporary employment	Dummy variable equals to 1 if there is a temporary (not fixed) employment contract in the main job, and 0 otherwise.
No contract	Dummy variable equals to 1 if there is no employment contract in the main job, and 0 otherwise.

(*Continued*)

Table A5.2 (Continued)

Variable	*Definition*
Job demand	It is the sum of dummy variables on a job's organisational characteristics. Higher values indicate worse working conditions.
Job hazard	It is the sum of dummy variables on a job's physical characteristics. Higher values indicate worse working conditions.
Subjected to age discrimination	Dummy variable equals to 1 if over the past 12 months at work the person has been subjected to age discrimination, and 0 otherwise.
Subjected to ethnicity discrimination	Dummy variable equals to 1 if over the past 12 months at work the person has been subjected to discrimination linked to race, ethnic background or colour, and 0 otherwise.
Subjected to gender discrimination	Dummy variable equals to 1 if over the past 12 months at work the person has been subjected to discrimination on the basis of her/his gender, and 0 otherwise.
Subjected to discrimination for religion	Dummy variable equals to 1 if over the past 12 months at work the person has been subjected to discrimination linked to religion, and 0 otherwise.
Subjected to discrimination for disability	Dummy variable equals to 1 if over the past 12 months at work the person has been subjected to discrimination linked to disability, and 0 otherwise.
Firm with at least 250 employees	Dummy variable equals to 1 if the company or organisation has at least 250 employees, and 0 otherwise.
Agriculture (reference group)	Dummy variable equals to 1 if Agriculture, forestry and fishing (NACE Revision 2, 1 digit), and 0 otherwise.
Manufacturing	Dummy variable equals to 1 if Mining and quarrying; Manufacturing; Electricity, gas, steam and air conditioning; Water supply, sewerage, waste management (NACE Revision 2, 1 digit), and 0 otherwise.
Construction	Dummy variable equals to 1 if Construction (NACE Revision 2, 1 digit), and 0 otherwise.
Trade	Dummy variable equals to 1 if Wholesale and retail trade; Transportation and storage; Accommodation and food service activities (NACE Revision 2, 1 digit), and 0 otherwise.
Finance	Dummy variable equals to 1 if Financial and insurance activities (NACE Revision 2, 1 digit), and 0 otherwise.
Information and communication	Dummy variable equals to 1 if Information and communication (NACE Revision 2, 1 digit), and 0 otherwise.
Estate	Dummy variable equals to 1 if Real estate activities (NACE Revision 2, 1 digit), and 0 otherwise.
Administration and education	Dummy variable equals to 1 if Administrative and support services, public administration and defence;

(*Continued*)

Table A5.2 (Continued)

Variable	*Definition*
	Education (NACE Revision 2, 1 digit), and 0 otherwise.
Profession	Dummy variable equals to 1 if Professional, scientific and technical workers; Administrative and support service; Public administration and defence (NACE Revision 2, 1 digit), and 0 otherwise
Other	Dummy variable equals to 1 if other professions – Arts, entertainment and recreation; Other service activities; Activities of households; Activities of extraterritorial organisations (NACE Revision 2, 1 digit), and 0 otherwise.
Manager	Dummy variable equals to 1 if Managers (ISCO-08), and 0 otherwise.
Professional	Dummy variable equals to 1 if Professionals (ISCO-08), and 0 otherwise.
Technician	Dummy variable equals to 1 if Technicians and associate professionals (ISCO-08), and 0 otherwise.
Clerical support	Dummy variable equals to 1 if Clerical support workers (ISCO-08), and 0 otherwise.
Service and sales	Dummy variable equals to 1 if Service and sales workers (ISCO-08), and 0 otherwise.
Other occupational group (reference group)	Dummy variable equals to 1 if Skilled agricultural, forestry and fishery workers; Craft and related trades workers; Elementary workers; Armed forces (ISCO-08), and 0 otherwise.
Country groups by area	
Continental	Dummy variable equals to 1 if Austria, Belgium, France, Germany, Luxembourg or Switzerland, and 0 otherwise.
United Kingdom and Ireland	Dummy variable equals to 1 if Ireland or United Kingdom, and 0 otherwise.
Southern	Dummy variable equals to 1 if Cyprus, Italy, Spain, Greece, Portugal, Malta or Turkey, and 0 otherwise.
Nordic	Dummy variable equals to 1 if Norway, Sweden, Finland, Denmark or the Netherlands, and 0 otherwise.
Baltic	Dummy variable equals to 1 if Estonia, Latvia or Lithuania, and 0 otherwise.
Central Eastern (reference group)	Dummy variable equals to 1 if Bulgaria, Croatia, Czech Republic, Poland, Hungary, Romania, Slovakia, Slovenia, Montenegro, FYROM, Serbia or Albania, and 0 otherwise.
WHO-5 items* (question Q87 – EWCS)	
I have felt cheerful and in good spirits	Categorical variable. It goes from 1 (all of the time) to 6 (at no time). It has been rescaled, so higher values indicate a better condition.

(*Continued*)

Table A5.2 (Continued)

Variable	*Definition*
I have felt calm and relaxed	Categorical variable. It goes from 1 (all of the time) to 6 (at no time). It has been rescaled, so higher values indicate a better condition.
I have felt active and vigorous	Categorical variable. It goes from 1 (all of the time) to 6 (at no time). It has been rescaled, so higher values indicate a better condition.
I woke up feeling fresh and rested	Categorical variable. It goes from 1 (all of the time) to 6 (at no time). It has been rescaled, so higher values indicate a better condition.
My daily life has been filled with things that interest me	Categorical variable. It goes from 1 (all of the time) to 6 (at no time). It has been rescaled, so higher values indicate a better condition.

Table A5.3 Descriptive statistics by age and gender (%)

	<50		50+	
	M	F	M	F
Age	35.43	35.87	55.89	55.62
Secondary school diploma	0.51	0.49	0.49	0.51
University degree	0.31	0.38	0.28	0.29
Unpaid work	36.42	53.01	35.84	51.42
Work-life balance	0.78	0.83	0.84	0.88
Part-time employment	0.1	0.32	0.12	0.38
Temporary employment	0.14	0.15	0.07	0.08
No contract	0.08	0.06	0.05	0.05
Observations	11,334	11,923	4,951	5,471

6 Assessment of Extended Working Life in Albania on Various Dimensions of Well-Being from a Gender Perspective

Merita (Vaso) Xhumari and Megi Xhumari

Context analysis

The assessment of extended working life across different dimensions of well-being from a gender perspective in Albania is conducted in the context of the reforms and challenges that Albania is facing in its difficult road to becoming a market economy, remodelling the welfare state and being a European Union candidate country. Extended working life has not been a topic in political or media discourse, apart from measures introduced to increase the retirement age and some employment promotion programs for women. However, Albania's transformation of its economic and social systems has strongly impacted individuals' choices in this regard, making it an interesting case for analysing the gendered impacts of extended working life on the well-being of older workers, in order to support evidence-based policies.

In 1993, following the model of other ex-socialist countries, there were changes from a paternalistic model to a human rights model of social welfare with parametric reforms of the social insurance system (Xhumari, 2011). The parametric changes included unifying and increasing retirement age (the age at which workers are eligible to receive the contributory pension in Albania) from 45–50 to 55 years for women, depending on the occupational category, and from 50–55 to 60 years for men, apart from those who had worked in agricultural cooperatives; these have been decreased from 60 for women to 55 and from 65 for men to 60 years to be standardised with the rest. Unification of the pension system is to be a gradual process and is planned to be completed by 2056. Another parametric change was unifying and increasing the required social insurance period from 20/25 to 35 years to be entitled to a full old-age pension (Law no. 7703, dated 11.05.1993). Until 1993, the retirement age varied from 45 years old (for miners and others) to 65 years old (men working in agricultural cooperatives), depending on the categorisation of occupations and on the status of employment, whether in state-owned enterprises or in agricultural co-operatives. Thus two inherited social insurance schemes, one for employees working in state-owned enterprises mainly in urban areas (Law no. 4171, dated 13.09.1966), that provides what was called a "state pension", and another for those working in agricultural cooperatives in rural areas (Law 4976, dated

DOI: 10.4324/9781003145325-6

29.06.1972) who receive what was called a "cooperative pension".[1] This is only one aspect of the differences in the way of living between urban and rural areas in Albania, especially for women who are predominantly to be found working in agriculture, compared to men.

In 1991, an early retirement scheme was introduced (Decree no. 7464, dated 31.01.1991), as an instrument of the Government for dealing with the massive unemployment of older workers who were within five years from their formal retirement age. Until 1989, the employment rate was almost 100 per cent, with about 890 thousand employees in state-owned enterprises, and with about 550 thousand in agriculture cooperatives. In 1990, the unemployment rate was 8.5 per cent of the labour force, and by 1992 it had increased to 26.5 per cent (UNDP, ILO and Ministry of Labour, Emigration and Ex-Persecuted, 1995, p. 24). In this context, the early retirement scheme artificially increased the number of pensioners, while the pensioner-to-social insurance contributors' ratio (dependency ratio of the pension system) reached a critical point (1:1), which remains almost the same today (SII, 2021). The unintended consequences nowadays are apparent as the pension reforms have not been integrated with active labour market policies and adequate skills development for young people, as well as for older workers. Both these categories remain vulnerable groups in the labour market.

The life course paradigm, as a multidimensional approach, takes into consideration many dimensions of an individual's life through different trajectories such as education, employment, and retirement in a societal context (institutions, legislation, social norms and so on). From this perspective, policies should aim to allow young workers, being the older workers of tomorrow, and other vulnerable groups to be able to work in conditions that allow them to continue working until retirement age, which is likely to increase in the coming years (EU-OSHA, Cedefop, Eurofound and EIGE, 2017).

In Albania, the limited capacity of the government to regulate the labour market, along with the impact of regional and global crises, has led to low employment rates, long-term unemployment and informal employment in the labour market. The unregulated migration from rural to urban areas brought cheaper labour, as the rural population did not have many opportunities to work on the land that was distributed to them from cooperatives in 1991 (Law no. 7501, dated 19.07.1991). The land given to the rural population for use has changed their status, from being employees in agriculture cooperatives to being self-employed in agriculture. However many of them, not being owners of their land, and in some cases because of conflicts with former land owners before the socialist period, preferred to move to urban areas or abroad for better employment and life opportunities. This situation distorted labour relations in the fragile private sector, which is characterised by informal employment and temporary contracts.

The employment structure nowadays consists of 45.7 per cent in paid employment, while 32.3 per cent are self-employed and 22 per cent are contributing family workers. About 31 per cent of women as compared to 18 per cent of men are contributing family workers (INSTAT, 2019b). This illustrates the prevalence of small family businesses in the Albanian labour market. Informal self-employment and unpaid family work are widespread in agriculture, particularly among young men and older women. Although more than half of the employment increase in 2018 involved women, they continued to be under-represented in full-time employment with a 40.2 per cent employment rate, as compared to an employment rate of 54.6 per cent for men of working age (18–64). Unemployment remains a significant challenge for the 40+ age group, which represents 64 per cent of registered job seekers. About 70 per cent of registered unemployed are long-term unemployed (World Bank Group & Wiiw, 2019).

Demographic projections show a clear trend of an increasing old-age dependency ratio increasing from 20.5 older people per 100 people of working age in 2019 to 35 in 2031; while the youth dependency ratio will remain at 25.0 young people per 100 people of working age (INSTAT, 2019a). The fertility rate declined from three births per woman in 1990 to 1.6 in 2018. Above the age of 40 there are already more women than men at each age cohort. Life expectancy at birth has increased from 72 years in 1990 to 78 years in 2018 (80 and 76 years among women and men, respectively) (INSTAT, 2021b). Such demographic trends need to be reflected in policies on ageing, especially directed towards women who form the majority of the population aged above 40 years old.

In 2019, the Albanian population was 2,854,191 inhabitants, and about 1,684,135 Albanian migrants live outside its territory (884,719 males and 799,416 females), mainly as a result of emigration after 1990; 76 per cent of emigrants are of working age (15–64). In 2019, for the first time, the increase in women migrants (2.7%) was higher than that of men (2.6%) (INSTAT, 2020b). The main causes of emigration are high levels of unemployment in Albania and better employment opportunities and incomes abroad. For women, family reunification is also considered to be one of the main factors (INSTAT, 2014, p. 9). Emigration has had a direct impact on the labour market, on the sustainability of the PAYG pension system, and on family support of the older population and the well-being of Albanian families. While remittances accounted for about 28 per cent of Gross Domestic Product (GDP) in 1993, this has gradually declined to 9.6 per cent of GDP in 2019 (World Bank, 2019). This trend shows a pressing need for labour market policies and pension reforms to provide adequate incomes and living standards, as support from family members living abroad will further reduce for the older population. The expectation of older people to be supported by their emigrant family members seems to be gradually decreasing. This is even more significant in the context of a drastic reduction of the replacement rates of pensions, from 70 per cent of average wages in the beginning of 1990 to 40 per cent in recent years. Changes in family structure, as more young couples live separately from their parents, urbanisation and mobility has led to changes in how and where people live including residing in unknown neighbourhoods. All these factors are weakening traditional connections and supports to the older population. As the National Action Plan on Ageing 2020–2024 states, "This speedy demographic transition the country has experienced, has been accompanied by both a decrease in the size of family units and an ever-declining tradition of supporting the elderly. In addition, unlike most of the countries in the region, Albania has not inherited a traditional and integrated system of social and health care for the elderly" (DCM No. 864, dated 24.12.2019).

In 2019, the level of "at risk of poverty" for the age group 65 years and older was 12.9 per cent for males and 14.8 per cent for females; the level is higher for the age group 18–64, with 22.3 per cent of males and 23.3 per cent of females being at risk of poverty. The risk of poverty rate for employed individuals aged 18 and above is estimated at 14.6 per cent, while it is 28.7 per cent for the inactive population. There is also a difference when comparing households without dependent children (14.2%) to households with dependent children (27.2%). In general, referring to this indicator, Albania (23.0%) has a lower rate than the other Western Balkan countries, Montenegro (24.5%), Serbia (23.2%), and Romania (23.8%), while it is considerably higher than the EU average (28 countries) at 16.8 per cent (INSTAT, 2021a, p. 2). Promoting active ageing is a pressing need to reduce the risk of poverty for women and to increase their well-being across the life course.

Methodologically, this chapter is based on a desk review of the legal framework, strategies, policy documents, studies and statistical reports on pensions, labour markets, education and training. The life course perspective is used for assessing complex factors influencing extended working life such as education, employment, work-life balance and pension policies. Statistical data from INSTAT on demographic projections, Labour Force Survey (LFS) and enterprise surveys are complemented with data from Eurostat and the World Bank on labour market indicators. The Eurofound EWCS 2015 and EQLS 2016 surveys are used for analysing age and gender patterns in work-life balance (Eurofound, 2017, 2019). The Gender Equality Index report is used for assessing gender gaps.

The analysis addresses questions on how pensions, labour market, education and Vocational Education and Training (VET) policies, as well as regulated working relations in Albania, deal with extended working life from a gender perspective. For each policy domain, the key relevant reforms are presented in order to provide insights into how strategically Albania addresses specific dimensions of extended working life from a gender perspective.

The chapter is structured as follows: the above context analysis is followed by discussion on pension reforms, which are considered to be passive policies for extending working life. The focus then turns to the active labour market policies which have been implemented in recent years and then on education and training. Job satisfaction and family obligations are analysed as important factors that influence workers' decisions for continuing employment, especially for women; and finally future policy directions are discussed.

Passive policies for extending working life

In 1993, the social security system was adapted to the new social needs of the complex changes in the labour market, social structure and migration trends by unifying the rights and obligations of all categories of the economically active population. Pension policy was used to give an "ad hoc" solution to massive unemployment through early retirement. The early old-age pension, calculated at 60 per cent of the average best wages of the last three years of employment, as well as the low retirement age for certain professionals (especially those working in textiles, metallurgy, mining and other economic sectors that closed after the structural economic reforms in the beginning of the 1990 aimed at creating a market economy), artificially increased the number of pensioners. This was calculated by the ILO at 182[2] per cent of the population aged 65+ (ILO, 2005); and at 140 per cent by the World Bank (World Bank, 2006). During 1994–2002, the burden of the pension cost was transferred to the surviving labour force by doubling social insurance contributions to 42.5 per cent of the gross wage, out of which 31.7 per cent was for pensions, divided between employers and employees (Law no. 7703, dated 11.05.1993).[3]

From the reform of 2002 until today, pensioners are offered the right to receive their pension and to continue working and paying contributions. If people do not receive their pension but continue working and paying contributions past retirement age, their amount of pension is increased by 0.5 per cent for each month; but if they ask for early retirement, their amount of pension is reduced by 0.6 per cent for each month (Law no. 7703, dated 11.05.1993). What has been the result? In 2017, about 11 per cent of women pensioners (above 60 years old) and 13.6 per cent of men pensioners (above 65 years old) extended working life beyond retirement age. In 2019, these shares had increased to 15 and 17.2 per cent, respectively. In 2019, most men (63.8%) who extended working life above retirement age belonged to the category "Own-account workers", while about 55.5 per cent of the women who extended working life belonged to the category "Contributing family workers". In relation to the causes of economic inactivity, in general, women remain out of the labour force mostly because they are engaged in unpaid work at home (18.%), while only one per cent of men declare "working in the home" as the reason behind their economic inactivity (INSTAT, 2020a, p. 71).

In 2020, referring to the types of old-age pension, retired women receiving a rural pension make up two-thirds (66.5%) of total rural pension recipients. This means that women predominate in having agriculture as their main economic activity, a sector with the lowest incomes compared to other economic activities. In 2020, the average monthly rural old-age pension (9,295 ALL,[4] which is approximately €75) was more than half of the average monthly urban old-age pension (15,732 ALL; €130). Even among urban old-age pensions, the average pension for women was 20 per cent lower than for men, because of their lower contribution period (26.9 years for women compared to 31.3 years for men). This reflects the fact that women are more likely to be outside the formal labour market, while both men and women are required to accumulate 37 years of insurance contributions to be eligible for a full old-age pension (SII, 2021). The average net replacement rate for old-age pensions in Albania (the individual net pension entitlement divided by net pre-retirement average earnings) was about 40 per cent. While this is in accordance with the International Labour Organisation (ILO) minimum standard of pensions (40%, Convention, 102/1952), currently, the EU minimum living standard is defined as 60 per cent of average income (European Commission, 2010).

During the period 1993–2020, the average real retirement age increased by ten years, from 53 to 63 years of age. Women's average retirement age remains five years earlier than men, and their average length of time for being in receipt of a pension is six years longer than for men (25.6 years, compared to 19.3 years) (SII, 2021) due to their longer life expectancy compared to men. In Albania, the paradox is that stipulating the retirement age by law is taken more as a right for employers to lay off employees, rather than as a right of employees to decide to retire. One consequence of these recent developments therefore appears to be less room for individual choice and opportunities for extending working life. This is also perhaps because representatives of social partners at the governing body of the Social Insurance Institute (SII), such as trade unions, have raised the question of early retirement for certain categories of workers such as miners, but they have never discussed the potential of people wanting to extend working life.

Active labour market policies

Extending working lives should not be limited to policies such as increasing retirement age and insurance period, but should also encompass employment promotion services, employers' incentives to offer work flexibility for the transition to retirement and training opportunities during the life course. Since 1995, active labour market policies have been formalised with Law no. 7995, dated 20.09.1995 which identified both the youngest age group (15–29) and the 55+ group as among the vulnerable population categories that need targeted employment services due to their high unemployment rates (INSTAT, 2019b).

Table 6.1 shows that between 2018 and 2019, labour force participation increased more among women than among men at all age groups, perhaps as a result of employment promoting programmes targeting women's inclusion in the

Table 6.1 Labour force participation rate by age and gender in 2018–2019 (%)

Age-group	*Men*		*Women*		*Total*	
	2018	*2019*	*2018*	*2019*	*2018*	*2019*
Total(15+)	67.6	68.0	51.4	53.0	59.4	60.4
15–24	43.4	43.2	27.6	30.2	35.8	36.7
25–29	88.1	88.3	68.3	75.3	78.3	82.0
25–54	90.7	90.6	75.6	77.4	83.0	83.9
55–64	78.5	79.4	49.1	50.8	63.7	65.2
65+	19.0	19.8	10.4	11.7	14.5	15.6

Source: INSTAT, Labour Force Surveys 2018, 2019, www.instat.gov.al.

workforce. However, in 2019 there was still a gender gap in total labour force participation of 15 per cent, especially in the age-group 55–64, where it is almost double, with a difference of 28.6 percentage points.

The World Bank emphasised a gender gap in employment rates where women continue to have 15 per cent lower employment rates compared to men. In 2018, the employment rate was 46 per cent for women aged 55–64, compared to 54 per cent for all women of working age; this compares to 71 per cent for men aged 55–64.[5] Part-time employment of women was 25 per cent, compared to 15 per cent for men; while the share of women who are self-employed is 25 per cent, compared to 42 per cent for men (World Bank Group & Wiiw, 2019, pp. xi, xiii, 81). The share of women who are employed part-time and self-employed is the same, while men have more opportunities to be employed full-time or to be self-employed in their own businesses and to extend their working life. Referring to the employment of the registered unemployed age group 50+ by employment agencies, they account for only 14 per cent of total employees in 2018 (NESA, 2019). This suggests that if older employees lose their job, they find it difficult to get back to work and employment agencies have not been successful in finding jobs for unemployed older workers. That fact is confirmed also by the perception of the older population of job insecurity, which is higher compared to other age groups, according to the EQLS (2016) and EWCS (2015) surveys.

The Gender Equality Index for the domain of work in Albania is 67.6 and is lower than the average for the EU28 by only 4.4 points. Albania performs better than the EU average in terms of participation in the labour market, but less so in terms of the segregation and quality of work. The full-time equivalent employment rate was 40.2 per cent for women and 54.6 per cent for men. A gender gap is visible according to the indicator that measures the duration of working life in Albania: for women, this is 31.2 years (compared to 33.4 years in the EU28) and for men it is 40.5 years (compared to 38.3 years in the EU28) (EIGE, MoHSP, INSTAT & World Bank, 2020). If we compare these indicators with those of social insurance, there is a difference. The registered insurance period of women who received an old-age pension in 2020 was 26.9 years, while that of men was 31.3 years. The difference between the years of employment and pension contribution suggests that informal economic activities in Albania are an important source of income for many families. It is important to know that everybody of working age has an opportunity to contribute to a pension even though they are not in formal employment through the voluntary social insurance scheme, which is a complementary scheme for compulsory social insurance (Law no. 7703, date 11.05.1993, Art.3). Voluntary social insurance offers an opportunity also for Albanian emigrants who live abroad, if they want to be covered by the Albanian social insurance system, to do so.

New typologies of private sector employment, such as part-time work, self-employment, family businesses, seasonal jobs, remote working and online working, have opened opportunities for people to extend working life beyond retirement age. While permanent and full-time jobs are generally considered "good quality", part-time or temporary/seasonal jobs may be considered as a bridge to full employment for women, as women represent 69 per cent of those who are long-term unemployed. However, high levels of youth unemployment, informal employment, low wages, lack of adequate skills and insufficient public services create difficulties for women's employment. The low activity rates of women are also related to low levels of education, the need to care for family and reliance on remittances (World Bank Group & Wiiw, 2019, pp. xv, 5).

The ILO integrated approach which combines economic policies with targeted measures addressing labour market demand and supply through education and training is orienting recent reforms in Albania. In 2017, employment, VET and SIIs were transferred from the responsibility of the Ministry of Labour and Social Welfare to the Ministry of Economy and Finance. In this context, the National Employment and Skills Agency (NESA) has been reorganised to strengthen its capacity to develop periodic surveys of enterprises of their employees, working conditions and training needs (DCM no. 554, dated 31.07.2019). The representation of employers and trade unions at the Governing Council of NESA is expected to develop a fruitful social dialogue.

The National Strategy on Employment and Skills 2014–2020 (extended to 2022) and specific measures in the National Action Plan for Women Entrepreneurs 2014–2020 aim to improve women's position in the labour market, increasing their employment and reducing women's role as contributory family workers. It aims for greater economic empowerment, particularly of women who are employed in the agriculture sector, through subsidising self-employed women and the provision of social/public services that are currently limited in rural areas (DCM, no. 659/2019).

Recently, the World Bank assessed that gender gaps in education and health have almost disappeared in Albania. Nevertheless, women face more obstacles than men throughout their lives in building a successful career or starting a business. A World Bank policy financing loan was therefore provided to improve women's access to assets, to enhance job opportunities and to strengthen gender-informed policy (World Bank Albania, 2020).

Employment promotion programmes for specific categories of women, such as those in households with children under 18 years old who have a higher level of being at risk of poverty, support employers by subsidising social insurance contributions and some wages, up to the level of minimum wage, for six months for new jobs that are offered to women who fall into these categories (DCM no. 27, dated 11.01.2012). Unemployed women who are looking for a job continue to benefit from employment promotion programmes more than men. The number of unemployed women jobseekers increases with age, while the data show the opposite for men (INSTAT, 2020a, p. 73).

Employment depends heavily not only on employment services, but also on the spectrum of economic activities. Male employees predominate in the mining and quarrying industry (89.7% of all employees), while women (73.7%) are more likely to be in the human health and social work activities sector. Women's employment in processing industries is 59 per cent of the total. The average hourly gender pay gap in this sector was 6.8 per cent, while among employees in the mining and quarrying industry and related activities, the gender pay gap is highest at 35.1 per cent. In processing industries, food services and agriculture where women are in the majority, wages are below the average level. However, in administrative and support service activities, where female employees predominate, women get paid 11.5 per cent more than men. The average hourly earnings per employee are highest in financial and insurance activities, with a difference between men (609ALL; €4.82) and women (571ALL; €4.52). Gender inequality in earnings is higher for full-time employees at 7.1 per cent, where women account for 49.2 per cent of workers, so there is a considerable proportion of women with lower wages compared to men. For part-time employees, of whom 57.5 per cent are women, the average wages of women are 1.5 per cent higher compared to men's wages (INSTAT, 2018a, pp. 9–12).

Along with the overall gender gap in earnings, there are notable age differences. The gender gap in hourly wages is highest in the 40–49-year age group – women 282ALL (€2.23) men 318ALL (€2.52). For the age group 50–59 years, there is a slight decline in earnings for both sexes, but it increases again for the group aged 60 years and over (women 314ALL (€2.48); men 333ALL (€2,63)) (INSTAT, 2018a). Women employed at 60 years and over with high earnings may include those with a title as professor, who have a higher retirement age of (68 years), with the possibility to be further extended (Law no. 80/2015, Art.65). But this professor category is dominated by men. For example, if we consider the case of the University of Tirana, which is the biggest and the oldest university in Albania, where women with the title "professor" comprise only 13.3 per cent of the total female academic staff, while the percentage of men who are professors comprise about 25.4 per cent of male academic staff (www.unitir.edu.al). This suggests that some social, cultural, economic or institutional barriers may have limited females' careers. The difference in earnings may also reflect women's greater engagement in family work including raising children which prevents them from pursuing a management career or taking on leading positions.

Education and training

The dynamic of labour market demand has increased the need for qualified labour to respond to a competitive open market. The known correlation between employment and education has increased the interest in and opportunities for education in Albania, with private schools becoming available at all levels of education over the past decade. Major progress was made towards increasing access to education and school enrolment rates at all levels, particularly for girls. Nevertheless, the education system is still behind in responding to labour market needs due to the increased demand for qualified employees; education and training needs to be compatible also with the regional and global labour market demand.

The proportion of people engaged in adult learning or training in Albania is quite low at ten per cent, in both work and non-work-related training (Eurofound, 2019), while the EU objective for participation in "Education & Training 2020" was at least 15 per cent. The concept of training and lifelong learning combines education with work activity and creates opportunities especially for women and older workers to adjust their skills and competencies to be able to extend their working life. In Albania there are not many opportunities for training offered by the educational system or by employers. Since 2013, the idea of schools as multifunctional community centres open to people of all ages has been introduced. Universities can also offer short-term training courses since the last reform (Law no. 80/2015, Art.81). However, the higher education institutions have not used such opportunities to offer training as a form of life-long learning programme (Albanian Government, 2021).*

LeTSGEPs' Horizon 2020 project is assisting the University of Tirana to design a Gender Equality Plan in the context of the requirement announced by the EU for any applicant for Horizon Europe 2021–2027 projects.[6] The Gender Equality Plan (GEP) 2021–2022 of the University of Tirana aims to enhance women's career in leadership positions as a gender gap in the 50+ age group was identified given the higher prevalence of men in management and leadership, although 60 per cent of academic staff and students are women. The GEP has a broader vision to change the traditional culture, and above all to change the outlook of students and the younger generation in respecting gender equality principles in all aspects of society. The integration of gender dimensions in teaching and research and developing online courses on gender equality will increase awareness of the topic among the most educated population. However, in addition to the GEP to comply with the European Commission requirements for Horizon Europe 2027 projects, more needs to be done to prompt changes from "within" the university to support women to progress their careers and to facilitate work-life balance.

In fulfilment of the United Nations (UN) Agenda 2030 SDG4 "Ensuring inclusive and equitable quality education and promoting lifelong learning opportunities for all", and the EU integration process, the National Strategy on Education 2021–2026 is based on a lifelong learning paradigm, which includes all stages of learning, from preschool to the period after retirement and covers all forms of learning, "formal, non-formal and informal" (Albanian Government, 2021, p. 7). The Action Plan on Ageing 2020–2024 designed for the first time by the Albanian Government aims also to support older women and men to be integrated into society, to enable a long, healthy and active life, to extend working life and maintain the ability to work, and to promote lifelong learning. It also aims to create a "University of Older Age" as part of a collaboration between state institutions and civil society organisations aimed at "Learning throughout life" (DCM, no. 864/2019). Lifelong learning is considered an important component of the new strategic vision in education 2021–2026 and special attention is paid to VET (Law no. 15/2017).

Job satisfaction and family obligations

Along with the reform of the social insurance system, employment policies, education and training opportunities, other factors that will affect possibilities for extending working life are job satisfaction and family obligations. The age and gender differences in employment activity and earnings among other factors are related to work-life balance, affordable services and family support. The Eurofound EWCS and EQLS surveys, which were administered in Albania for the first time in 2015 and 2016 respectively, indicated that there is a difficult employment position for women aged 50 years and older, reporting high levels of job insecurity, low wages, low job satisfaction and tension between employers and workers (Eurofound, 2017; Eurofound, 2019). Such perceptions are also reflected by the Albanian LFS which shows that 31 per cent of women are unpaid contributing family workers, as compared to 18 per cent of men (INSTAT, 2019b). In this context, women require more support to be able to combine employment with caring and other unpaid contributions to the family, in order to avoid the risk of being formally unemployed or having to make an early exit to retirement.

The EWCS (2015) results for Albania show gender differences regarding the question "if people will be able to continue current jobs until 60 years of age". The level of positive respondents at 72 per cent is high for the 50+ age group in employment, but for all age groups of women, it is lower at 61 per cent for all women, compared to 67 per cent for all men. Regarding the question: "How satisfied are you with working conditions in your main paid job?" eighteen per cent of those in the age group 50–64 responded "Not at all satisfied" and 36 per cent responded "Not very satisfied". Therefore, more than half of all older workers do not have adequate working conditions to motivate them to extend their working life. In response to the question regarding current employment "Does the work involve tiring or painful positions?" fifty per cent of male and 47 per cent of female older workers answered "Between 1/4–3/4 of the time", while 24 per cent of women and 20 per cent of men gave the answer "Almost all of the time" (Eurofound, 2017).

In addition, according to the EQLS (2016), 86 per cent of women reported being too tired from work to carry out household jobs, in comparison to 64 per cent of men. Similarly, 67 per cent of women reported having difficulties fulfilling family responsibilities because of work, in comparison to 49 per cent of men (Eurofound, 2019). The Albanian LFS also shows that among the reasons for not taking up employment by women of working age were their engagement in domestic chores (22%) and early retirement (40%) (INSTAT, 2017). Apart from the need to improve workplace conditions, training and work-time arrangements, changes in cultural norms are also needed to make the gender division of household duties more equal.

The Gender Equality Index in the domain of time use for Albania is 48.1, indicating very unbalanced responsibilities regarding care for family members and unpaid household work. While women carry most of these responsibilities, they do not participate as much as men in social activities that are important for their well-being and quality of life. The share of persons reporting that they care for their children or grandchildren, older people or people with special needs every day is 51.1 per cent for women and 24.6 per cent for men. The difference is even more prominent where everyday cooking and housework are concerned, as this kind of activity is performed by 87.8 per cent of women and by only 16.1 per cent of men. On the other hand, women spend less time in sporting, cultural or other leisure activities outside of their home (EIGE, MoHSP, INSTAT & World Bank, 2020, p. 18).

The EQLS (2016) shows a gender gap regarding the health of Albanians that should be taken into account when considering implications for maintaining working capabilities and functional skills. Older women reported a higher risk of depression (57%) than men (33%). Promoting activities to help mitigate depression, such as sports, is recommended given that only 12 per cent of Albanians take part in sports or physical exercise, compared to the EU28 average of 42 per cent. In Albania, 40 per cent of respondents from rural areas and 20 per cent of the urban population report that they find it difficult to access recreational or green areas (Eurofound, 2019).

Work-life balance improvements have recently been introduced by the Labour Code (2015), for instance, by limiting the working week to a maximum of 48 hours, providing more flexible working arrangements, and recognising telework and work from home as on a par with other types of employment. Flexibility based on the ability of women and men to get an hour or two off during working hours to perform activities related to family care has also been made possible. New mothers have the right to request paid rest time during the working day and at least four months of unpaid annual leave for parents is now also possible. Social insurance provides paid 365 days of maternity leave, and in 2017 the right of fathers to take paternity leave after the first 63 days of mandatory leave for mothers was also recognised. Traditionally, public primary schools offer classes until 13:00, so grandparents often take care of children if both parents have full-time jobs. Otherwise, usually the mother stops working at some point to take care of the children. In Albania, there is no support from either public or private employers for childcare services.

Improving access to childcare and introducing child and family benefits as part of the social protection system similar to those in many EU and Western Balkan countries is recommended to facilitate work-life balance.

Policy reflections

New social risks such as informal employment, part-time and seasonal employment, long-term unemployment and trends of population ageing, emigration, changes in family and culture, have led to the need for new societal interventions. Traditional society linked to a standard full-time worker who lives in a traditional family, where older and younger generations co-reside and support each other, is gradually disappearing. Social protection, employment services, education and labour relations need to be adjusted to keep pace with societal changes. "This situation is amplified even more by the higher levels of emigration of the young people and middle-aged individuals, which makes it necessary to treat the issues of the ageing of population as amongst the main priorities of the Albanian Government", was emphasised in the National Action Plan on Ageing 2020–2024 (DCM, No. 864, dated 24.12.2019).

Parametric reforms of the social insurance system to increase the retirement age and the insurance period have had a direct impact on extending the working life by ten years, despite the pension replacement rate being almost halved from 70 per cent in 1990 to about 40 per cent in 2020. From a life-course perspective, this is likely to exacerbate older women's disadvantage in terms of their economic independence, as they are more likely to work in the informal sector, part-time and as contributing family workers. Consequently, women typically have lower wages and pensions and a higher likelihood of being at risk of poverty in retirement, because women live for a longer period, due to their higher life expectancy compared to men.

The analysis of different indicators from various sources, combining administrative data with citizens' perceptions, confirms decreasing standards of living for those in the age group 50+, especially women. As the EWCS (2015) and EQLS (2016) surveys demonstrate, societal action is needed to address inequalities and differences between generations, women and men, and between urban and rural dwellers. In the context of high levels of tension between employers and employees, there is a need for social dialogue regarding the hardships that women and older age groups experience such as a high risk of depression, feeling tired from work, difficulties in work-life balance, insecurity in keeping their jobs until retirement and income inadequacy. Strengthening families' capacities through increasing access to and improving the quality of public services is an important way to promote women's employment, work-life balance and income adequacy. The persistent gender gap in employment, wages and pensions shows that employment services, education, VET and pension policies should be diversified to specific individual needs, according to age, gender and urban-rural differences.

Most countries in the Western Balkans have recently engaged in labour market flexibilisation and minimum wage increases; however, a major reform of the entire system of labour taxation and social insurance might serve as the most promising avenue for the revitalisation of regional labour markets. Introducing a progressive labour taxation system, especially at low wage levels, could boost formal employment and increase net labour income (World Bank Group & Wiiw, 2019, p. xiii). In this context, the Albanian government has introduced a progressive tax system for wages and other income and exempted minimum wages from taxes, which is a direct benefit for women.

The way in which incentives for extending working life introduced by the social insurance reforms are implemented shows that there is less room for individual choice and opportunities for extending working life, as it is largely the employer's decision, in both the public and private sector. As the formal retirement age is used by employers to force older employees to exit the labour market without taking into consideration their expectations and capabilities to continue their active working life, full-time or part-time, it is important to note that the implementation of the National Action Plan for Ageing 2020–2024 will promote positive attitudes towards older employees, and to combat age discrimination in the workplace (DCM, No. 864, dated 24.12.2019). The representatives of social partners at the decision-making bodies of SII, NESA and trade unions, have not discussed the potential of people wanting to extend working life. About 13 per cent of pensioners continue their working life mainly through being self-employed, a proportion that is likely to increase in the future. However, to have a clear understanding of their situation, some questions on peoples' expectations on extended working life need to be included in the Albanian LFS that is administered quarterly by INSTAT. More data will assist researchers to perform in-depth analysis on the gender implications of measures for extending working life.

These findings could provide an additional impetus to re-examine income inequalities and work-life balance, especially in the context of the critical situation of COVID-19. The economy is likely to suffer from both a demand shock, due to the closure of small family businesses, and a labour supply shock, as a result of the restricted measures due to social distancing. Employment, education and VET systems as well as labour relations should be adapted to provide more flexibility, adequate skills and competencies different from traditional education, to match demand and labour supply, and above all to proceed with future technological, structural and cultural changes. The Labour Code could offer more flexibility in choices for working online from home and in promoting training in the working place. Referring to the recent employment promotion programme for employers, those who develop skills through in-job training will be subsidised by the government; such policy measures are expected to increase women's employment prospects. Lifelong learning will create an environment for self-fulfilment and will help advance job skills and flexibility for older workers in their transition to retirement.

Extending the coverage of compulsory social insurance to unpaid and contributing family workers and of voluntary public social insurance to those self-employed in agriculture to obtain more than the minimum level of pensions will enhance the adequacy of benefits, as about 90 per cent of old-age pensions are at minimum levels. The unequal distribution of employment and other public services to the rural and urban population might be diminished with the administrative-territorial reform of 2015 that merged small (rural) communes and (urban) municipalities into 61 large municipalities. In addition, local government units have been granted more competencies in terms of providing social welfare services and making sure they are both available and working. This includes the decentralisation of essential public services delegated to regional bodies (employment, VET and social insurance) and to local governments (social assistance and social services). However, the increased competencies need to be accompanied by additional human and financial resources, as this will ensure the provision of good quality services and effective social welfare.

Gender-responsive budgeting as part of the Public Finance Management Strategy 2014–2020, from central government (Law no. 57/2016) is extended to local government (Law no. 68/2017) including annual and mid-term budget programming (Albanian Government 2019). At least one policy objective should be gender-based and should measure gender-related outputs and outcomes. Public institutions are asked to provide gender-based disaggregated data. There are 34 gender-responsive budgeting programs for the period 2019–2021, which include funds for increasing women's entrepreneurship, especially in agriculture. The Gender Equality Index for Albania is 60.4 points, seven points lower than the EU28 average (EIGE, MoHSP, INSTAT & World Bank, 2020). Since 2004, a special law on gender equality imposes changes to all legal frameworks such as the introduction of the right to paternity leave, although in 2018 there were only six per cent of fathers out of total beneficiaries from this right (SII, 2019, p. 29). It means that mentalities, traditions and people's behaviour do not change immediately with the establishment of the law, but it takes time. Policy driven by the National Strategy on Gender Equality 2016–2020 aims above all at the economic empowerment of women and at developing societal awareness of gender equality (DCM, No. 733, dated 20.10.2016). One of its objectives was the reduction of women's unpaid domestic work by increasing access to and the quality of social services for children, older people and others in need of care, but there is no evaluation of whether this objective is fulfilled. The National Policy and Action Plan on Ageing 2020–2024 also emphasised the objective of providing supportive motivating work environments for people before their retirement and fostering lifelong learning (DCM, no. 866, dated 24.12.2019).

Harmonising policies, coordinating efforts and increasing the effectiveness of existing resources are necessary. Increasing the capacity development of all stakeholders and implementation of an integrated planning system for social protection, employment, education and vocational training are important policy goals. The Albanian National Strategy for Development and Integration (NSDI) II (extended to 2022) has defined as the main objectives of expanding employment opportunities, enhancing the quality of education, consolidating social protection and building an inclusive society (UN, 2018, p. 41). The Integrated Planning System implemented in the NSDI aims towards coherence between objectives in the economy, employment, education and social protection; however, their coordination remains a challenge. Regular evaluation through research and monitoring instruments will enable successful implementation of the strategic objectives and evidence-based policy.

Notes

1 These two types of pensions have differences not only in eligibility criteria, but above all in the amount of benefits, where the "cooperative pension" is very low compared to "state pension". In the reform of 1993, the two existing schemes were unified into one social insurance system and for a transitional period the differences were gradually diminished. In the official statistical reports after 1993, the terminology used to show the existing differences was "urban pension" for the category of "state pensions" which means for all those whose right to a pension is related to the period of employment in state-owned enterprises, and "rural pension" for "agriculture cooperative members' pensions".

2 182 per cent may look absurd, but the official retirement ages in Albania started from 45 years old, which with the new Law 7703, dated 11.05.1993 has been gradually increased, a process that continues today.
3 The amount of social insurance contributions was gradually reduced and today it is 24.5 per cent of the gross wage, out of which 21.6 per cent for pensions, 0.3 per cent for employment injuries, 0.3 per cent for sickness, 1.4 per cent for maternity/paternity benefits and 0.9 per cent for unemployment.
4 ALL is the international code for the Albanian Lek.
5 Take into consideration that in 2018 the retirement age of women was 60 years and of men 65 years.
6 www.letsgeps.eu

References

Albanian Government (2019). *Public finance management strategy 2019–2022*, available at: http://www.financa.gov.al/wp-content/uploads/2020/06/PFM-Strategy-2019-2022-ENG.pdf (accessed December 20, 2020).

Albanian Government (2021). *National strategy on education 2021–2026*, available at: https://arsimi.gov.al/wp-content/uploads/2021/05/Draft-Strategjia-per-Arsimin-2021-2026-1.pdf (accessed September 21, 2021).

Council of Europe (2018). *Recommendation on key competences for lifelong learning*. Official Journal of the European Union 2018/C 189/01, available at: https://eur-lex.europa.eu/legal-content/EN/TXT/PDF/?uri=CELEX:32018H0604(01)&rid=7 (accessed 20 December 2020).

Decision of the Council of Ministers (DCM) No. 151, dated 19.02.2020 "*On the National Plan for European Integration (NPEI) 2020–2022*," available at: https://qbz.gov.al/eli/vendim/2020/02/19/151 (accessed 25 September 2021).

Decision of the Council of Ministers (DCM) No. 864, dated 24.12.2019 "*On the adoption of the 2020–2024 National Policy Document on aging and the national action plan for its implementation*," available at: http://acpd.org.al/wp-content/uploads/2021/01/PLANI-KOMB%C3%8BTAR-I-VEPRIMIT-MBI-MOSHIMIN-Anglisht.pdf (accessed 20 September 2021).

Decision of the Council of Ministers (DCM) no. 659/2019. "*National strategy for employment and skills 2019–2022*," available at: https://www.financa.gov.al/wp-content/uploads/2020/10/Publikim_EN_Strategjia-Komb%C3%ABtare-p%C3%ABr-Pun%C3%ABsim-dhe-Aft%C3%ABsi-2019-2022.pdf (accessed 25 September 2021).

DCM no. 554, dated 31.07.2019 "*On the establishment, manner of organization and functioning of the National Employment and Skills Agency," available at:* https://qbz.gov.al/

Decision of the Council of Ministers No. 733, dated 20.10.2016 "*National Strategy on Gender Equality and Action Plan (NSAPGE) 2016–2020*", available at: https://albania.un.org/sites/default/files/2020-05/no.46-%20National%20Strategy%20and%20Action%20Plan%20on%20Gender%20Equality%202016-2020.pdf (accessed 1 February 2022).

DCM no.193, 02.04.2014 "*On employment promotion program through in-job training*," available at: https://qbz.gov.al/

DCM no. 27, dated 11.01.2012" *On employment promotion program for women of special groups*," amended by the DCM no. 73, dated 27.1.2016, *available at:* https://qbz.gov.al/

EIGE, MoHSP, INSTAT & World Bank (2020). *Gender Equality Index for the Republic of Albania*, available at: http://www.instat.gov.al/media/6661/gender_equality_index_for_the_republic_of_albania_2020.pdf (accessed 20 December 2020).

Eurofound (2017). *European Working Conditions Survey 2015*, available at: https://www.eurofound.europa.eu/sites/default/files/ef_publication/field_ef_document/ef1634en.pdf (accessed 5 November 2020).

Eurofound (2019). *Life and society in the EU candidate countries*. Luxembourg: Publications Office of the European Union, available at. https://www.eurofound.europa.eu/sites/default/files/ef_publication/field_ef_document/ef18032en.pdf (accessed 4 January 2020).

European Commission (2010). *EUROPE 2020 A strategy for smart, sustainable and inclusive growth*, Brussels. https://ec.europa.eu/eu2020/pdf/COMPLET%20EN%20BARROSO%20%20%20007%20-%20Europe%202020%20-%20EN%20version.pdf

European Commission (2016). *From university to employment: Higher education provision and labour market needs*. Luxembourg: European Commission.

Eurostat (2019). *Key figures on enlargement countries*, available at: https://ec.europa.eu/eurostat/web/products-statistical-books/-/ks-go-19-001 (accessed 13 November 2021).

EU-OSHA, Cedefop, Eurofound and EIGE (2017). *Joint report on towards age-friendly work in Europe: A life-course perspective on work and ageing from EU Agencies*, Luxembourg, available at: https://www.cedefop.europa.eu/files/2220_en.pdf (accessed 15 January 2021).

ILO (2005). *Social security spending in South Eastern Europe: A comparative review*, ISBN 92-2-117855-2 (print). Hungary: ILO Budapest.

INSTAT (2014). *Return migration and reintegration in Albania 2013*, available at: http://www.instat.gov.al/en/themes/demography-and-social-indicators/migration-and-migrant-integration/publications/2014/return-migration-and-reintegration-in-albania-2013/ (accessed 18 September 2021).

INSTAT (2017). *Labour Force Surveys 2011–2017*, available at: http://www.instat.gov.al/al/temat/tregu-i-punës-dhe-arsimi/punësimi-dhe-papunësia/#tab3 (accessed 18 December 2020).

INSTAT (2018a). *Structure of Earning Survey*, available at: http://www.instat.gov.al/en/themes/labour-market-and-education/structure-of-earnings-survey/publications/2020/structure-of-earnings-survey-ses-2018/ (accessed 20 December 2020).

INSTAT, Institute of Public Health, and ICF (2018b). *Albania Demographic and Health Survey 2017–18*, Tirana, Albania, available at: https://dhsprogram.com/pubs/pdf/FR348/FR348.pdf (accessed 12 December 2020).

INSTAT (2019a). *Projections of the population 2019–2031*, available at: http://www.instat.gov.al/en/themes/demography-and-social-indicators/projection/publications/2019/projections-of-the-population-2019-2031/ (accessed 12 January 2021).

INSTAT (2019b). *Labour Force Survey*, available at: http://www.instat.gov.al/en/themes/labour-market-and-education/employment-and-unemployment-from-lfs/publication/2020/press-release-labour-market-2019/ (accessed 20 December 2020).

INSTAT (2020a). *Women and men in Albania*, available at: http://www.instat.gov.al/en/themes/demography-and-social-indicators/gender-equality/publication/2020/women-and-men-in-albanian-2020/ (accessed 7 January 2021).

INSTAT (2020b). *Diaspora e Shqipërisë në shifra*, available at: http://www.instat.gov.al/media/7848/diaspora-ne-shifra-2020.pdf (accessed 1 February 2022)

INSTAT (2021a). *Income and living conditions in Albania*, 2019, available at: http://www.instat.gov.al/en/themes/social-condition/income-and-living-conditions-in-albania/publication/2021/income-and-living-conditions-in-albania-2019/ (accessed 18 September 2021).

INSTAT (2021b). *Demographic indicators*, available at: http://www.instat.gov.al/al/temat/treguesit-demografikpercentC3percentAB-dhe-socialpercentC3percentAB/popullsia/#tab2 (accessed 4 January 2021).

Law no. 68/2017 "*On Local Government Finances*."

Law no. 15/2017 "*On Vocational Education and Training in the Republic of Albania*."

Law no. 57/2016 For some amendments and additions to the Law No. 9936, dated 26.6.2008 "*On the Management of the Budgetary System in the Republic of Albania*."

Law no. 80/2015 "*On Higher Education and Science Research in Higher Education Institutions in the Republic of Albania*."

Law no. 139/2015 "*On local self-governance*."

Law no. 136/2015 "*Labour Code in the Republic of Albania*."

Law no. 115/2014, dated 31.07.2014 "*On territorial-administrative division of the local governance units in the Republic of Albania*."

Law no. 10 139, dated 15.5.2009 "*On supplementary state pensions of employees in higher education institutions, Centre for Albanological studies, Academy of Sciences and all other public research institutions in the Republic of Albania who have a science title*."

Law no. 9442, dated 16.11.2005 on ratification the ILO Convention 102/1952 "*On Minimum Standards of Social Protection*."

Law no. 9198, 01.07.2004 "*On Gender Equality in the Society*," repealed by Law no. 9970, 24.07.2008 dated "*On Gender Equality in the Society*," amended.

Law no. 7995, dated 20.09.1995 "*On Employment Promotion*," changed by Law No. 15/2019.

Law no. 7703, dated 11.05.1993 "*On Social Insurance in the Republic of Albania*," amended.

Law no. 7501, dated 19.07.1991 "*On the Land*," amended.

Law no. 7494, dated 02.07.1991 "On approval of the Decree no. 7464, dated 31.01.1991 "On some ammendments of the Law no. 4171, dated 13.09.1966 "*On State Social Insurance of the Popular Republic of Albania*", and the Law 4976, dated 29.06.1972 "*On pensions of the agriculture cooperatives' members*". Law 4976, dated 29.06.1972 "*On pensions of the agriculture cooperatives' members*."

Law no. 4171, dated 13.09.1966 "*On State Social Insurance of the Popular Republic of Albania*."

NESA (National Employment and Skills Agency) (2018). *Annual report*, available at: http://shkp.gov.al/publikime-shkp/ (accessed 15 January 2021).

NESA (National Employment and Skills Agency) (2019). *Statistics 2010–2018*, available at: http://www.shkp.gov.al/statistika-ne-vite-publikimi/ (accessed 13 January 2021).

SII (Social Insurance Institute) (2019). *Annual Report 2018*, available at: http://www.issh.gov.al/wp-content/uploads/2019/09/raport2018.pdf (accessed 19 September 2021).

SII (Social Insurance Institute) (2021). *Annual Report 2019–2020*, available at: http://www.issh.gov.al/wp-content/uploads/2021/05/LIBER-STATISTIKASH-2019-2020.pdf (accessed 13 September 2021).

UN (2018). *Albania report on the harmonization of sustainable development goals with existing sectoral policies*, available at: https://www.un.org.al/sites/default/files/Albania%20Report%20on%20the%20Harmonization.pdf, (accessed 12 January 2021).

UNDP, ILO and Ministry of Labour, Emigration and Ex-Persecuted (1995). *Improvement and development of wage policies in Albania*, Tirana.

World Bank (2006). *Albania Social Insurance Review*, Report No. 37594-AL.

World Bank (2019). *Personal remittances received (% of GDP) – Albania*, available at: https://data.worldbank.org/indicator/BX.TRF.PWKR.DT.GD.ZS?locations=AL (accessed 20 December 2020).

World Bank Albania (2020). available at: http://pubdocs.worldbank.org/en/392601587075676027/Albania-Snapshot-Apr2020.pdf (accessed 1 May 2020).

World Bank Group & Wiiw (Vienna Institute for International Economic Studies) (2019). *Western Balkans Labour Market Trends*, available at: https://www.seejobsgateway.net/event/launching-western-balkans-labor-market-trends-2019 (accessed 20 December 2020).

Xhumari, M. (2011). *Pension trajectories in Western Balkans 1990–2010*. UNFPA Tirana, Pegi, ISBN 978-9928-124-24-1.

7 Care for Dependent People and Extending Working Life in Poland

Justyna Wiktorowicz, Izabela Warwas, and Piotr Szukalski

Introduction

The policy of extending working life has been a significant outcome of the debate concerning the economic sustainability of ageing populations (Maltby, 2011). People are healthier and live longer today than in previous years (Edge et al., 2017), thus economic activity can continue for longer. Moreover, in many countries, the share of beneficiaries of old-age pensions is higher than the share of the population aged 65 and over and Poland is no exception (Eurostat, 2020). Determinants of economic activity are varied and have both institutional and organisational characteristics, but in many cases the most important are those related to the individual situation of older workers. One of them is the responsibility of taking care of someone, which is known to vary by location of residence due to differences in the level and scope of the institutional infrastructure which supports the carers of dependents. Additionally, cultural conditions influence who should be cared for and to what extent, as well as the level of interest of employers in implementing measures aimed at achieving a balance between work and private life. The latter is greater in companies with more developed Human Resource Management (HRM) systems, which are usually located in large cities due to the attractiveness of their location, while in rural areas having dependents might be a greater barrier to working than in bigger towns, especially for women.

The aim of this chapter is to assess to what extent the duty to care for dependent people in the family affects the economic activity of men and women in Poland including variations by place of residence. Secondly, the role of social policy and of organisations in extending economic activity is considered.

Our chapter has the following structure: first, the main features of extending working life proposed in the literature are described; then an empirical analysis of the significance of care responsibilities for extending working life in Poland is conducted; thirdly, we describe how social policy and employers respond to the needs of employees aged 50+ in relation to care responsibilities, and extending working life in Poland. The chapter ends with conclusions and recommendations.

DOI: 10.4324/9781003145325-7

Extending working life and its determinants

Determinants of extending working life are divided into pull factors (embeddedness in the pension system) and push factors (different measures at the organisation level, such as collective employment agreements, seniority wages and HRM, or measures related to the situation of the labour market) (de Preter et al., 2013; van Oorschot & Jensen, 2009), as well as stay factors (including Active Labour Market Policies and lifelong learning) (Hofäcker, 2015). Regarding pull factors – the pension system in Poland has changed in recent decades. A major reform introduced in 1999 replaced the former system by introducing a more flexible mixed system combining defined benefit and defined contribution schemes (Kohlbacher et al., 2018). Besides the general pension system, there are two separate systems: one for farmers (which provides benefits for 15% of recipients) and special public pension schemes for those in uniformed services, judges and public prosecutors (4%). Pension system reform from 1999 was justified first of all by demographic trends and their consequences for public finances, and prolonging working life was perceived as the appropriate response to the ageing of population. It was important because the economic activity of Poles aged 50+ was, and still is, low. In 2010 the average effective retirement age was 59.5 years (60.2 for men and 59.0 for women), and 75 per cent of men and one-third of women retired before statutory pension age (60 for women and 65 for men). In 2015 this average had reached 61.6 years, whereby over one-third of men and 5 per cent of women retired early. In 2019 it was 62.1 (64.6 for men and 60.7 for women), and only 11.9 per cent of men and 1.3 per cent of women retired before statutory pension age (ZUS, 2020). However, half of Poles aged 55–64 are still inactive – in 2019 the activity rate for men was 63.7 per cent and for women it was 39.5 per cent (GUS, 2020b). Thus, an increase is visible in the past decade, especially in the case of men. The most important changes in the pension system were in this context the limitation of provisions for early retirement – in the general pension system they do not exist from 2011 onwards. The second important issue is related to the changes that were made in the statutory pension age. Initially, from 1999 it was set at the level of 60 years for women and 65 years for men. Pension reforms stated by regulation from 2012 (Ustawa, 2012) increased the statutory retirement age – gradually by four months per year. This regulation, being in force from 1 January 2013, provided that statutory pension age should have reached 67 for men by 2020 and for women by 2040. However, this reform was stopped in 2017, when – due to electoral promises of the Peace and Justice party reflecting expectations of its electorate – statutory pension age returned to the previous level – with a much lower pension age for women (60) than for men (65). It should be stressed that an increasing number of people are retiring with a defined contribution pension scheme which stimulates people to work longer to increase the amount of their pension.

The effectiveness of pull factors is reduced by many individual factors. At the individual level, gender and health are key dimensions of extending working life (Ní Léime et al., 2020; McNair et al., 2004; Naegele & Bauknecht, 2013) but other components of human capital – higher skills and education levels are also related to prolonging economic activity (see e.g. Khan et al., 2014; Maltby, 2011; Silcock, 2013). The "devaluation" of the competencies of older workers and their lower ICT skills are problematic. Location, which shapes the availability of job offers and standards of HR management, is also an important factor.

Care responsibilities are also mentioned as affecting extending working life (Porcellato et al., 2010; de Preter et al., 2013; Reeuwijk et al., 2013; van Solinge & Henkens, 2007). Women are under pressure to enter a period of economic inactivity when they take care of their home, children or other family members in need of care (Contreras et al., 2013; Kryńska et al., 2013; European Commission, 2021). Care is one of the most important reasons for leaving the labour market, especially for older women. In 2019, the share of individuals not seeking a job because of family and household responsibilities among economically inactive people aged 55–64 was 11.4 per cent, for women it was 13.3 per cent, and this level was similar for rural and urban areas (GUS, 2020b). In addition, three million employees had a dependent adult in the family who required regular care. The obligation to care for dependent parents involved 10 per cent of those surveyed with care responsibilities, the care usually concerned one parent (79%) (Baszun et al., 2020). Thus, the need for greater support for caregivers – from both the institutional and organisational perspective – is high. According to the Polsenior study, 47 per cent of people aged 55–59 declared that they provide at least some extent of permanent help in caring for their parents, 21 per cent for their spouses, and 17 per cent for their grandchildren (Szatur-Jaworska, 2012). In other European countries the situation is similar but of course the extent of burden depends also on the welfare regime and on demographic conditions – longevity, fertility and health status (Herlofson & Brandt, 2020).

Are care responsibilities a barrier to extending working life in Poland?

Data and methods

The stated intention of our research was not easy to transform into operationalised measures. When seeking the data best reflecting the approach we adopt in the proposed statistical model, we used individual data from a study of the population aged 16+ from the last edition of the Social Diagnosis (SD) – SD2015 – survey (http://diagnoza.com). SD was a large-scale study undertaken in Poland every two years from 2002 until 2015, after which the SD study was discontinued. The database consists of n = 35,279 individuals representative of all Poles aged 16 and above. The SD survey is one of the largest Polish surveys which describes respondents' lifestyle, system of values, social attitudes and relations.[1] We restricted the sample to persons aged 50–64 (n = 5,728), which we consider to be representative of the "sandwich generation". In this group, 59.5 per cent of people were economically active. The share of women was 52.7 per cent. Taking into consideration the place of residence, 38.3 per cent of people aged 50–64 declared that they lived in rural areas, 13.9 per cent in small towns, 20.2 per cent in medium-sized towns and 27.7 per cent in cities. Detailed sample structure and descriptive statistics are presented in Appendix 7.1. Additionally, selected data from official public statistics were used for the assessment of institutional support for caregivers. We decided to use data on taking care of children and other dependants to describe the needs of caregiving employees. Additionally, data on unmet care needs were used to describe the underdevelopment of institutional support, and data on the type and size of place of residence as an indirect measure of the scale of implementation of measures aimed at providing support for caregivers.

Care measurement

An ex-post operationalisation of the data is required to measure how care responsibilities affect employment. In this chapter, the following variables were created (see also Table 1): (1) unpaid care for disabled adults or older people (*V1*); (2) part-time work due to the inability to provide adequate care to children (*V2*) or a sick or disabled person (*V3*); (3) not seeking employment due to caring for: children (*V4*), disabled or older persons (*V5*); (4) not taking up employment in the two years preceding the study due to caring for: children (*V6*) or disabled or older persons (*V7*). Care responsibilities in the work context were measured using the bivariate variable *C1* (*care responsibilities* – version 1). *C1* = 1 when at least one situation described by *V1* – *V7* variables indicates care responsibilities. This measurement is not perfect, as it ignores active, full-time employees who care for children (including disabled children) or older people. The scale of care for older people can be indirectly estimated on the basis of the question: "Have you felt responsible in recent months for the well-being of your parents or older relatives and their care?" (*V8*). The variable *C2* (*care responsibilities* – version 2) measures the care responsibility in a broader sense. *C2* = 1 when one or more of V1-7 or "often felt responsible for wellbeing" was chosen. V9 variable informs of having children (regardless of their age and level of independence). The distribution of these variables by gender is presented in Table 7.1.

Statistical analysis methods

In statistical analysis descriptive statistics, as well as the chi-squared test of independence comparison by gender, was used. To analyse the relationship between care responsibilities (measured by the *C1* variable) and extending working life of Poles aged 50–64, logistic regression models were constructed. The bivariate economic activity (*EA*) variable was used as the output variable, *EA* = 1 for economically active people (workers, self-employed, farmers, unemployed), *EA* = 0 for economically inactive people. Independent variables are apart from the *C1* variable, other individual factors of extending working life indicated earlier. First, variables describing human capital were used – the level of education, the active use of at least one foreign language, lifelong learning,

Table 7.1 Care responsibilities of Poles by age and gender (%)

Abbr.	*Specification*		*Below 50+*				*50–64*				*Total*
			T	*W*	*M*	*Sig.* [b]	*T*	*W*	*M*	*Sig.* [b]	
V1	Care for the disabled or the elderly in total		5.8	6.6	5.1	***	12.6	15.1	9.9	***	8.0
	in which: Care for a disabled adult		5.3	5.8	4.8	*	11.8	13.9	9.4	***	7.4
V2	The reason for part-time work	care for an elderly, sick or disabled person	0.0	0.1	0.0	*	0.1	0.1	0.1	ns	0.1
V3		child care	0.6	1.3	0.0	***	0.1	0.1	0.0	ns	0.5
V4	The reason for not seeking employment by currently inactive persons	care for an elderly, sick or disabled person	0.5	0.8	0.1	***	1.0	1.5	0.5	***	0.6
V5		child care	3.2	6.3	0.1	***	0.2	0.2	0.1	ns	2.3
V6	Leaving work in the last two years in order to care for:	elderly or disabled person	0.7	1.2	0.2	***	1.4	2.0	0.7	***	0.9
V7		children	5.5	10.8	0.1	***	0.9	1.5	0.2	***	4.1
C1	**Care responsibilities (version 1)** [c]		**11.7**	**18.1**	**5.2**	***	**13.3**	**16.2**	**10.0**	***	**12.2**
V8	Often responsible for care and well-being of parents and elderly family members		10.3	11.8	8.8	***	17.6	19.9	15.2	***	12.6
C2	**Care responsibilities (version 2)** [d]		**19.8**	**26.8**	**12.5**	***	**24.7**	**28.1**	**21.0**	***	**21.3**
V9	Having dependent children		49.7	55.5	43.7	***	33.7	30.4	37.4	***	44.6

Notes

a The number of people from a given sub-sample (by columns) was assumed to amount to 100%. T – total, W – women, M – men.

b Gender differences: * $p < 0.05$, ** $p < 0.01$, *** $p < 0.001$.

c Care responsibilities (version 1): at least one situation described by *V1 – V7* took place.

d Care responsibilities (version 2): at least one situation described by *V1 – V8* took place.Source: own calculations based on the Social Diagnosis individual data.

digital inclusion (*WWI* indicator, measuring the number of activities done via the Internet; range (1–26)), as well as health condition – *HCI* (measured by the number of illnesses often experienced in the last month; range (1; 15)). Additionally, marital status, gender, age, income and place of residence were included. A logistic regression equation was estimated using the maximum likelihood estimation method. The logistic regression models were considered correct if (1) in the omnibus test of model coefficients $p < \alpha$; (2) in Hosmer-Lemeshow test $p > \alpha$; (3) Nagerkelke's pseudo R^2 counts for most of models ca. 0.4 (between 0.25 and 0.51 for particular models); (4) quality of classification is relatively high, in particular, the percentage of correct qualifications for $y = 1$ and count R^2 is high (Hosmer et al., 2013). The initial list of independent variables was the same in each model. The calculations are performed in PS IMAGO SPSS 4.0 (Version 4.0, Predictive Solutions, Krakow, Poland).

Care responsibilities in the job context – the situation of women and men in Poland

People aged 50–64 as caregivers

People aged 50–64 experience more strongly than younger people that care responsibilities have a limiting impact on their working lives. To a lesser extent, this limiting influence applies to working time, and more often to not taking up employment at all. In a narrower sense (*C1*), such duties were estimated for 13.3 per cent of people in this group, more often for women (16.2%) than for men (10%) – compared to 11.7 per cent of people aged less than 50 (Table 7.1). In Poland, women aged 50–64 are the most heavily burdened with care responsibilities, often concerning two generations (children and parents or spouses and parents), which significantly reduces their economic activity. Care for people with disabilities or for older people is the biggest burden in the case of 15.1 per cent of women aged 50–64 (compared to 9.9% for men in this age group and only 5.8% for people aged under 50, where this is the case for 6.6% of women in this group). Additionally, one in five women aged 50–64 often feels a sense of responsibility for providing care to and for the well-being of parents or older relatives. Thus, more broadly (*C2*), care responsibilities concern 28 per cent (for women aged less than 50, this percentage is 11.8%). In addition, nearly one in three women aged 50–64 has dependent children.

As illustrated by Figure 7.1, care responsibilities (both versions) concern to a slightly lesser extent rural as compared to urban dwellers. In a narrower sense (*C1* – version 1), individuals living in small and medium-sized towns are particularly burdened with care responsibilities, and also the largest gender differences are recorded here – women are twice as likely as men to perform care responsibilities. In a broader sense (*C2* – version 2), residents of large and medium-sized towns (again, more often women) are the most heavily burdened.

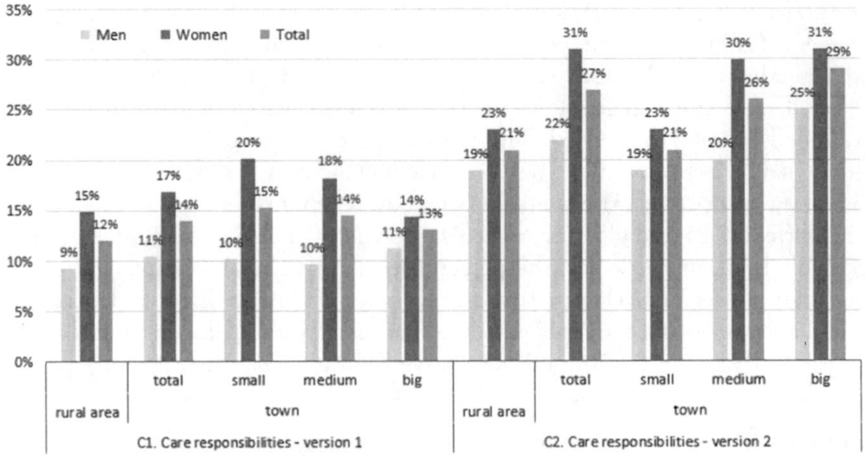

Figure 7.1 Care responsibilities.

Determinants of extending working life – significance of care duties

The analysis of logistic regression results (Tables 7.2–7.4) confirms that care responsibilities (measured by *C1* variable) are, ceteris paribus, an important factor in influencing extending working life for Poles aged 50–64 – people not having caring duties are approximately 1.5 times more likely to be employed than those with such responsibilities. Analysis by gender (models 2 and 3, Table 7.2) indicates that care responsibilities are important in the case of women – women who do not have such responsibilities compared to those having such duties are approximately 1.8 times more likely to be employed. For men the effect size is smaller, but also men with care responsibilities are more likely to be employed than men without such duties (approx. 1.2 times). This relation is important for people living in areas with less than 100 thousand inhabitants, and the effect is lower for people living in cities (Table 7.3). On the other hand, for people aged 50–64 in medium-sized towns this relationship is the strongest – caregivers are almost three times likely to be economically active than non-caregivers (versus ca. 1.5 for rural areas and small towns). Taking into consideration both criteria, i.e. place of residence and gender (Table 7.4), we confirm that the impact of care duties is higher for women than for men in most areas; only in medium-sized towns it is an even stronger determinant of extending working life for men than for women (OR 3.5). Although for the total population aged 50–64 in cities, care duties have a rather small effect for economic activity, for women this relation is in cities similarly strong as in other areas.

For Poles aged 50–64 almost all factors from the initial list are significant for extending working life. The higher the age, income, health condition, level of education and ICT skills, as well as for those in couples, being active in lifelong learning, knowing other languages, the higher the odds of extending working

Table 7.2 Logistic regression estimation results – care responsibilities as a factor of extending working life for people aged 50–64 (total, and by gender)

Description	*People aged 50–64*								
	Total			*Women*			*Men*		
	Model 1			*Model 2*			*Model 3*		
	OR	*90% CI*	*p*	*OR*	*90% CI*	*p*	*OR*	*90% CI*	*p*
Level of education (Ref.: at most secondary education)			<0.001			0.002			<0.001
basic vocational	1.18	(1.00–1.38)	0.094	1.29	(1.02–1.64)	0.078	1.06	(0.84–1.33)	0.680
secondary	1.55	(1.29–1.83)	<0.001	1.68	(1.31–2.14)	<0.001	1.34	(1.03–1.75)	0.072
tertiary	2.32	(1.80–2.94)	<0.001	1.87	(1.34–2.61)	0.002	2.77	(1.87–4.11)	<0.001
Qualifications improved (Ref.: not improved)[1]	4.62	(3.26–6.58)	<0.001	5.09	(3.14–8.26)	<0.001	5.04	(2.93–8.66)	<0.001
Knows foreign language(s) (Ref.: knows no foreign language)	1.24	(1.05–1.46)	0.034	1.31	(1.04–1.66)	0.056	1.12	(0.88–1.42)	0.443
Not a caregiver (Ref.: is a caregiver)	**1.51**	**(1.30–1.76)**	**<0.001**	**1.79**	**(1.47–2.19)**	**<0.001**	1.21	(0.94–1.55)	0.216
With spouse or partner (Ref.: others)	1.21	(1.08–1.38)	0.009	1.15	(0.98–1.36)	0.157	1.33	(1.10–1.61)	0.015
Income (th. PLN)	1.46	(1.39–1.58)	<0.001	1.89	(1.70–2.11)	<0.001	1.29	(1.19–1.40)	<0.001
Age (Ref.: 50–54)			<0.001			<0.001			<0.001
55–59	0.49	(0.43–0.56	<0.001	0.41	(0.34–0.49)	<0.001	0.60	(0.49–0.73)	<0.001
60–64	0.10	(0.08–0.11)	<0.001	0.05	(0.04–0.07)	<0.001	0.16	(0.13–0.19)	<0.001
HCI	0.90	(0.87–0.94)	<0.001	0.95	(0.90–1.00)	0.084	0.84	(0.79–0.89)	<0.001
WWI	1.01	(1.00–1.02)	0.006	1.01	(1.01–1.02)	0.005	1.00	(0.99–1.01)	0.788
Male (Ref.: female)	2.05	(1.82–2.28)	<0.001	n.a.	n.a.	n.a.	n.a.	n.a.	n.a.

(Continued)

Table 7.2 (Continued)

Description	*People aged 50–64*								
	Total			*Women*			*Men*		
	Model 1			*Model 2*			*Model 3*		
	OR	*90% CI*	*p*	*OR*	*90% CI*	*p*	*OR*	*90% CI*	*p*
Place of residence (Ref: large cities)[2]			<0.001			0.005			<0.001
rural areas	1.18	(0.96–1.29)	0.068	1.10	(0.89–1.35)	0.459	1.13	(0.92–1.39)	0.342
small town (below 20 th.)	0.81	(0.66–0.93)	0.048	0.73	(0.56–0.93)	0.035	0.84	(0.65–1.08)	0.265
medium-sized town (20–100 th.)	0.75	(0.62–0.85)	0.002	0.77	(0.62–0.96)	0.048	0.67	(0.53–0.84)	0.004
Constant	0.55		0.001	0.37		<0.001	1.60		0.088
p in the omnibus test of model coefficients	$\chi^2(16)=1759.8$, p<0.001			$\chi^2(15) = 1160.4$; p<0.001			$\chi^2(15) = 531.8$; p<0.001		
Nagelkerke R^2	0.359			0.429			0.250		
Percentage correct (for y = 1)	83.6%			81.2%			86.9%		

Source: own calculations based on the Social Diagnosis individual data.

Notes

1 in the last year

2 over 100,000 inhabitants

OR – odds ratio of being employed for 50–64 age groups, p – probability in Wald test, 90% CI – 90% confidence interval for odds ratio

Table 7.3 Logistic regression estimation results – care responsibilities as a factor of extending working life for people aged 50–64 by place of residence

Description	*People aged 50–64 by place of residence*											
	Rural areas			*Small towns*			*Medium-sized towns*			*Cities*		
	Model 4			*Model 5*			*Model 6*			*Model 7*		
	OR	*90% CI*	*p*	*OR*	*90% CI*	*p*	*OR*	*90% CI*	*p*	*OR*	*90% CI*	*p*
Level of education (Ref.: at most secondary education)			0.003			0.063			0.840			<0.001
basic vocational	1.24	(0.99–1.53)	0.109	1.46	(0.89–2.39)	0.207	0.98	(0.64–1.50)	0.949	0.88	(0.57–1.34)	0.612
secondary	1.64	(1.26–2.14)	0.002	2.00	(1.21–3.31)	0.024	1.14	(0.74–1.74)	0.617	1.29	(0.85–1.96)	0.321
tertiary	2.64	(1.57–4.44)	0.002	2.70	(1.35–5.40)	0.018	1.09	(0.64–1.88)	0.786	2.74	(1.68–4.47)	<0.001
Qualifications improved (Ref.: not improved)[1]	10.38	(3.04–35.48)	0.002	5.37	(2.31–12.51)	0.001	4.06	(2.06–7.99)	<0.001	4.33	(2.54–7.37)	<0.001
Knows foreign language(s) (Ref.: knows no foreign language)	0.87	(0.63–1.20)	0.477	1.25	(0.79–1.99)	0.421	1.17	(0.83–1.65)	0.465	1.78	(1.33–2.38)	0.001
Not a caregiver (Ref.: is a caregiver)	**1.50**	**(1.17–1.94)**	**0.008**	**1.54**	**(1.02–2.32)**	**0.081**	**2.55**	**(1.83–3.56)**	**<0.001**	1.13	(0.83–1.53)	0.523
With spouse or partner (Ref.: others)	1.36	(1.11–1.67)	0.014	1.88	(1.31–2.69)	0.004	1.08	(0.83–1.39)	0.644	1.03	(0.82–1.29)	0.855
Income (th. PLN)	1.44	(1.28–1.62)	<0.001	2.16	(1.56–2.98)	<0.001	1.45	(1.26–1.66)	<0.001	1.42	(1.28–1.58)	<0.001
Age (Ref.: 50–54)			<0.001			<0.001			<0.001			<0.001
55–59	0.48	(0.39–0.59)	<0.001	0.44	(0.30–0.64)	<0.001	0.45	(0.34–0.60)	<0.001	0.50	(0.38–0.67)	<0.001

(*Continued*)

Table 7.3 (Continued)

Description	*People aged 50–64 by place of residence*											
	Rural areas			*Small towns*			*Medium-sized towns*			*Cities*		
	Model 4			*Model 5*			*Model 6*			*Model 7*		
	OR	90% CI	*p*	OR	90% CI	*p*	OR	90% CI	*p*	OR	90% CI	*p*
60–64	0.09	(0.07–0.12)	<0.001	0.06	(0.04–0.09)	<0.001	0.12	(0.09–0.17)	<0.001	0.09	(0.07–0.12)	<0.001
HCI	0.90	(0.85–0.96)	0.005	0.79	(0.70–0.88)	<0.001	0.90	(0.83–0.98)	0.030	0.94	(0.87–1.01)	0.176
WWI	1.00	(0.99–1.01)	0.939	0.99	(0.99–0.98)	0.505	1.02	(1.01–1.03)	0.002	1.02	(1.01–1.03)	0.009
Male (Ref.: female)	2.23	(1.87–2.67)	<0.001	2.16	(1.56–2.98)	<0.001	1.54	(1.20–1.97)	0.004	2.23	(1.78–2.79)	0.269
Constant	0.78		0.411	0.18		<0.001	0.41		0.024	0.67		
p in the omnibus test of model coefficients	$\chi^2(13) = 663.6$; $p<0.001$			$\chi^2(13) = 313.3$; $p<0.001$			$\chi^2(13) = 307.7$; $p<0.001$			$\chi^2(13) = 522.1$; $p<0.001$		
Nagelkerke R^2	0.354			0.441			0.313			0.388		
Percentage correct (for y = 1)	84.1%			81.7%			78.5%			86.5%		

Source: own calculations based on the Social Diagnosis individual data.

Notes
1 in the last year
2 over 100,000 inhabitants
OR – odds ratio of being employed for 50–64 age groups, p – probability in Wald test, 90% CI – 90% confidence interval for odds ratio

Table 7.4 Logistic regression estimation results – care responsibilities as a factor of extending working life for people aged 50–64 by gender and place of residence

Description	*People aged 50–64*											
	Women			*Men*			*Women*			*Men*		
	OR	*90% CI*	*p*	*OR*	*90% CI*	*p*	*OR*	*90% CI*	*p*	*OR*	*90% CI*	*p*
Place of residence	*Rural areas*						*Small towns*					
Number of model	Model 8			Model 9			Model 10			Model 11		
Level of education (Ref.: at most secondary education)			0.028			0.150			0.418			0.103
basic vocational	1.23	(0.90–1.68)	0.282	1.29	(0.95–1.76)	0.166	1.85	(0.93–3.65)	0.139	1.24	(0.56–2.75)	0.657
secondary	1.54	(1.09–2.18)	0.041	1.82	(1.18–2.78)	0.022	1.52	(0.78–2.97)	0.302	2.55	(1.06–6.12)	0.079
tertiary	3.16	(1.59–6.28)	0.006	1.54	(0.68–3.46)	0.381	2.20	(0.85–5.65)	0.171	2.61	(0.80–8.52)	0.183
Qualifications improved (Ref.: not improved)[1]	16.34	(2.12–126.13)	0.025	7.11	(1.54–32.96)	0.035	4.15	(1.42–12.12)	0.029	16.09	(1.27–204.22)	0.072
Knows foreign language(s) (Ref.: knows no foreign language)	1.36	(0.86–2.15)	0.271	0.55	(0.34–0.90)	0.045	1.22	(0.63–2.36)	0.621	0.92	(0.43–1.95)	0.851
Not a caregiver (Ref.: is a caregiver)	**1.77**	**(1.27–2.47)**	**0.005**	1.23	(0.81–1.87)	0.422	**2.22**	**(1.23–3.98)**	**0.026**	0.87	(0.44–1.72)	0.731
With spouse or partner (Ref.: others)	1.59	(1.19–2.11)	0.009	1.15	(0.84–1.57)	0.476	1.82	(1.11–3.00)	0.048	2.25	(1.23–4.12)	0.027
Income (th. PLN)	1.66	(1.36–2.02)	<0.001	1.35	(1.15–1.58)	0.002	3.32	(2.26–4.89)	<0.001	1.65	(1.25–2.16)	0.003
Age (Ref.: 50–54)			<0.001			<0.001			<0.001			<0.001
55–59	0.39	(0.29–0.51)	<0.001	0.63	(0.46–0.86)	0.014	0.46	(0.28–0.76)	0.011	0.36	(0.19–0.67)	0.007
60–64	0.07	(0.05–0.10)	<0.001	0.12	(0.09–0.17)	<0.001	0.03	(0.02–0.06)	<0.001	0.08	(0.04–0.16)	<0.001
HCI	0.91	(0.83–0.98)	0.052	0.89	(0.81–0.98)	0.047	1.12	(0.92–1.37)	0.352	0.61	(0.50–0.74)	<0.001
WWI	1.01	(0.99–1.02)	0.440	0.99	(0.97–1.01)	0.330	1.01	(0.99–1.04)	0.420	0.98	(0.95–1.00)	0.078
Constant	0.39		0.026	3.34		0.007	0.06		<0.001	1.44		0.670
p in the omnibus test of model coefficients	$\chi^2(12)$ = 361,6; p<0.001			$\chi^2(12)$ = 241,0; p<0.001			$\chi^2(12)$ = 199,1; p<0.001			$\chi^2(12)$ = 130,4; p<0.001		
Nagelkerke R^2	0.381			0.276			0.522			0.396		
Percentage correct (for y = 1)	78.4%			81.7%			77.9%			85.1%		
Place of residence	*Medium-sized towns*						*Cities*					

(*Continued*)

Table 7.4 (Continued)

Description	*People aged 50–64*											
	Women			*Men*			*Women*			*Men*		
	OR	*90% CI*	*p*	*OR*	*90% CI*	*p*	*OR*	*90% CI*	*p*	*OR*	*90% CI*	*p*
Number of model	Model 12			Model 13			Model 14			Model 15		
Level of education (Ref.: at most secondary education)			0.389			0.595			0.040			<0.001
basic vocational	1.40	(0.73–2.71)	0.397	0.61	(0.33–1.14)	0.194	1.27	(0.65–2.45)	0.557	0.67	(0.37–1.20)	0.259
secondary	1.69	(0.89–3.19)	0.177	0.67	(0.35–1.27)	0.301	2.21	(1.18–4.13)	0.037	0.72	(0.39–1.33)	0.376
tertiary	1.17	(0.53–2.59)	0.749	0.77	(0.33–1.76)	0.600	2.35	(1.17–4.71)	0.044	5.08	(2.19–11.77)	0.001
Qualifications improved (Ref.: not improved)[1]	5.85	(1.58–21.63)	0.026	3.80	(1.67–8.67)	0.008	4.27	(2.12–8.59)	<0.001	5.60	(2.13–14.74)	0.003
Knows foreign language(s) (Ref.: knows no foreign language)	1.44	(0.87–2.37)	0.235	0.93	(0.57–1.54)	0.819	1.27	(0.83–1.92)	0.353	2.35	(1.52–3.63)	0.001
Not a caregiver (Ref.: is a caregiver)	**2.16**	**(1.41–3.29)**	**0.003**	**3.46**	**(1.95–6.14)**	**<0.001**	**1.54**	**(1.02–2.32)**	**0.086**	0.65	(0.39–1.10)	0.178
With spouse or partner (Ref.: others)	0.83	(0.59–1.18)	0.388	1.54	(1.02–2.34)	0.087	0.88	(0.64–1.19)	0.477	1.20	(0.83–1.76)	0.416
Income (th. PLN)	2.31	(1.76–3.02)	<0.001	1.22	(1.05–1.42)	0.032	1.72	(1.46–2.03)	<0.001	1.25	(1.08–1.44)	0.011
Age (Ref.: 50–54)			<0.001			<0.001			<0.001			<0.001
55–59	0.35	(0.24–0.53)	<0.001	0.50	(0.32–0.77)	0.009	0.37	(0.25–0.56)	<0.001	0.80	(0.52–1.24)	0.404
60–64	0.07	(0.04–0.10)	<0.001	0.21	(0.14–0.33)	<0.001	0.04	(0.02–0.06)	<0.001	0.22	(0.14–0.33)	<0.001
HCI	0.95	(0.86–1.05)	0.367	0.70	(0.58–0.84)	0.002	0.94	(0.85–1.04)	0.320	0.98	(0.87–1.10)	0.788
WWI	1.03	(1.01–1.04)	0.007	1.01	(0.99–1.03)	0.400	1.01	(1.00–1.02)	0.212	1.03	(1.01–1.05)	0.010
Constant	0.19		0.005	0.89		0.844	0.64		0.392	1.52		0.427
p in the omnibus test of model coefficients	$\chi^2(12)$ = 225.6; p<0.001			$\chi^2(12)$ = 91.0; p<0.001			$\chi^2(12)$ = 395.7; p<0.001			$\chi^2(12)$ = 161.1; p<0.001		
Nagelkerke R^2	0.397			0.222			0.487			0.298		
Percentage correct (for y = 1)	74.5%			85.2%			85.2%			89.5%		

Source: own calculations based on the Social Diagnosis individual data.

Notes

1 in the last year

2 over 100,000 inhabitants. OR – odds ratio of being employed for 50–64 age groups, p – probability in Wald test, 90% CI – 90% confidence interval for odds ratio

life. The odds ratio is, ceteris paribus, ca. 1.2 times higher in rural areas and by circa. 20 per cent lower in smaller towns than in cities (model 1). Men aged 50–64 are approximately twice as likely as women to be employed. The list of factors that are important for being employed is similar for women (model 2) and men (model 3) analysed in total (without disaggregation by type of place of residence – models 2 and 3 in Table 2), meanwhile marital status, knowing foreign language(s) and level of digital inclusion have a stronger effect for women than men. The results between women and men are different when the analysis was carried out by type of place of residence (Table 7.4). Marital status is important especially for men in small and medium-sized towns and for women in rural areas and small towns. In each subpopulation income is the important factor – its meaning is higher for women than for men (with each additional thousand Złoty of income women are approximately 1.8 times likely to be economically active, while for men OR 1.3) and in small towns (OR circa. 2) than in other areas. The greater importance of income for women than for men is typical for each type of urban area and the biggest difference is for smaller towns (Table 7.4).

Model results also confirm the role of human capital (the level of education, lifelong learning, ICT skills and health). The higher the human capital, the higher the probability of working at the age of 50–64. This conclusion applies for all workers, for each gender, place of residence (Tables 7.2 and 7.3), as well as when both criteria are taken into consideration (Table 7.4). In rural areas and small and large towns, it is imperative to improve qualifications and level of education, and in medium towns and cities, Information and communications technology (ICT) skills and foreign language skills are also important (Table 7.3) – ICT skills especially for women in medium-sized towns and men in cities, and languages for men in cities (Table 7.4).[2] This could be related to specific conditions in local labour markets, which may be more "exacting" in bigger towns.

In conclusion, the analysis confirms that Poland is a country where care responsibilities limit the economic activity of people aged 50 or over, especially women living in rural areas and in towns with less than 100,000 inhabitants.

Institutional and organisational support for extending the working lives of caregivers

Role of social policy

It is an important goal of social policy to decrease the likelihood of pushing people aged 50 or over out of the labour market as a result of their care responsibilities. On the other hand, since care responsibilities in Poland are increasingly combined with employment and "working caregivers" do not give up work but combine care with employment (Program Solidarność Pokoleń, 2013), work-life balance (WLB) measures are also important, especially in the workplace.

Social policy at the national and local level could indirectly affect women's propensity to work. Access to affordable, good-quality childcare or dependent older adult care is a crucial factor affecting decisions about entering/withdrawing from the labour market. The importance of this is extremely visible at certain life-course stages, which are related to a high probability of taking on family caring duties. The two typical stages when family duties determine a chance to be economically active are early parenthood with children of pre-school age and later adulthood, i.e. the period when individuals are aged 50–60 and their parents (or parents-in-law) are usually expected to be supported with care. At the same time, the latter group can be burdened with taking care of their grandchildren if parents of the children want to work and there is no affordable institutional childcare. The double burden of the so-called sandwich generation is likely to be a factor enhancing their labour market withdrawal. The Diagnosis 50+ study, the only comprehensive study to date of mature adults in the labour market in Poland, shows that childcare absorbs men and women, mostly those aged 45–59 who are responsible for grandchildren and older people – this mostly affects women. In addition, general caring for dependent people takes on average six hours a day for one-quarter of Poles aged 45+ (Kryńska et al., 2013).

The burden of the challenges associated with belonging to the "sandwich generation" is more pronounced in the case of rural areas and small towns due to the higher percentage of very old people living in depopulated, peripheral and poor rural areas (Szukalski, 2020), a higher probability of being a dependent older person needing family support (Urbaniak et al., 2018), and more traditional expectations regarding duties related to the social role of grandparents, more specifically grandmothers (Grotowska-Leder & Roszak, 2016). In rural areas, seniors use institutional care less often than in towns, and their children, daughters-in-law or sons-in-law take care of them more often than elsewhere. This is the result of, among other things, the long-term underdevelopment of social infrastructure (a lack or scarcity of nursing homes as well as crèches or kindergartens) (Małe dziecko, 2006; GUS, 2020a; MRPiPS, 2020). For example, older institutional care infrastructure is poorer in less urbanised areas – in rural municipalities there are on average: 1.3 facilities, fewer than 1 (0.66) care homes with an average of 85 places, and only 0.37 facilities providing around-the-clock care for the disabled, chronically ill or older people. In urban municipalities, these statistics are higher – respectively, 3.8 facilities, 1.56 care homes with on average 235 places, but the number of facilities providing around-the-clock care is also low – on average 0.54[3] (BDL, 2019). Similar trends are observed regarding institutional care for children. In 2019, in urban areas, 89.1 per cent of children could avail of institutional care (kindergartens, pre-primary classes), while in rural areas only 64.2 per cent children could do so (GUS, 2020a). Furthermore, over half of these are pre-primary sections in primary schools, dedicated to six-year-old children. In urban municipalities (mostly big or medium-sized towns), the mean share of children aged 3–5 years in kindergartens is much higher – 97 per cent (BDL, 2019). The same is the case for full-time nurseries which are located almost exclusively in towns and cities with specific part-time nurseries ("kluby dziecka") dedicated to rural areas. The two aforementioned reasons are intertwined – the underdevelopment is related to lower interest in using public support and traditional expectations are reinforced by a lack of access to institutional help. As a result, women aged 50+ living in areas with underdeveloped social services are sometimes forced to withdraw from the labour market to take care of their grandchildren or parents (in-law).

Policymakers at the national, regional and local levels declare their awareness of problems related to childcare but issues of adult dependent care are not yet a popular topic. In official documents and policies, institutional assistance addressed to parents with young child(ren) is mentioned but the issue of older adults caring for family members is much less emphasised. The issue was distinctly mentioned in "Solidarity of Generations" (Program Solidarność pokoleń, 2013), a governmental programme aimed at increasing the economic activity of older people, where Priority 3.3. was devoted to systematic solutions decreasing the burden related to the care of family members (the development of institutional care for children and other dependent family members, job-sharing). Also, a recent national strategy document "Strategy for Responsible Development" (SOR, 2017) underlines the importance of incentives promoting the increased economic activity of people aged 50+ but even this document does not use the term WLB. The problem was described in detail in "Policy toward the elderly" (Polityka, 2018), but no systematic policy solutions were specified in the document.

Organisational support – the role of WLB measures

Employers can make a significant contribution to reducing the negative impact of the lack of sufficient supply, scope or quality of care services so that people aged 50 or over would be able to continue their careers. As mentioned earlier, they can do this through the implementation of WLB programmes. A low level of WLB can negatively influence both employees and organisations (Karkoulian et al., 2016). The balance between work and private life, including family life, is receiving increasing attention from companies and from researchers (McCarthy et al., 2010), and its importance – especially in the context of care – increased during a pandemic.

WLB programmes allow for the mitigation of conflicts between work and family responsibilities, among others, through maintaining job security by retaining employees who face difficulties in reconciling family and professional duties. WLB programmes are the practices offered to employees that go beyond the applicable law (labour code) and constitute a coherent, complementary set of deliberately selected measures. To a large extent, this is due to a personnel strategy which provides a justification for the business strategy and organisational culture and which responds to changes in the environment (Warwas, 2020). Some companies narrow down the implemented programmes to the issue of balance between work and family, discussing activities in the field – Corporate Family Responsibility

(CFR) (Perotin & Robinson, 2000). WLB and CFR, as a fundamental part of internal Corporate Social Responsibility (CSR) (Peng et al., 2014), allow us to build a society in which women and men enjoy the same opportunities and can help create economic, social and ethical value, thus making possible a more just, productive and sustainable society (Liden et al., 2013). The benefits of the use of WLB practices include higher satisfaction with work-family balance, greater productivity and better quality of life.

As far as Polish organisations are concerned, only a small number of empirical studies on the planning and implementation of policies and practices aimed at maintaining WLB in Polish companies can be seen despite the fact that the issue of WLB has been present in scientific discourse in Poland for almost 20 years (Borkowska, 2003). It is therefore difficult to estimate the real effects of employers' actions in this area. Previous research indicates that as many as 81 per cent of companies have neither developed nor implemented a WLB policy, and most of their solutions in this area (not necessarily through comprehensive WLB programmes) are aimed at women, especially mothers of young children (Gross-Gołacka, 2020). Compared to other countries, Poland ranks rather low – the WLB index calculated by the OECD in the framework of the Better Life Index is 6.8 on a 10-point scale (http://www.oecdbetterlifeindex.org/countries/poland/). Thus, Poland is one of the countries that do not facilitate this balance, and almost 40 per cent of Poles believe that the balance in their lives is maintained at below-average level (Cieślak-Wróblewska, 2019). In the case of the signatories of the Diversity Charter, i.e. organisations distinguished in the area of HRM, the expectations of employees (42% of responses) are the main reason for taking action in this area, and almost a third of respondents indicate that such measures "have been a key element of the company's organisational culture since its establishment" (Gross-Gołacka, 2020). The 2017 Small-Medium Enterprise (SME) study indicates that WLB instruments are not used very often in small and medium-sized companies in Poland. Among the solutions directly related to care responsibilities, only 23 per cent of employers confirm offering additional unpaid leave to meet the need to care for dependent persons, and only 10 per cent pointed to medical benefits for parents or in-laws. Training for managers in WLB was offered by 12 per cent of companies (Wiktorowicz & Warwas, 2017). There is a worryingly large discrepancy between employers' provision and employees' expectations. It varies from one WLB instrument to another: employer-funded crèches/kindergartens are attractive to 56 per cent but available to only 6 per cent of employees; workplace crèches/kindergartens (respectively, are attractive to 53% but available to only 3%), co-financing of care services (care vouchers) (attractive to 51%, but available to only 5%) and extra days off for adult care (attractive to 48% but available to 5%) (Baszun et al., 2020). Similar conclusions on childcare services are indicated in the research conducted by Pracuj.pl (2018) – the five most desirable benefits for parents are provided by about 20 per cent of the companies employing them, and the most unmet is the need for crèches and kindergartens in the workplace, which is expected by 71 per cent of those surveyed while only 9 per cent have access to such services.

Conclusions and final remarks

The issue of extending working life has been discussed in the literature and in the social policy arena for years, but the issues related to measures regarding the provision of care for dependent people are still not a priority in this context in Poland. Balancing professional and family life is at the forefront of transformations in the world of work and is possibly the biggest challenge for families in the 21st century (European Commission, 2019). Our empirical analysis shows that limitations of the economic activity of Poles aged 50–64 are more strongly related to care duties than for younger Poles. To a lesser extent, this limiting influence applies to working time, and more often to not taking up work at all. Poland differs in comparison with other EU countries, where the percentage of women employed part-time is circa three times higher (PARP, 2020). Women aged 50–64 are the most heavily burdened with care responsibilities in Poland, often caring for two generations (this confirms earlier findings – Kryńska et al., 2013). The early retirement of women was and still is often caused by care responsibilities (Kotowska et al., 2010; Perek-Białas & Stypińska, 2010; PARP, 2020). Three-quarters of employees confirm that they have in their own environment people who are not able to combine care responsibilities with work – most often this concerns women quitting work to care for a child (62%) or dependent adults (30%) (Baszun et al., 2020). Our study confirms that in general in Poland the impact of care responsibilities on extending working life is significant in the case of women – this confirms earlier findings (Contreras et al., 2013; European Commission, 2021). Taking into consideration place of residence, care duties are significant for economic activity in rural areas and small- and medium-sized towns. Only in medium-sized towns is the impact of care responsibilities as significant for women as for men. As we discussed, the reasons for this situation are both institutional and organisational in character.

These results clearly confirm the need to implement measures that would support people of pre-retirement age in their decisions to continue their professional careers. Taking into account the past practices of Polish organisations, as well as the still insufficient interest on the part of social policymakers, these issues should be of greater concern to the various stakeholders in this area. WLB appears to be an exclusive practice implemented by Human Resource (HR) leaders (Gross-Gołacka, 2020). In SMEs, the country's dominant companies, WLB solutions are not used very often (Wiktorowicz & Warwas, 2017). Moreover, there is a large gap between the degree of dissemination of these policy measures and the expectations of employees, as the demand for such solutions is met only to a small extent (Baszun et al., 2020; www.pracuj.pl).

It seems that place of residence is an important determinant of access to care facilities. In spite of expectations, the relationship is not clear. Generally, the less populated the place of residence is, the less developed is the institutional care system due to financial restrictions (the institutions are financed by local governments whose budgets are closely related to the incomes of the inhabitants) and to more traditional expectations regarding family responsibilities in the case of care for children and other dependent persons. At the same time, HR leaders introducing WLB techniques are typically located in big towns and cities due to the overrepresentation of foreign companies in such well-developed areas and due to the existence of larger companies that are more prone to CSR implementation.

As the research presented above shows, changes in the uptake of the WLB approach in Poland are slow and selective. Acceleration and dissemination require a critical review of applied solutions. An interesting benchmark may be solutions proposed in "Secondo Welfare"[4] (Ferrera & Maino, 2014; Maccioni & Prandini, 2019). Polish experience confirms that local governments play an important role in this multi-stakeholder approach. Their role is especially the development of care infrastructure – ensuring access to childcare facilities (crèches, kindergartens) and adult care facilities (day care facilities, hospices), co-financing of services and facilities (subsidised or free crèches and kindergartens, cheaper or free public transport), as well as the organisation of nursing care and counselling, including services for dependent adults (in-home care and care outside of the home, transport) (Baszun et al., 2020). It also seems necessary to promote care-sharing, i.e. the sharing of care responsibilities, including more broadly institutional daycare. It is also important to provide caregivers with psychological or therapeutic support (Wiktorowicz, 2016).

Summarising both institutional and organisational measures can and should stimulate extending working life by supporting the balance between care duties and work. WLB is more and more frequently treated as a useful tool to solve problems emerging from demographic change and population ageing due to the perception of individual and societal needs, which are life-course in-built (European Commission, 2021). There are, however, many obstacles to implementing the above-mentioned approach and research about care for dependent people and extending working life in Poland adds to the discussion.

Notes

1 More details: Czapiński and Panek (2015).

2 The estimated models are characterised by good statistical properties, including the relatively high Nagerkelke R^2. The high quality of the classification indicates that the identified determinants make it possible to predict to a large degree the extension of working life in the population aged 50–64 in Poland.

3 The difference partially could be explained by higher percentage of the elderly (65+: 20,5% vs 15,8% at the end of 2020) and the oldest old (85+: 2,3% vs 1,9%) in urban areas in comparison to the rural ones (BDL, 2022), partially by stronger family ties in rural societies, and partially by economic factors, i.e. lower incomes of rural communes per capita, affecting affordability of maintaining the facilities. The most important problems with access to social services are observed in peripheral rural areas with depopulation, age structure deformation and obsolete economic structure (Szukalski, 2020).

4 The adjective "second" has a triple connotation: temporal (these are forms of provision that are grafted on the trunk of the "first", state-based welfare edifice that was built during the 20th century); functional (second-line provisions and initiatives are

typically a complementary addition to, not a replacement of, first-line and state-based provisions); financial (the secondo welfare typically mobilises extra, non-public resources, made available by a wide range of economic and social actors) (Ferrera & Maino, 2014).

References

Baszun, R., Zamęcki, A., & Joniewicz, T. (2020). *Praca zawodowa a pełnienie ról opiekuńczych przez kobiety i mężczyzn w Polsce*, Warsaw: Forum Odpowiedzialnego Biznesu, http://odpowiedzialnybiznes.pl/wp-content/uploads/2020/08/FOB_Praca-zawodowa-a-pełnienie-ról-opiekuńczych-przez-kobiety-i-mężczyzn-w-Polsce.pdf.

Bank Danych Lokalnych, Database of the Statistics Poland. https://bdl.stat.gov.pl/bdl/start<https://scanner.topsec.com/?d=2120&r=show&u=https%3A%2F%2Fbdl.stat.gov.pl%2Fbdl%2Fstart&t=84936ea1d45655d2514595c81e08f4496f455825>

Borkowska, S. (2003). *Programy praca-życie a efektywność firm*. Warsaw: Wydawnictwo IPiSS.

Cieślak-Wróblewska, A. (2019). *Przygnębiający obraz work-life balance*, Rzeczpospolita, 24.03.2019, https://www.rp.pl/Praca/303249948-Przygnebiajacy-obraz-work-life-balance.html (retrived 15.12.2020)

Contreras, N., Martellucci, E., & Thum, A.-E. (2013). *Extending working life in Belgium*. CEPS Working Document, No. 386.

Czapiński, J. & Panek, T. (Eds), (2015). Social Diagnosis 2015. Objective and subjective quality of life in Poland. *Contemporary Economics*, 9(4). http://www.diagnoza.com/pliki/raporty/Diagnoza_raport_2015.pdf

de Preter, H., van Looy, D., & Mortelmans, D. (2013). Individual and institutional push and pull factors as predictors of retirement timing in Europe: A multilevel analysis. *Journal of Aging Studies*, 27(4), 299–307.

Edge, C. E., Cooper, A. M., & Coffey, M. (2017). Barriers and facilitators to extended working lives in Europe: a gender focus. *Public Health Reviews*, 38, Article no. 2. 10.1186/s40985-017-0053-8.

European Commission (2019). *Work-life balance for all: Best practice examples from EU Member States*. Luxembourg: Social Agenda, KE-04-19-351-EN-N.

European Commission (2021). *Green paper on ageing. Fostering solidarity and responsibility between generations*, COM(2021) 50 final, Brussels, 27.1.2021, https://ec.europa.eu/info/sites/info/files/1_en_act_part1_v8_0.pdf.

Eurostat (2020). Social protection statistics – pension expenditure and pension beneficiaries, Data extracted: October 2020. https://ec.europa.eu/eurostat/statistics-explained/index.php?title=Social_protection_statistics_-_pension_expenditure_and_pension_beneficiaries#Pension_beneficiaries_in_the_EU. Eurostat [lfsa_argan], https://ec.europa.eu/eurostat/data/database.

Ferrera, M. & Maino, F. (2014). *Social Innovation Beyond the State. Italy's Secondo Welfare in a European Perspective*. Working Paper-2 Welfare. http://secondowelfare.it/allegati/ferrera_maino_wp2_2014_2wel.pdf.

Funk, L. (2004). *Employment opportunities for older workers: A comparison of selected OECD countries*. DICE Research Report.

Gross-Gołacka, E. (2020). *Jak wygląda zarządzanie różnorodnością i work-life balance w Polsce?*. http://odpowiedzialnybiznes.pl/artykuly/jak-wyglada-zarzadzanie-roznorodnoscia-i-work-life-balance-w-polsce/

Grotowska-Leder, J. & Roszak, K. (2016). *Wzory wsparcia w rodzinach trzypokoleniowych. Na przykładzie mieszkańców dwóch gmin województwa świętokrzyskiego*. Lodz: Wydawnictwo Uniwersytetu Łódzkiego.

GUS (2020a). *Oświata i wychowanie w roku szkolnym 2019/2020*. Warsaw: Statistics Poland. https://stat.gov.pl/obszary-tematyczne/edukacja/edukacja/oswiata-i-wychowanie-w-roku-szkolnym-20192020,1,15.html.

GUS (2020b), *Labour force survey in Poland IV quarter 2019*. Warsaw: Statistics Poland.

Hashim, J. & Wok, S. (2011). *Competence as a moderator of older workers' trainability and performance*. Department of Business Administration, Economics & Management Sciences, International Islamic University Malaysia, 1–22.

Herlofson, K. & Brandt, M. (2020). Helping older parents in Europe: The importance of grandparenthood, gender and care regime. *European Societies*, 22(3). https://www.tandfonline.com/doi/full/10.1080/14616696.2019.1694163.

Hofäcker, D. (2015). In line or at odds with active ageing policies? Exploring patterns of retirement preferences in Europe. *Ageing and Society*, 35(7), 1529–1556.

Hosmer, D. W. Jr., Lemeshow, S., & Sturdivant, R. X. (2013). *Applied logistic regression*. New Jersey: John Wiley & Sons Inc. http://www.oecdbetterlifeindex.org/countries/poland/

Karkoulian, S., Srour, J., & Sinan, T. (2016). A gender perspective on work-life balance, perceived stress, and locus of control. *Journal of Business Research*, 69(11), 4918–4923, 10.1016/j.jbusres.2016.04.053.

Khan, M. R., Rutledge, M. S., & Wu, A. Y. (2014). *How do subjective longevity expectations influence retirement plans?*, Working Paper 2014-01. Chestnut Hill, MA: Center for Retirement Research at Boston College.

Kryńska, E., Krzyszkowski, J., Urbaniak, B., & Wiktorowicz, J. (Eds) (2013). *Diagnosis of the current situation of women and men aged 50+ on the labour market in Poland*. Lodz: University of Lodz. https://dspace.uni.lodz.pl/xmlui/handle/11089/3567.

Kohlbacher, F., Warwas, I. and Mollenhauer, H. (2018). "The productive ageing society of Japan and Poland and its impacts on productivity and prosperity", in Flynn M., Li Y., and Chiva A. (Eds.) *Managing the Ageing Workforces in the East and the West*, Emerald Publishing.

Kotowska, E. I., Matysiak, A., Styrc, M., Paillhe, A., Solaz, A., Vignoli, D., Vermeylen, G., Anderson, R. (2010). *Second European Quality of Life Survey: Family life and work*. Luxembourg: Office for Official Publications of the European Communities, 1–96.

Liden, R., Wayne, S., Liao, C., & Meuser, J. (2013). Servant leadership and serving culture: Influence on individual and unit performance. *Academy of Management Journal*, 57(5), 1434–1452. 10.5465/amj.2013.0034.

Macchioni, E. & Prandini, R. (2019). Work–life balance measures of working carers and well-being satisfaction within couple relationships: The result of an Italian policy looking through the gender lens. *Social Sciences*, 8, 109. 10.3390/socsci8040109.

McCarthy, A., Darcy, C., & Grady, G. (2010). Work-life balance policy and practice: Understanding line manager attitudes and behaviors. *Human Resource Management Review*, 20, 158–167. 10.1016/j.hrmr.2009.12.001.

Maltby, T. (2011). Extending working lives? Employability, work ability and better quality working lives. *Social Policy and Society*, 10(3), 299–308.

Małe dziecko w Polsce. Raport (2006). Warszawa: Fundacja Rozwoju Dzieci. https://www.frd.org.pl/wp-content/uploads/2016/02/raport_o_sytuacji_edukacji_elementarnej.pdf.

MRPiPS (2020). *Informacja o sytuacji osób starszych w Polsce za rok 2019*. Warsaw: Ministerstwo Rodziny, Pracy i Polityki Społecznej. https://www.gov.pl/web/rodzina/informacja-o-sytuacji-osob-starszych-w-polsce-za-rok-2019.

McNair, S., Flynn, M., Owen, L., Humphreys, C., & Woodfield, S. (2004). *Changing work in later life: A study of job transitions*. Surrey: Centre for Research into the Older Workforce, University of Surrey.

Naegele, G., & Bauknecht, J. (2013). *WP3: Conceptual framework. Task 1 of wp3*. http://mopact.group.shef.ac.uk/wp-content/uploads/2013/10/D3.1-Extending-working-lives-conceptual-framework.pdf (retrieved 15.05.2015).

Ní Léime, A., Ogg, J., Rašticová, M., Street, D., Krekula, C., Bédiová, M., & Madero-Cabib, I. (Eds) (2020). *Extended Working Life Policies. International Gender and Health Perspectives*. Cham: Springer Open. 10.1007/978-3-030-40985-2.

Peng, Y-S., Dashdeleg, A-U., & Chih, H. L. (2014). National culture and firm's CSR engagement: A cross-nation study. *Journal of Marketing & Management*, 5(1), 38–49.

Perek-Białas, J., & Stypińska, J. (2010). Łączenie pracy i opieki nad osobą starszą – wpływ na jakość życia opiekuna. In Kałuża, D., Szukalski, P. (Eds). *Jakość życia seniorów w XXI wieku. Ku aktywności*. Lodz: Wydawnictwo Biblioteka.

Perotin, V., & Robinson, A. (2000). Employee participation and equal opportunities practices: Productivity effect and potential complementarities. *British Journal of Industrial Relations*, 38(4), 557–583.

PARP (2020). *Analiza luki zatrudnienia oraz wynagrodzeń kobiet i mężczyzn*. Warsaw: Polish Agency for Enterprise Development.

Phillipson, C. H., & Smith, A. (2005). *Extending working life: A review of the research literature*. Research Report No. 299, London: Department for Work and Pension.

Polityka społeczna wobec osób starszych 2030. Bezpieczeństwo - Uczestnictwo – Solidarność (2018). Uchwała nr 161 Rady Ministrów z dnia 26 października 2018 r. w sprawie przyjęcia dokumentu Polityka społeczna wobec osób starszych 2030. Bezpieczeństwo – Uczestnictwo – Solidarność, http://www.monitorpolski.gov.pl/mp/2018/1169/M2018000116901.pdf.

Porcellato, L., Carmichael, F., Hulme, C., Ingham, B., & Prashar, A. (2010). Giving older workers a voice: Constraints on the employment of older people in the North West of England. *Work, Employment & Society*, 24(1), 85–103.

Pracuj.pl (2018). *Rodzice w pracy, Życie na pełen etat. Raport Pracuj.pl*. https://prowly-uploads.s3.amazonaws.com/uploads/4091/assets/62837/Rodzice_w_pracy_%C5%BBycie_na_pe%C5%82ny_etat_-_Raport_Pracuj_pl.pdf (retrieved 10.01.2021).

Program Solidarność pokoleń (2013). *Działania dla zwiększenia aktywności zawodowej osób w wieku* 50+. Uchwała Nr 239 Rady Ministrów z dnia 24 grudnia 2013 w sprawie ustanowienia Programu Solidarność pokoleń. Działania dla zwiększenia aktywności zawodowej osób w wieku 50+, Dz.U. z dn. 4 lutego 2014, poz. 115, https://archiwum.mpips.gov.pl/seniorzyaktywne-starzenie/program-solidarnosc-pokolen/.

Reeuwijk, K. G., de Wind, A., Westerman, M. J., Ybema, J. F., van der Beek, A. J., & Geuskens, G. A. (2013). 'All those things together made me retire': Qualitative study on early retirement among Dutch employees. *BMC Public Health*, 13(1), 516.

Silcock, D. (2013). Extending working lives. *Pensions*, 17, 229–235.

Sinclair, D., Watson, J., & Beach, B. (2013). Working longer: An EU perspective. ILC-UK. http://www.ilcuk.org.uk/files/Working_longer_an_EU_perspective.pdf (retrieved 4.04.2019).

Social Diagnosis (2015). http://www.diagnoza.com/index-en.html.

SOR (2017). *Strategia na rzecz odpowiedzialnego rozwoju do roku 2020 (z perspektywą do 2030 r*. https://www.gov.pl/documents/SOR

Szatur-Jaworska, B. (2012). Sytuacja rodzinna i więzi rodzinne ludzi starszych i osób na przedpolu starości. In Mossakowska, M., Więcek, A., & Błędowski, P. (Eds), *Aspekty medyczne, psychologiczne, socjologiczne i ekonomiczne starzenia się ludzi w Polsce*, Warszawa: Termedia, http://gerontologia.org.pl/wp-content/uploads/pliki/ol/polsenior.pdf.

Szukalski, P. (2020). Przestrzenne zróżnicowanie starości demograficznej we współczesnej Polsce. *Demografia i Gerontologia Społeczna. Biuletyn Informacyjny*, 7. http://hdl.handle.net/11089/33028

Urbaniak, B., Krzyszkowski, J., Przywojska, J., Wiktorowicz, J., & Lisek-Michalska, J. (2018). *Potrzeby osób w wieku 60+ z terenu województwa łódzkiego. Raport końcowy*. Lodz: Regionalne Centrum Polityki Społecznej. https://dspace.uni.lodz.pl/xmlui/handle/11089/25535

Ustawa z dnia 11 maja 2012 r. o zmianie ustawy o emeryturach i rentach z Funduszu Ubezpieczeń Społecznych oraz niektórych innych ustaw, Dz. U. z dnia 6 czerwca 2012 r., poz. 637.

van Oorschot, W. & Jensen, P. H. (2009). Early retirement differences between Denmark and The Netherlands. A cross-national comparison of push and pull factors in two small European welfare states. *Journal of Aging Studies*, 23(4), 267–278.

van Solinge, H. & Henkens, K. (2007). Involuntary retirement: The role of restrictive circumstances, timing, and social embeddedness. *Journals of Gerontology: Social Sciences*, 62B(5), S295–S303.

Warwas, I. (2020). Włączenie jako wartość dla organizacji. In *Odwaga i równowaga, czyli work-life balance po polsku*, Warsaw: Forum Odpowiedzialnego Biznesu, 19–25, http://odpowiedzialnybiznes.pl/wp-content/uploads/2020/05/FOB_Odwaga-i-rownowaga.pdf.

Wiktorowicz (2016). Równowaga praca-życie a wydłużanie aktywności zawodowej. *Przedsiębiorczość i Zarządzanie*, T. XVII, Z. 4(Cz. 2), 201–213.

Wiktorowicz, J. & Warwas, I. (Eds) (2017). Utrzymanie w zatrudnieniu pracowników dojrzałych. *Warunki do wdrożenia modelu STAY w małych i średnich przedsiębiorstwach*, Lodz: Uniwersytet Łódzki. http://stay.uni.lodz.pl/zal/STAY_raport_diagnostyczny.pdf.

Whiting, E. (2005). The labour market participation of older people. *Labour Market Trends*, 113, 285–296.

ZUS (2020). *Ważniejsze informacje z zakresu ubezpieczeń społecznych 2019 r.* Warsaw: Zakład Ubezpieczeń Społecznych, June 2020.

8 The Relationship between Self-rated Health and Employment during the Recent Economic Crisis; The Case of Spain

Antía Domínguez-Rodríguez, Jeroen Spijker, and Amand Blanes-Llorens

Background

The recent economic crisis affected different domains of society in Spain, just as in other European countries. This had particular repercussions for the labour market and population health, which impacted the daily life of many citizens (Banks et al., 2006; García-Gómez, 2011; Kalwij & Vermeulen, 2005). The literature is still unclear about the precise relationship between economic crisis and health status at the population level, as national and international studies have shown contradictory results. Some studies on health and economic crises indicate that, contrary to what might be expected, in times of recession, health does not worsen but actually improves and then deteriorates during the subsequent economic recovery (Gerdtham & Ruhm, 2006; Ruhm, 2000, 2007; Tapia Granados, 2014; Virtanen et al., 2005). Explanations for this include greater social support, improvements in certain health-related behaviours, such as the increase in hours of sleep or free time that can be devoted to healthy activities such as physical exercise, as well as the reduction in risk factors. Regarding the latter, these include less consumption of tobacco and alcohol due to personal budget constraints and less exposure to work-related and traffic accidents and air pollution as a result of a decline in economic activity (Dávila Quintana & González López-Valcárcel, 2009; Karanikolos et al., 2013; Tapia Granados, 2014). However, other studies (Díaz Olalla, 2013; La Parra & Álvarez-Dardet, 2014; Stuckler & Basu, 2013) alert us to health concerns and other human costs that an economic crisis can cause, through for instance job insecurity, job loss or governmental austerity measures in social welfare and health care. Such effects also depend on other factors, including the duration or intensity of the crisis, the severity and timing of budget cuts (Espino Granado, 2014; Gili et al., 2012; Rocha Bones et al., 2010). In the case of Spain, health worsened among those with a disadvantaged socioeconomic position during the 2008–2014 financial crisis, in particular the long-term employed and the economically and socially deprived. This was especially the case with self-perceived health, mental health, certain infectious diseases and lifestyle changes, including an increase in the intake of

DOI: 10.4324/9781003145325-8

toxic substances (Cortès-Franch & González López-Valcárcel, 2014; López del Amo González et al., 2018; Urbanos-Garrido & Lopez-Valcarcel, 2015).

One key element in the negative health effect of the financial crisis appears to be a reduction in family income and subsequent impoverishment, which, below a certain critical threshold, affects health. Indeed, while between 2008 and 2014 the risk of poverty and/or social exclusion (AROPE) in the total population aged 16+ increased "only" by 5 percentage points to 29 per cent, it did so by 18 percentage points in the case of the unemployed, reaching a level of 60 per cent (INE (Instituto Nacional de Estadistica), 2018).[1] Moreover, the health effect of poverty is exacerbated when combined with low educational attainment. For instance, it can lead to a deterioration in the quality of the diet (and the lower educated have, on average, less knowledge on health-damaging behaviour), which, if sustained in the long term, increases the risk of obesity (Dávila Quintana & González López-Valcárcel, 2009).

Regarding evidence of the impact of the economic crisis on health in Spain, the unemployed, the low educated and those with low incomes and older people are population groups that have been most vulnerable to the effects of the crisis, as they tend to accumulate disadvantaged situations. That said, having medium or high levels of education is known to have mitigated the adverse effects of the crisis on health (Cortès-Franch & González López-Valcárcel, 2014). Also noteworthy is the different way that unemployment, family income and education influenced self-perceived health (SPH) of men as compared to that of women in Spain during the last economic crisis (Calzón Fernández et al., 2017). The authors concluded that this was likely due to gender roles, as the effect of unemployment on SPH was clearer in men, while low levels of education and income observed a greater impact on women. Education also has a cumulative effect on health, as was recently attested by Martín et al. (2019) who showed that healthy life expectancy[2] in Spain in 2012 was more than twice as high among highly educated women aged 65 (13.5 years) than among low educated women of the same age (6.7 years).

As mentioned earlier, there is also reliable evidence that suggests that an economic crisis can lead to health improvements. In the case of Spain, Spijker et al. (2018) observed this for several health indicators in the population aged 50 and over in the Spanish Autonomous region of Catalonia between 2006 and 2010–12, especially SPH. SPH is a sensitive indicator of health differences between relatively similar populations in terms of objective health (Idler & Benyamini, 1997). Moreover, and unexpectedly, the social gap decreased, which was generally due to a greater improvement among the lower social groups. However, in the case of the difference between the employed and the unemployed, this was explained by the fact that the latter's composition became much more heterogeneous. For instance, being unemployed during an economic boom when almost everyone is working (the unemployment rate among 50–64-year-olds in 2006 was just 5.9%) is much more likely to be due to health reasons than when people with high-status and well-paid jobs are also being laid-off or fired, as occurred during the economic crisis (the unemployment rate for the same age group reached 20.3% in 2013). Importantly, however, despite this apparent decline in health differences, the non-employed (unemployed or inactive) always performed less well in the different health indicators studied than the employed.

On the other hand, the same study showed an increasing risk of poor mental health and medicine intake among 50–64-year-olds during the same period of economic downturn (Spijker et al., 2018). In a multivariate analysis that included, among other variables, household social class, income and size, educational level and private medical insurance coverage, the employed variable explained most of the variance (Spijker & Zueras, 2018). The authors suggested that for this age group, being so close to retirement, the possibility of becoming unemployed produces additional stress during an economic crisis. Similar results have been observed in other Spanish studies (Bartoll et al., 2014; Fernandez et al., 2015; Gili et al., 2012). For instance, Gili et al. (2012) showed that the recession has significantly increased the frequency of mental health disorders among individuals experiencing unemployment and mortgage payment difficulties.

Employment status affects health, but health can also affect employment status, as people who report poor physical and/or mental health are significantly less likely than those in good health to be employed and to find a job when unemployed or inactive, even when other variables known to affect employment status are controlled for (Mackenbach et al., 1994; Webber et al., 2015). This association can also be modified by changes in economic cycles and is mediated by sociodemographic variables, including educational level and marital status (Domínguez-Rodríguez & Blanes-Llorens, 2019). In addition, in recent decades, the work and job experiences of women have seen vast changes, as younger female cohorts obtained higher educational levels and increased their participation in the labour market (Torns, 1995). Moreover, this currently still takes place, despite the economic crisis and regardless of health status and other individual and household factors (Domínguez-Rodríguez & Blanes-Llorens, 2019). Nevertheless, having a good state of health remains an important factor for staying on in the labour market, and more so for women than for men (Prieto et al., 2002).

Conversely, having poor health status at older ages is an important trigger for labour market exit and there are also other factors that can hasten older workers in exiting early from the labour force. Obvious examples include age (being close to retirement age), partner status (individuals with a partner are more likely to transition to retirement, especially if the partner is already retired), educational level (the lower educated are more likely to retire), not having children in the household, as well as (early) retirement legislation (Debrand & Sirven, 2009; Kalwij & Vermeulen, 2005).

Thus, being aware of the extensive amount of job losses during the last economic crisis and, concurrently, considering the possible health differences according to employment status[3] and other variables known to affect both health and labour force participation among individuals who are in the later stages of their career (ages 50–64), in this chapter we aim to answer the following three research questions. In doing so, we will also highlight any gender differences:

- how does employment status (employed, unemployed and inactive) differ according to health status?
- has the economic crisis penalised people with a worse health status more in relation to their participation in the labour market?
- besides health, are there other factors associated with a change in the labour force participation of older men and women between the peak of the economic boom (2006) and the end of the economic crisis (2014)?

Data and method

The 2006 Spanish National Health Survey (ENSE) and the 2014 European Health Survey for Spain (EESE) were used for the analysis. Both surveys are carried out by the National Institute of Statistics (INE), together with the Spanish Ministry of Health. The purpose of these surveys is to obtain information on the health and well-being of individuals. The sample size for the population aged 16 years and older living in private dwellings who responded to the survey for adults is 29,478 in 2006 and 22,842 in 2014. The corresponding values for the target population (ages 50–69) are 8,298 and 7,226 people respectively. The variables included in the study and their respective categories are provided in Table 8.1.

In order to answer the first two research questions, only descriptive analysis is used, but logistic regression is employed for the third analysis. This statistical tool permits us to estimate, among the economically active population, the probability of being employed according to different health statuses and simultaneously control for as well as test the effect of other independent variables, known to influence the employment status of women.

Our dependent variable in the third analysis is employment status, which is dichotomised into employed (1) and unemployed (0). In other words, the inactive population is excluded from the analysis. The reason behind this decision is because we are interested in the employability of the active workforce during two quite distinct periods: at the height of the economic boom and at the height of the economic crisis. Including the inactive would in this case make comparison quite difficult, given the large number of job losses that led to permanent labour exit (especially pre-retirement). Another justification for only considering the economically active is the relatively large proportion of women who do not participate in the workforce, which makes gender comparison more difficult.

With respect to the health indicator, we analyse self-perceived health because it is considered to be a valid indicator of health status in middle-aged populations (Miilunpalo et al., 1997). The initial five categories are recoded into three (good, fair and bad health) as there are relatively few cases with "very bad" health, especially when crossed with other independent variables, while the "good" and "very good" categories were combined to keep the scale symmetrical.

Table 8.1 Variables included in the study and the relative importance (%[a]) of each category according to sex and survey year (Spain, ages 50–69)

	2006		*2014*	
	Men	*Women*	*Men*	*Women*
Employment status				
Employed	51.9%	27.8%	48.7%	35.5%
Unemployed	7.1%	5.0%	14.5%	10.2%
Inactive	41.0%	67.2%	36.8%	54.4%
Self-assessed health				
Good health	60.2%	47.5%	68.6%	60.9%
Fair health	28.0%	37.9%	22.5%	27.1%
Bad health	11.8%	14.6%	8.9%	12.0%
Socioeconomic variables				
Educational attainment				
Primary or less	62.3%	74.2%	57.2%	63.6%
Secondary and professional training	21.9%	14.9%	25.3%	20.5%
Tertiary	15.1%	10.0%	17.5%	15.9%
Missing	0.7%	0.9%	0.0%	0.0%
Social Class				
Directors, managers and professionals	20.1%	18.0%	20.3%	19.1%
Intermediate occupations and self-employed	24.6%	23.3%	19.4%	19.2%
Supervisors/skilled/semi-skilled workers, incl primary sector	41.7%	40.4%	49.8%	44.6%
Unskilled workers	12.7%	15.4%	9.9%	14.7%
Does not answer	0.9%	2.9%	0.5%	2.3%
Other covariables				
Living arrangement				
Alone	7.1%	7.5%	10.9%	12.2%
With partner	26.1%	28.5%	31.4%	30.5%
With partner and children	46.8%	37.4%	44.3%	34.5%
Single parent	2.0%	7.5%	4.5%	10.8%
Other	17.9%	19.1%	8.8%	12.0%
Control variable				
Age				
50–54	29.6%	27.5%	31.1%	29.3%
55–59	26.3%	25.9%	26.7%	25.7%
60–64	25.8%	24.1%	22.5%	22.2%
65–69	18.3%	22.5%	19.7%	22.8%
Total weighted sample N[b](%)	**3909** (47.5%)	**4329** (52.5%)	**3484** (48.2%)	**3741** (51.8%)

Source: ENSE 2006 and EESE 2014.

Notes

a Weighted proportions.

b The sum of the weighted samples for men and women equals the unweighted overall sample.

In the multivariate analysis, this variable is introduced first together with age, which is used as a control variable (Model 1).

Regarding the modelling strategy, the other independent variables are introduced stepwise into the model, starting with education (Model 2). The ten educational attainment categories in 2006 and nine in 2014 were recoded into three groups based on the International Standard Classification of Education (ISCED): (1) (Less than) primary or lower secondary (compulsory education; ISCED 0–2); (2) Upper secondary and professional training (ISCED 3–4); and (3) Tertiary education (ISCED 5–6). We hypothesise that the higher the educational level, the higher the odds to be employed.

We then included two household variables (Model 3). The first was the social class of the head of household,[4] whereby we first reduced the original six categories into four: (1) Directors, managers and professionals; (2) Intermediate occupations and self-employed workers; (3) Supervisors, qualified technicians and primary sector and semi-skilled workers; (4) Unskilled workers. Here we hypothesise that there is a social class gradient in being economically active. We subsequently included type of household. In 2014 there was a question on the type of household respondents lived in, with eight possible categories. However, as this question did not exist in 2006, we reconstructed the typologies based on the household questionnaire on the relationship with the head of household and co-residence with the remaining members of the household. These were then recoded into five categories: (1) Single-person household; (2) Couple only; (3) Couple with children; (4) Single parent; (5) Other. As the participation of Spanish men in the labour market is unaffected by their life cycle stage (Carrasco & Mayordomo, 2005), while Spanish women with a retired partner are known to have a lower probability of remaining in employment or returning to work following a spell of inactivity (Jiménez-Martín et al., 2006), we hypothesise that 50–69-year-old active women who live as a couple are least likely to be employed.

Finally, in the 2006 sample, only relatively few cases (0.7%) provided no information on the dependent variable (employment status) and the principal independent variable (health status). These were therefore excluded, leaving us with a final sample of 15,463 cases (8237 in 2006 and 7226 in 2014). For the multivariate analysis, the missing values of both educational level and social class (respectively, 0.8% and 2.% of the 2006 sample) are maintained.

Results

To answer the first research question, results show clear differences in health status according to employment status among both men and women and in both years that were studied table 8.3. Over the course of the eight-year period between 2006 and 2014, the proportion of good health increased in all categories, while that of fair and bad health declined, although there are several specific patterns worth noting. Firstly, the proportion of men in good health is higher than for women, irrespective of employment status. Secondly, in the case of men, in 2006 the employed had the best health (68%), with similar levels among the unemployed and inactive (respectively, 55% and 51%). However, while by 2014 health had improved among all three employment statuses, it had done so the most among the employed (+10 percentage points), followed by the unemployed (+7), while the proportion of the inactive in good health only increased by 3 percentage points, thus leading to a much clearer employment gradient in health. Thirdly, in the case of women, this health gradient was already apparent in 2006 with regard to the proportion in good health (among the employed, unemployed and inactive, respectively, 57%, 48% and 43%) and even increased moderately over time as the proportion in good health increased by, respectively, 14, 8 and 7 percentage points. Lastly, gender differences in health declined slightly among all employment status categories.

To gain insight into whether the economic crisis affected the labour force participation of the least healthy people more than others, we compare the distribution of the three labour force activity statuses according to health status, by year and sex (Table 8.3). Among men in good health, most are employed. This is the case in both years (59% in 2006 and 57% in 2014). At the same time, the proportion of unemployed doubled from 7% in 2006 to 14% in 2014 and the proportion of healthy but inactive men declined from 35% to 30%. Regarding women in good health, in 2006 there were proportionally more inactive than employed women (61% vs. 34%), but the difference declined substantially over the eight years (to 47% inactive and 43% employed). In contrast, while among men with a fair health status, the same proportion was inactive in 2006 as employed (46%), women were close to three times more likely to be inactive (71%) than employed (25%). Among both sexes few with fair health were unemployed (8% of men; 5% of women). However, by 2014 the proportions of employed men in fair health had declined by eight percentage points over the studied period, while the proportion unemployed increased by seven percentage points to 16% as a result of the economic crisis. In the case of women, the proportion unemployed also increased between the two periods (6 percentage points), but also that of the employed (4 percentage points). Concerning the third health category, bad health, 60% were inactive in 2006, increasing to 62% in 2014. More noteworthy, however, and confirming our premise that the economic crisis was particularly detrimental in terms of employment for those in bad health, is that the proportion employed declined from 32% to 20% and, conversely, the proportion unemployed increased from 7% to 18%. This occurred despite health actually improving during this period among the unemployed (Table 8.2). A similar pattern was also observed for women, although changes were less severe, thereby reducing gender differences. Nevertheless, there were still proportionally more women in bad health who were inactive than their male counterparts.

An interesting result, however, is that if we put aside the inactive population aged 50–69 as they are not active on the labour market because they are either retired, disabled, homemakers or engaged in care duties, gender differences in the proportion employed almost disappear, even when crossed with health status (Table 8.4). Indeed, particularly during the economic crisis economically active

Table 8.2 Distribution of health status according to labour force activity of 50–69-year-olds, by sex and year (%)

	Employed		*Unemployed*		*Inactive*		**Total**	
	2006	2014	2006	2014	2006	2014	**2006**	**2014**
Male								
Good health	67.93	78.15	55.51	62.67	51.19	53.93	**60.18**	**67.00**
Fair health	24.67	18.06	32.52	25.39	31.37	30.18	**27.97**	**23.58**
Bad health	7.40	3.79	11.96	11.93	17.44	15.89	**11.85**	**9.42**
Total	100.00	100.00	100.00	100.00	100.00	100.00	**100.00**	**100.00**
Female								
Good health	57.26	70.90	47.92	56.16	43.47	50.66	**47.53**	**58.40**
Fair health	33.75	23.27	34.72	29.54	39.87	31.96	**37.91**	**28.63**
Bad health	9.00	5.83	17.36	14.30	16.66	17.38	**14.56**	**12.97**
Total	100.00	100.00	100.00	100.00	100.00	100.00	**100.00**	**100.00**

Source: ENSE 2006 and EESE 2014. Proportions are based on the weighted samples.

Table 8.3 Distribution of the population according to labour force activity of 50–69-year-olds, by health status, sex and year

	Good health		*Fair health*		*Bad health*		**Total**	
	2006	*2014*	*2006*	*2014*	*2006*	*2014*	**2006**	**2014**
Male								
Employed	58.56	56.83	45.75	37.30	32.43	19.60	**51.88**	**48.71**
Unemployed	6.53	13.58	8.23	15.64	7.15	18.39	**7.08**	**14.52**
Inactive	34.91	29.59	46.02	47.06	60.42	62.01	**41.04**	**36.77**
Total	100.00	100.00	100.00	100.00	100.00	100.00	**100.00**	**100.00**
Female								
Employed	33.50	43.06	24.75	28.83	17.18	15.93	**27.81**	**35.47**
Unemployed	4.99	9.78	4.54	10.50	5.91	11.22	**4.95**	**10.18**
Inactive	61.50	47.15	70.71	60.68	76.91	72.85	**67.24**	**54.36**
Total	100.00	100.00	100.00	100.00	100.00	100.00	**100.00**	**100.00**

Source: ENSE 2006 and EESE 2014. Proportions are based on the weighted samples.

Table 8.4 Proportion of the economically active who are employed, according to health status by sex and year. Ages 50–69

	Male		*Female*	
	2006	*2014*	*2006*	*2014*
Good health	89.96	80.71	87.03	81.48
Fair health	84.75	70.46	84.51	73.30
Bad health	81.93	51.59	74.42	58.68
Total	**86.59**	**77.04**	**85.28**	**77.71**

Source: SENSE 2006 and EESE 2014. Proportions are based on the weighted samples.

women were slightly *more* likely to work than similar men, especially if they had bad health (59% vs. 52%).

Therefore, to answer our third research question that concerns whether other factors besides health also affect labour force participation among the economically active, we only analysed the 50–64-year age group.[5] Men and women are also analysed separately, given their frequently different labour force trajectories. The results, based on multivariate logistic regression, are provided in Tables 8.5 and 8.6. The probabilities and the 95 per cent confidence intervals of being employed are shown for those active in the labour market according to different characteristics.

The first thing that is important to highlight is that, despite the differences in work trajectories between men and women, the effect of the crisis goes in the same direction, albeit that some, mainly minor, gender differences according to specific characteristics are observed.

In Model 1 we analyse the effect of health status, controlling for age. Results show that the proportion employed by sex and year follows similar trends in men and women: the better the health status, the higher the rates, but the probability of being employed significantly decreased in all health states as a result of the crisis. That said, and as the descriptive results already showed, the impact of the crisis is more accentuated for those in a poor state of health, especially among men. In men, the probability dropped from 0.82 in 2006 to 0.52 in 2014 and in women from, respectively 0.74 to 0.58 in 2014. In addition, while in 2006 the differences in being employed between health statuses were only significant between bad and good health in the case of women, in 2014 the percentage employed was significantly higher in each successive health status (i.e. also between good and fair health and between fair and bad health) in both men and women.

Perhaps surprisingly, this health gradient is only marginally reduced (but remains statistically significant) when adding the variables educational attainment (Model 2), household social class and living arrangement (Model 3). That said, the effect of adding the other variables on the proportion employed is most visible in 2014 among women and those with worse health, increasing from 0.58 (Model 1) to 0.64 in (Model 3).

Table 8.5 Predicted probabilities (and 95 per cent confidence interval) of the active population aged 50–64 being employed in Spain in 2006 and 2014 according to health status, educational attainment, household social class and living arrangements. Results from the binomial logistic regression. Men

		Model 1						*Model 2*						*Model 3*					
		2006			*2014*			*2006*			*2014*			*2006*			*2014*		
		Pr.	*L*	*U*	**Pr.**	*L*	*U*	**Pr.**	*L*	*U*	**Pr.**	*L*	*U*	**Pr.**	*L*	*U*	**Pr.**	*L*	*U*
Self-assessed health																			
	Good health	**0.90**	0.88	0.91	**0.81**	0.79	0.83	**0.89**	0.88	0.91	**0.80**	0.78	0.82	**0.90**	0.88	0.91	**0.80**	0.78	0.82
	Fair health	**0.85**	0.82	0.87	**0.71**	0.66	0.75	**0.85**	0.82	0.88	**0.73**	0.69	0.76	**0.85**	0.82	0.87	**0.73**	0.69	0.77
	Bad health	**0.82**	0.77	0.88	**0.52**	0.43	0.60	**0.83**	0.78	0.88	**0.55**	0.47	0.63	**0.82**	0.77	0.88	**0.57**	0.49	0.65
Edu. attainment																			
	Primary or less							**0.87**	0.85	0.88	**0.69**	0.66	0.72	**0.88**	0.86	0.90	**0.72**	0.69	0.75
	Secondary and professional training							**0.85**	0.82	0.88	**0.81**	0.78	0.84	**0.82**	0.79	0.86	**0.80**	0.77	0.83
	Tertiary							**0.95**	0.93	0.97	**0.93**	0.90	0.95	**0.93**	0.90	0.97	**0.90**	0.87	0.94
Social class																			
	Directors, managers and professionals													**0.88**	0.85	0.92	**0.85**	0.81	0.89
	Intermediate occupations and self-employed													**0.95**	0.93	0.97	**0.82**	0.78	0.86
	Supervisors/skilled/semi-skilled workers, incl primary sector													**0.88**	0.86	0.90	**0.76**	0.73	0.78
	Unskilled workers													**0.73**	0.68	0.78	**0.64**	0.58	0.73
	Does not answer													**0.95**	0.79	1.12	**0.47**	0.18	0.95
Living arrangement																			
	Alone													**0.73**	0.66	0.80	**0.74**	0.69	0.80
	With partner													**0.87**	0.84	0.90	**0.81**	0.78	0.84
	With partner and children													**0.92**	0.90	0.93	**0.77**	0.75	0.80
	Single parent													**0.82**	0.71	0.92	**0.67**	0.58	0.75
	Other													**0.83**	0.79	0.86	**0.73**	0.67	0.79
	N	1676			1991			1670			1991			1670			1991		
	Adjusted R^2	0.021			0.026			0.031			0.077			0.114			0.096		

Source: ENSE 2006 and EESE 2014.

Note: All models are controlled for age. Pr = Probability; L = Lower endpoint; U = Upper endpoint. Results are based on the weighted samples.

Table 8.6 Predicted probabilities (and 95 per cent confidence interval) of the active population aged 50–64 being employed in Spain in 2006 and 2014 according to health status, educational attainment, household social class and living arrangements. Results from the binomial logistic regression. Women

	Model 1						*Model 2*						*Model 3*					
	2006			*2014*			*2006*			*2014*			*2006*			*2014*		
	Pr.	*L*	*U*	**Pr.**	*L*	*U*	**Pr.**	*L*	*U*	**Pr.**	*L*	*U*	**Pr.**	*L*	*U*	**Pr.**	*L*	*U*
Self-assessed health																		
Good health	**0.87**	0.85	0.89	**0.81**	0.79	0.83	**0.86**	0.84	0.89	**0.80**	0.78	0.83	**0.86**	0.83	0.88	**0.80**	0.77	0.82
Fair health	**0.85**	0.81	0.88	**0.73**	0.68	0.77	**0.86**	0.82	0.89	**0.75**	0.71	0.79	**0.86**	0.83	0.89	**0.76**	0.72	0.80
Bad health	**0.74**	0.67	0.81	**0.58**	0.50	0.67	**0.75**	0.69	0.82	**0.62**	0.54	0.70	**0.77**	0.71	0.83	**0.64**	0.57	0.71
Edu. attainment																		
Primary or less							**0.82**	0.79	0.84	**0.70**	0.67	0.73	**0.83**	0.81	0.86	**0.74**	0.71	0.77
Secondary and profesional training							**0.90**	0.86	0.93	**0.75**	0.71	0.79	**0.89**	0.85	0.93	**0.76**	0.72	0.80
Tertiary							**0.90**	0.87	0.94	**0.94**	0.92	0.96	**0.86**	0.81	0.92	**0.91**	0.87	0.94
Social class																		
Directors, managers and professionals													**0.92**	0.89	0.96	**0.88**	0.83	0.92
Intermediate occupations and self-employed													**0.88**	0.84	0.91	**0.83**	0.79	0.87
Supervisors/skilled/semi-skilled workers, incl primary sector													**0.81**	0.77	0.84	**0.72**	0.69	0.75
Unskilled workers													**0.80**	0.75	0.86	**0.75**	0.70	0.80
Does not answer													**0.85**	0.73	0.98	**0.76**	0.51	1.02
Living arrangement																		
Alone													**0.87**	0.81	0.93	**0.82**	0.76	0.87
With partner													**0.82**	0.78	0.87	**0.69**	0.65	0.74
With partner and children													**0.87**	0.84	0.89	**0.81**	0.78	0.84
Single parent													**0.89**	0.84	0.94	**0.80**	0.75	0.85
Other													**0.82**	0.78	0.86	**0.75**	0.69	0.80
N	1733			1709			1733			1709			1733			1709		
Adjusted R^2	0.018			0.022			0.042			0.074			0.063			0.102		

Source: ENSE 2006 and EESE 2014.

Note: All models are controlled for age. Pr=Probability; L = Lower endpoint; U=Upper endpoint. Results are based on the weighted samples.

With regard to the effect of educational attainment, the crisis increases the educational gap in employability as the proportion employed substantially declined among the lowest educated (down, respectively 16 and 9 percentage points between 2006 and 2014 among low educated men and women in Model 3).[6] At the same time, the proportion employed remained high among the tertiary educated men (equalling 0.90 in 2014) and increased by 0.05 in the case of women to 0.91, while the decline in employment among the economically active secondary school and professionally trained was only statistically significant among women.

Turning to household social class (Model 3), among each category the probability of being employed was negatively impacted by the crisis. However, statistically significant declines are only observed among men who lived in a household where the head of household occupies an intermediate occupation or is self-employed (the probability decreases from 0.95 in 2006 to 0.82 in 2014) and among supervisors/skilled/semi-skilled workers including in the primary sector (from 0.88 in 2006 to 0.76 in 2014). In the case of women, declines in employment of 4–9 percentage points are observed in all four social class categories, although only the result for supervisors/skilled/semi-skilled workers is statistically significant. Finally, by type of household the impact of the crisis on those who are economically active is more visible among men than among women, particularly when men do not live alone (e.g. from 0.92 to 0.77 for those who live alone and from 0.82 to 0.67 for single fathers). In the case of women, the largest drop in the proportion employed took place among those who live as a couple without children (from 0.82 to 0.69) although the decline observed for coupled women with children was also significant.

As bad health and labour force exit are positively associated with age, Figure 8.1 shows the Model 3 results of the predicted probabilities of the active population being employed by health status for both sexes and single ages. As one can observe, the crisis has penalised the probability of being employed for both economically active men and women among all health states and all but ages 62 to 64. We assume that the latter exception occurred because the economic crisis led to increases in both voluntary and involuntary early retirements. One is also able to observe that while in 2006 health differences in the likelihood of being employed were small (especially in the case of 50–56-year-old men and between women with good and fair health), in 2014 there was a much clearer and wider health gradient, irrespective of age. In the case of men with a bad health status the probability of being employed was, on average for all ages, 0.21 lower than men with a good health status. In the case of women, the gap was 0.14. Finally, gender differences indicate a slightly higher employment rate among younger men in 2006. Nevertheless, the crisis penalised men more than women, particularly for those with fair or bad health, for whom in 2014 the proportion employed was at almost every age lower than in the case of women (Figure 8.1).

In terms of the explanatory power of the models, adding education tripled the R^2 of the male and female models for 2014 from about 2–3 per cent to 7–8 per cent, while the increase in explained variance in the 2006 model was just 1–2 per cent. On the other hand, adding social class and living arrangements to the 2006 model

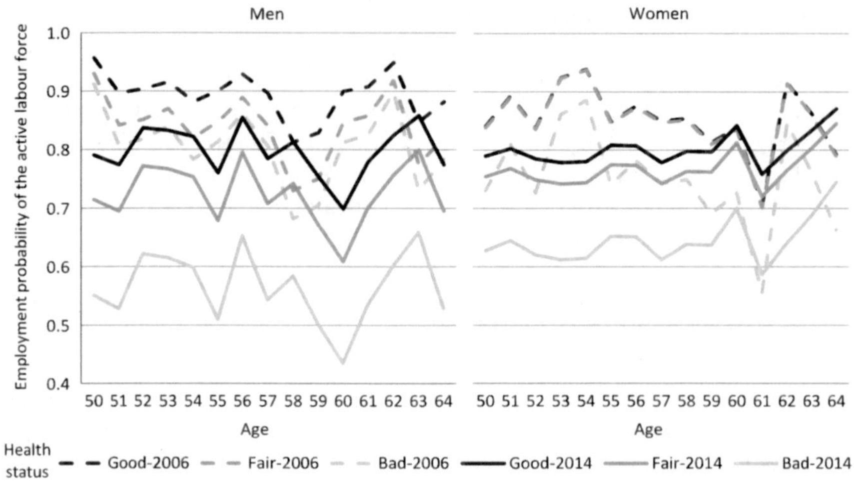

Figure 8.1 Predicted probabilities of the active population aged 50–64 being employed in Spain in 2006 and 2014 by sex, age and health status in 2006 and 2014. Results from the binomial logistic regression

Source: ENSE 2006 and EESE 2014.

Note: Results are based on the weighted samples.

for men explained an additional 8 per cent of the variance in the probability of the active population being employed (from 3% to 11%) but just 2% more in the case of women (from 4% to 6%). Regarding the male and female 2014 models, the difference in R^2 was just 2–3%.

Discussion

In this study, we analysed how labour force participation among 50–69 year-olds differed according to health status in Spain just before (in 2006) and at the end (in 2014) of the Great Recession, whether the economic crisis penalised people with a worse health status more in terms of their participation in the labour market and whether, besides health, there are other factors associated with a change in labour force participation during the studied period.

Summarising the results, we have shown that, while the trend in labour force activity among men remained stable and increased for women due to a cohort effect, the probability of economically active men and women being employed declined between the two periods. Regarding the results according to health status, the least healthy were most affected and proportions changed little after controlling for educational attainment, household social class and living arrangements, thus indicating that health status had a strong independent effect on being employed during the economic crisis. Results were similar for men and women, although having a bad health status affected men more than women.

A possible explanation for this is that men are more likely to highlight health problems and pressures from employer as reasons for (early) retirement than women, often via disability, long-term sickness or unemployment benefits (Fernández et al., 2008; García-Pérez et al., 2013). Conversely, one possible reason why especially women in bad health were slightly *more* likely to work than similar men at the height of the financial crisis is because of an economic need to compensate for their partner's job loss. In addition, given women's more discontinuous work profile, their pension is set to be lower if they retire (early) than their partners who tend to have (had) a more continuous work profile (Spijker et al., 2020). Although gender discrimination has decreased in recent years, one can still speak of a triple form of gender discrimination in Spain, that is, a higher rate of non-employment, a shorter working life and later access to their pensions in order to have enough years of contribution to the state pension scheme, especially if women are low educated (Domínguez-Rodríguez et al., 2020).

Thus, returning to our first research question, we can confirm that health status has a clear effect on employment status, as the lowest employment rates were observed for those with the worst health status and the highest among those in good health. Regarding the second research question, the economic crisis actually doubly penalised those with a bad health status, as health differences in the probability of being employed among those active in the workforce significantly increased between 2006 and 2014 (compare results of Model 1 of 2006 and 2014 in Tables 8.5 and 8.6). However, in this study we could not determine if the poor health status was due to the loss of employment or if poor health led to job loss, something which we leave for future research. We do think that the effect of the latter is likely to be small given that our results revealed health improvements among both the employed and unemployed during the studied period. In a study by Blundell et al. (2021) declines in health among 50–70-year-olds explained only 3% of the decline in employment in England and 15% in the United States. Britton and French (2020) obtained an estimate of 10% in the case of low-educated 50–70-year-old men in England.

Nevertheless, given the substantial differences in labour force participation according to health status, we recommend special attention to be paid to those sectors most vulnerable during times of crisis and especially those economically active without a good health status, irrespective of the causality of the events. In terms of the three other variables tested (re: third research question), all contained categories that observed a statistically significant higher or lower probability of being employed than one or more other categories. However, the highest educated who were active in the labour market stood out from the other categories for the fact that the economic crisis did not affect their employability at all, with very similar results for men and women (in terms of both absolute proportions and the educational gradient). On the other hand, the model results did bring to light an increasing role of education in explaining the variability in employment among the economically active and the decreasing role of social class, especially in the case of men. This could be the result of the economic crisis increasing the competition for higher-skilled occupations, thereby also displacing higher educated workers towards less-skilled occupations (Caparrós Ruiz, 2018).

Despite our interesting findings, some limitations of our study should be highlighted. Perhaps most importantly is the fact that it is virtually impossible to derive causal conclusions from analysis based on cross-sectional analysis due to the lack of information on what occurred first: health deterioration or unemployment. One possibility is for future research to explore the application of instrumental variable (IV) techniques, although finding a valid and strong IV may be hard due to the requirement of IVs to be correlated with the treatment variable (here SPH) but uncorrelated with the outcome (i.e. being employed) (Angrist & Pischke, 2014).

Notwithstanding, given the sharp increases in unemployment during the crisis period and the sharper decline in the employment rate among those in worse health, our results are in line with Prieto et al. (2002) who state that having good health is an important asset to have in order to remain in the labour market, especially in the case of women. On the other hand, according to the same authors, a recent health deterioration does not provoke an early labour market exit among men, something which we could not verify. Secondly, and inherent in this type of study, is that results are dependent upon the indicators used to measure health (Blundell et al., 2021; Britton & French, 2020) and socioeconomic status (Lundberg, 2008) and that the omission of other potentially explanatory variables or the correlation with unobservable characteristics can cause bias in the model's estimated probabilities (Ruhm, 2000). This is why education and social class were also included, although the latter variable was only available at the household level for both years. Nevertheless, there are other socioeconomic variables that may affect the probability of being employed, including type of contract (part-time vs. full-time employment, temporary vs. fixed/long-term contract). However, such information was not present in our data source. Future research could also look into the observed changes in the health status within the employment status category "inactive", as overall changes may be due to compositional changes within the inactive population. For instance, during the eight-year study period, the proportion of female homemakers aged 50–70 declined, while proportionally more inactive women in this age group had (pre)retired. Finally, when testing the effect of health on the probability of being employed, it would be interesting to test the effect of specific health problems, rather than only consider self-perceived health. We are nevertheless confident that our results are robust, as previous research has shown that whether using a single or multiple, subjective or objective, measure of health makes little difference to the estimates of the impact of health on employment (Blundell et al., 2021).

Acknowledgements

Jeroen Spijker gratefully acknowledges funding from the Spanish Ministry of Economy and Competitiveness under the "Ramón y Cajal" program (RYC-2013-14851) and the European Research Council (ERC-2019-CoG-864616,

HEALIN project, PI Iñaki Permanyer. The work also forms part of the R&D project "Sociodemografía del sistema público de pensiones y del cuidado de la población mayor dependiente" (CSO2016-77449-R) co-directed by Amand Blanes and financed by the same Spanish Ministry. Financial support was also received from the Catalan Government under the CERCA Program.

Notes

1 The indicator "at risk of poverty or social exclusion", abbreviated as AROPE, corresponds to the sum of persons who are either at risk of poverty, or severely materially deprived or living in a household with a very low work intensity (https://ec.europa.eu/eurostat/statistics-explained/index.php/Glossary:At_risk_of_poverty_or_social_exclusion_(AROPE)).
2 Healthy life expectancy refers to the number of years of "good" health someone can expect to live, if current health and mortality conditions continue to apply.
3 We are not able to ascertain any causal relationship between health (deterioration) and (change in) employment status as the analyses are based on cross-sectional data that does not provide information on the sequence of events. We elaborate on this limitation in the discussion.
4 Social class of the person interviewed was not available in the 2014 health survey. Although the head of household's social class usually corresponds to the (higher) status of the male partner, according to a study by Borrell et al. (2004) on social class differences in women's health in Barcelona, the effect on the social gradient in health is minor. Moreover, the authors state that using the "dominant social class" measure has several advantages: it is gender-blind, is not sexist and when the dominant social class is a less privileged class (e.g. manual worker) it means that both partners have an occupation equal to or lower than this measure.
5 It is interesting to note, however, that although just 2.0 per cent of 65 to 69-year-olds was active in the labour market (average for both years) 95.2 per cent of those were working.
6 The results of Model 2 are not commented on as the addition of the social class and living arrangement variables in Model 3 produced minor changes.

References

Angrist, J. D. & Pischke, J.-S. (2014). *Mastering'metrics: The path from cause to effect*. Princeton University Press.

Banks, J., Breeze, E., Lessof, C. & Nazroo, J. (2006). *Retirement, health and relationships of the older population in England: The 2004 English Longitudinal Study of Ageing (Wave 2)*. Institute for Fiscal Studies.

Bartoll, X., Palència, L., Malmusi, D., Suhrcke, M. and Borrell, C. (2014). The evolution of mental health in Spain during the economic crisis. *European Journal of Public Health, 24*(3), 415–418. doi:10.1093/eurpub/ckt208

Bentolila, S., García-Pérez, J. I. and Jansen, M. (2017). Are the Spanish long-term unemployed unemployable? *SERIEs*, *8*(1), 1–41.

Blau, D. M. & Gilleskie, D. B. (2001). The effect of health on employment transitions of older men. *Worker Wellbeing in a Changing Labor Market*. Emerald Group Publishing Limited, 35–65.

Blundell, R., Dias, M. C., Britton, J. and French, E. (2021). The impact of health on labor supply near retirement. *Journal of Human resources*, online before print. doi:10.3368/jhr.58.3.1217-9240R4

Borrell, C., Rohlfs, I., Artazcoz, L. and Muntaner, C. (2004). Inequalities in health related to social class in women. What is the effect of the measure used? *Gaceta Sanitaria*, 18, 75–82.

Britton, J. and French, E. (2020). Health and employment amongst older workers. *Fiscal Studies*, 41(1), 221–250. doi:10.1111/1475-5890.12213

Calzón Fernández S., Fernández Ajuria A., López del Amo González M. D. P. and Martín Martín J. J. (2017). Diferencias por sexo de la salud percibida antes y durante la crisis económica (2007 y 2011). [Sex Differences of Perceived Health before and During the Economic Crisis (2007 and 2011). Spain]. *Revista española de salud pública*, 91(21 de septiembre).

Caparrós Ruiz, A. (2018). Intergenerational occupational dynamics before and during the recent crisis in Spain. *Empirica*, 45(2), 367–393. doi:10.1007/s10663-016-9364-0

Carrasco, C. and Mayordomo, M. (2005). Beyond employment: Working time, living time. *Time & Society*, 14(2-3), 231–259.

Cortès-Franch, I. and González López-Valcárcel, B. (2014). Crisis económico-financiera y salud en España. Evidencia y perspectivas. Informe SESPAS 2014. *Gaceta Sanitaria*, 28(S1), 1–6.

Dávila Quintana, C. D. and González López-Valcárcel, B. (2009). Crisis económica y salud. *Gaceta Sanitaria*, 23(4), 261–265.

Debrand, T. & Sirven, N. (2009). *What are the motivations of pathways to retirement in Europe: Individual, familial, professional situation or social protection systems*. IRDES institut for research and information in health economics. Retrieved from https://econpapers.repec.org/RePEc:irh:wpaper:dt28

Diamond, P. (2007). *Top-heavy load: Trouble ahead for social security systems, Introduction by Peter A. Diamond*. Paper presented at the CESifo Forum.

Díaz Olalla, M. (2013). Efectos predecibles y ya constatables de los recortes del gasto social en el incremento de la mortalidad de la población española. *Salud*, 2000, 5–6.

Domínguez-Rodríguez, A. and Blanes-Llorens, A. (2019). El efecto de la salud en la actividad en los mayores de 50 años en España: 2006 y 2014. *Cuadernos de relaciones laborales*, 37(1), 177–202. doi:10.5209/CRLA.63825

Domínguez-Rodríguez, A., Zueras, P. and Miret Gamundi, P. (2020). The state retirement pension in Spain: A triple form of gender discrimination. *Revista Española de Investigaciones Sociológicas*, 170, 35–54.

Espino Granado, A. (2014). Crisis económica, políticas, desempleo y salud (mental). *Revista de la asociación española de neuropsiquiatría*, 34(122), 385–404.

Fernandez, A., Garcia-Alonso, J., Royo-Pastor, C., Garrell-Corbera, I., Rengel-Chica, J., Agudo-Ugena, J., … and Mendive, J. M. (2015). Effects of the economic crisis and social support on health-related quality of life: First wave of a longitudinal study in Spain. *British Journal of General Practice*, 65(632), e198–e203.

Fernández, J. J., Crego, A. and Alcover, C. M. (2008). Relaciones entre factores sociodemográficos, motivación hacia el retiro temprano y satisfacción en la vida postlaboral: análisis exploratorio en una muestra de prejubilados españoles. *Revista de Psicología del Trabajo y de las Organizaciones*, 24(3), 417–439.

García-Gómez, P. (2011). Institutions, health shocks and labour market outcomes across Europe. *Journal of health economics*, 30(1), 200–213.

García-Pérez, J. I., Jiménez-Martín, S. and Sánchez-Martín, A. R. (2013). Retirement incentives, individual heterogeneity and labor transitions of employed and unemployed workers. *Labour Economics*, 20, 106–120. doi:10.1016/j.labeco.2012.11.006

Gerdtham, U.-G. and Ruhm, C. J. (2006). Deaths rise in good economic times: Evidence from the OECD. *Economics & Human Biology*, 4(3), 298–316.

Gili, M., Roca, M., Basu, S., McKee, M. and Stuckler, D. (2012). The mental health risks of economic crisis in Spain: Evidence from primary care centres, 2006 and 2010. *European Journal of Public Health*, 23(1), 103–108. doi:10.1093/eurpub/cks035

Idler, E. L. and Benyamini, Y. (1997). Self-rated health and mortality: A review of twenty-seven community studies. *Journal of Health and Social Behavior*, 38(1), 21–37.

INE (Instituto Nacional de Estadistica). (2018). *Riesgo de pobreza o exclusión social (indicador AROPE) por relación con la actividad (personas de 16 y más años)*. Retrieved 15/11/2018, from INE (Instituto Nacional de Estadistica), http://www.ine.es/jaxiT3/Datos.htm?t=10008

Jiménez-Martín, S. M., Labeaga J. and Vilaplana Prieto C. (2006). A sequential model of older workers' labor force transitions after a health shock. *Health economics*, 15(9), 1033–1054. doi:10.1002/hec.1163

Kalwij, A. & Vermeulen, F. (2005). *Labour force participation of the elderly in Europe: The importance of being healthy*. IZA Institute of Labor Economics. Retrieved from https://ftp.iza.org/dp1887.pdf

Karanikolos, M., Mladovsky, P., Cylus, J., Thomson, S., Basu, S., Stuckler, D., Mackenbach, J. P. and McKee, M. (2013). Financial crisis, austerity, and health in Europe. *The Lancet*, 381(9874), 1323–1331. doi:10.1016/S0140-6736(13)60102-6

La Parra, D. and Álvarez-Dardet, C. (2014). Relación entre crisis económica y salud:¿ lo relevante son las políticas de austeridad? *Salud colectiva*, 10, 91–94.

López del Amo González, M. D. P., Benítez, V. and Martín-Martín, J. J. (2018). Long term unemployment, income, poverty, and social public expenditure, and their relationship with self-perceived health in Spain (2007–2011). *BMC Public Health*, 18(1), 133. doi:10.1186/s12889-017-5004-2

Lundberg, O. (2008). Commentary: Politics and public health – some conceptual considerations concerning welfare state characteristics and public health outcomes. *International Journal of Epidemiology*, 37(5), 1105–1108. doi:10.1093/ije/dyn078

Mackenbach, J. P., Van den Bos, J., Joung, I., Van de Mheen, H. and Stronks, K. (1994). The determinants of excellent health: Different from the determinants of iIl-health? *International Journal of Epidemiology*, 23(6), 1273–1281.

Martín, U., Domínguez-Rodríguez, A. and Bacigalupe, A. (2019). Desigualdades sociales en salud en población mayor: una aportación desde la salud pública al debate sobre el retraso de la edad de jubilación en España. *Gaceta Sanitaria*, 33(1), 82–84. doi:10.1016/j.gaceta.2017.10.010

Miilunpalo, S., Vuori, I., Oja, P., Pasanen, M. and Urponen, H. (1997). Self-rated health status as a health measure: The predictive value of self-reported health status on the use of physician services and on mortality in the working-age population. *Journal of Clinical epidemiology*, 50(5), 517–528.

Prieto, J., Romero, D. and Álvarez, S. (2002). Estado de salud y participación laboral de las personas mayores. *Papeles de Trabajo del Instituto de Estudios Fiscales*, 15/02. https://econpapers.repec.org/paper/hpewpaper/y_3A2002_3Ai_3A15.htm

Rocha Bones, K., Pérez, K., Rodríguez-Sanz, M., Borrell, C. and Obiols, J. E. (2010). Prevalencia de problemas de salud mental y su asociación con variables socioeconómicas, de trabajo y salud: resultados de la Encuesta Nacional de Salud de España. *Psicothema*, 22(3), 389–395.

Ruhm, C. J. (2000). Are recessions good for your health? *The Quarterly Journal of Economics*, 115(2), 617–650.

Ruhm, C. J. (2007). A healthy economy can break your heart. *Demography*, 44(4), 829–848.

Spijker, J., Bayona, J., Medina, A. & Menacho, T. (2018). *Atles de salut de la població de 50 i més anys a Catalunya*. Bellaterra: Centre d'Estudis Demogràfics.

Spijker, J., González, J. M. G. and Puga, D. (2020). Spain. In Ní Léime, Á., Ogg, J., Rašticová, M., Street, D., Krekula, C., Bédiová, M., and Madero-Cabib, I. (Eds.), *Extended Working Life Policies: International Gender and Health Perspectives*. Springer International Publishing, 427–437. 10.1007/978-3-030-40985-2_34

Spijker, J. and Zueras, P. (2018). Socioeconomic health inequalities in the Catalan population aged 50+ during the last economic crisis. *Revista española de salud pública*, 92(28 de noviembre), e1–e14.

Stuckler, D. & Basu, S. (2013). *Por qué la austeridad mata: El coste humano de las políticas de recorte*. Taurus.

Tapia Granados, J. A. (2014). La crisis y la salud en España y en Europa:¿ Está aumentando la mortalidad? *Salud colectiva*, 10(1), 81–91.

Torns, T. (1995). Mercado de trabajo y desigualdades de género. *Cuadernos de relaciones laborales*, 6, 81–92.

Urbanos-Garrido, R. M. and Lopez-Valcarcel, B. G. (2015). The influence of the economic crisis on the association between unemployment and health: An empirical analysis for Spain. *The European Journal of Health Economics*, 16(2), 175–184.

Virtanen, P., Vahtera, J., Kivimäki, M., Liukkonen, V., Virtanen, M. and Ferrie, J. (2005). Labor market trajectories and health: A four-year follow-up study of initially fixed-term employees. *American Journal of Epidemiology*, 161(9), 840–846. doi:10.1093/aje/kwi107

Webber, D. J., Page, D., Veliziotis, M. & Johnson, S. (2015). *Does poor health affect employment transitions? Project report*. Joseph Rowntree Foundation. Retrieved from http://eprints.uwe.ac.uk/27340

9 Decision to Extend Working Life in Turkey and Its Relation to Subjective Well-being: A Qualitative Analysis from a Gender Perspective

Hande Barlin, Nilufer Korkmaz Yaylagul, and Murat Anil Mercan

Introduction

Population ageing is bringing about changes in all walks of life, including the labour force. Indeed, working is a common theme discussed in active ageing literature (Rowe and Kahn, 1997; Walker and Maltby, 2012). Considering the healthy and successful ageing paradigm from a psycho-social perspective (Vanhoutte, 2014), working in later life has implications for an individual's subjective well-being (SWB).

SWB is a multifaceted, multidimensional concept central to the lives of individuals. The concept goes beyond momentary happiness and incorporates deeper constructs such as meaningfulness and life satisfaction that extends over time as well as self-actualisation. It includes both hedonic and eudemonic well-being. While hedonic well-being embodies affective-emotional and cognitive components (Kansky and Diener, 2021), eudemonic well-being relates to developing and realising an individual's potential (Vanhoutte, 2014). In the words of Diener et al. (2009) SWB, "emphasises an individual's assessment of his or her own life". Many factors play roles in the global SWB of an individual, including personal traits (Lucas and Diener, 2015), individual characteristics (Frey and Stutzer, 2010), life events (Gomaz et al., 2009) and genetic factors (Okbay et al., 2016). Furthermore, satisfaction in various life domains such as marriage and family, health, leisure and work (Diener et al., 2009) contributes to global SWB and vice versa (Schimmack, 2008). Each domain's importance in contributing to global SWB changes over the life course (Plagnol, 2010). For instance, health becomes a more important domain as people age. On the other hand, employment loses its significance (Plagnol and Scott, 2011). Most probably two forces interplay in this outcome. The first relates to lower labour force participation rates for older people compared to younger age groups and to the fact that many older people prefer to retire (Hsieh, 2005). The second relates to the findings that the relative importance of life domains changes with age (Bardo, 2017). Nonetheless, research (Graham, 2014; Nikolova and Graham, 2014) has shown that working can positively affect well-being in later life.

DOI: 10.4324/9781003145325-9

Working and working conditions are related to SWB regardless of age. Compared to those unemployed, people in employment have higher SWB (Winkelmann, 2009). The SWB of the employed is impacted by many factors, including employment type (Binder and Coad, 2011), organisational culture, characteristics of the workplace and established social relationships (Biggio and Cortese, 2013) as well as time arrangements (Golden et al., 2013). Older workers working voluntarily, both part- and full-time, report higher levels of SWB compared to retirees (Nikolova and Graham, 2014). Their physical and mental health tends to be better (Wahrendorf et al., 2017). Returning to work after an interruption also increases life satisfaction (Lux and Scherger, 2017). However, those wanting to extend their working lives after retiring from their career jobs and who could not find a job are found to have lower levels of life satisfaction (Dingemans and Henkens, 2014). Conversely, it has been argued that low-quality work in later life can produce adverse outcomes if older adults work out of obligation rather than by choice (Taylor, 2019).

As elsewhere in the world, the population in Turkey is also ageing. According to 2017 data, 32.5 per cent of adults between 60 and 64 years old and 13.8 per cent of adults who are 65 years and older participate in the labour force. There is a wide gender gap in terms of labour force indicators, such that while 19.2 per cent of men who are older than 65 are in paid employment, only 6.4 per cent of women work. In addition, like their younger counterparts, older women tend more to work in informal sectors and at part-time jobs, compared to men. Due to traditional low labour force participation rates of working-age women, older women are more likely to be dependent than self-sufficient (Mercan, 2020). Many older women face financial hardships consequent to the loss of their spouse (Yelboğa, 2018). Gender roles, low wages and incomplete careers (Demirbilek and Özgür, 2017) are reasons for lower female participation rates. Yet, social policies targeting older adults are limited, leaving older women dependent on their children and extended families (Sığın, 2016).

While providing job and training opportunities for older adults to participate in working life is among the government's national objectives (T.C. Cumhurbaşkanlığı Strateji ve Bütçe Başkanlığı, 2019), no tangible measures were devised towards this end. Similarly, research on the working life of older adults using primary data is very limited in Turkey. Perceived health status among workers aged between 45 and 64 is worse than that of their younger counterparts (Çağlayan and Etiler, 2015). Nonetheless, older workers are less stressed and do not take time off often (Korkut and Bulduk, 2021).

Most empirical research on SWB and working in later life is quantitative (Graham, 2014; Nikolova and Graham, 2014); qualitative studies are limited. There are none for Turkey. Against this background, based on a qualitative research design, this chapter investigates the late-life working experiences of Turkish individuals from middle and lower socio-economic backgrounds in relation to SWB. It analyses the motivations for extending working life and how working influences their SWB. The chapter also explores gender differences in these experiences.

Methodology

Employing a qualitative research methodology, the study is based on semi-structured, in-depth interviews with a cross-sectional design. Twenty people who are working in later life participated in the study.

Data collection

The interview guide was designed so that participants could freely tell their stories and express their feelings. The guide consisted of questions regarding participants' (1) socio-economic background, (2) life stories, (3) working experiences throughout their life, (4) decision to extend their working life and (5) experiences and opinions on working in later life. Pilot interviews were conducted for the interview guide to review the clarity and specificity of the questions. As the data were collected during the COVID-19 pandemic of 2020–2021, for the health and safety of the participants, in-depth interviews were either conducted over the phone or via web-based video calls (Zoom, WhatsApp and Facebook messenger) depending on the preference of the participant. Interviews lasted between 45 and 90 minutes and were audio-recorded.

Ethical considerations

Ethical approval for the study was obtained from the Gebze Technical University Ethics Committee. At the beginning of each interview, the research was explained to participants, and oral consent was recorded. The participants were anonymised, and they are referred to with codes in the text, which are composed of letters indicating their gender (M = male; F = female), age, socio-economic status (SES) (L = lower; M = medium) and queue number (e.g. M67M1).

Recruitment and participants

Participants were recruited using purposive sampling based on two criteria at the time of interview: (1) being older than 60 years and (2) actively working. Due to geographic convenience for the researchers, participants were recruited from Antalya, Mersin and Istanbul in Turkey. Recruitment was carried out through gatekeepers, including employers, civil society organisation members and the Third Age University coordinator at Akdeniz University.

Special attention was paid to ensuring diversity in gender, education level, SES and occupation. The sample was evenly split by gender and SES; six females, four males with lower SES and six males and four females with medium SES.[1] The age range varied between 61 and 83, and most participants continued to work following retirement. However, three of the female participants of lower SES were not yet entitled to retire as either they had delayed entry into the labour force or much of their employment was not registered and therefore did not contribute to pension entitlements. Among the participants, only two had an interrupted working life. These participants were also those who were not yet retired. Most of the participants worked in jobs for which they were qualified throughout their working lives. Most also continued to work in related jobs in later life. However, some participants changed careers following retirement (Table A9.1 in the Appendix).

The health status of the participants was generally good; most of them stated that they do not have chronological diseases such as diabetes, hypertension and circulatory diseases. Only one participant said that he had blood pressure and cardiovascular disease. Other participants mentioned rheumatoid arthritis, goitre and cervical disk hernia.

Data analysis

Data analysis included several stages. Thematic analysis was conducted in view of the SWB construct (Guest et al., 2012; Braun and Clarke, 2014). Interviews were transcribed verbatim by the researchers and their assistants. To get acquainted with the data, each transcription was read twice by researchers. For data analysis, NVivo12.0 was used. To ensure validity and reliability, coding was conducted by two independent researchers. Later codes were compared, and common codes identified by the researchers were used in the analysis. In the case of disagreement, the third researcher acted as a judge. All codes were grouped into categories, and, subsequently, categories were grouped into themes. Analysis was done in Turkish. Themes and quotations were translated into English by the first author during the drafting phase of the chapter.

Limitations

In the beginning researchers aimed to include participants from various income and education groups. However, participants from the highest income group (e.g. factory owners, CEOs of very large companies) could not be recruited. One reason is that potential participants from the highest income groups reached by the research team were unwilling to convey their personal experiences. The other reason for this is the COVID-19 restrictions, because of which face-to-face contacts could not be established with the respective gatekeepers. Contacts with gatekeepers for low- and medium-SES participants were established before the pandemic.

Findings

Four main themes emerge from the analysis: (1) motivations to extend working life; (2) current working experience; (3) outcomes of working; and (4) plans for future. The themes are robust across males and females as well as across participants from low and medium SES.

Motivations to extend working life

There are common themes regarding the decision to continue working in later life. Job satisfaction and financial relief are the motivation sub-themes most frequently referenced by participants. Other sub-themes discussed are getting out of the house, socialising, working as a habit, and remaining active.

Regardless of SES, most participants emphasise their job satisfaction. Participants, who attribute the utmost importance to working, express their positive sentiments towards working. For instance, F71L1, a cleaning lady, stresses that she does not get tired when she cleans the houses she loves.

> *When a person goes to the place, she loves ... when you do something. You never get tired. You don't feel [that you get tired] at all.* (F71L1)

On the other hand, financial necessity is shown as a primary motivational factor for people with lower SES. While nonfinancial motivational factors are also cited, most, if not all, work due to financial necessity. M70L2 works as a painter on demand. His household's only financial resource is his pension.

> *My earning is normal. Like every pensioner in Turkey. If I fared better in financial terms, would it be necessary for me to work? My pension is 2000TL. I pay 1000TL rent. How would we get by if I didn't work? Electricity bill, water bill ... I work, because I feel that I have to.* (M70L2)

However, for participants with medium SES, additional earnings were only a secondary motivational factor. Similar to M65M1, a graphic designer, many do not mention financial necessity if not explicitly asked.

> *Financial factors are not primary. They are only secondary or tertiary. Having an active lifestyle, meeting new people and having conversations are more important factors.* (M65M1)

Yet, as the conversation develops, many with medium SES admit that combining their pension and salary improves their standard of living. They state that financial motivation is as important as nonfinancial factors. M73M1 draws attention to the role his additional salary plays in maintaining his standards of living.

> *Now let me tell you the truth. I have a pension of 3500 TL [i.e.192 € authors' conversion into euros]. We have a house. We have a car. But it is very difficult to live on this pension. Because I earn an additional salary; I can lead a more comfortable life.* (M73M1)

Apart from job satisfaction and financial relief, other factors also act as motivations to extend working life. For instance, for some, working has become a habit, which they cannot let go.

> *Even thinking of quitting makes me uncomfortable. I would psychologically feel empty. I started working at 6 years old. ... Subtract 6 years from my age, I have been working for 67 years.* (M73M1)

M69M1, an engineer, beautifully summarises three other motivations for working – socialising, remaining active, and *getting out of the house.*

> *If I stay at home, I will get older. I will feel old. To be active, to have dialogue with others, to be in contact with others is important.* (M69M1)

Indeed, getting out of the house is a factor, especially discussed by male participants regardless of SES. Work provides an escape from possible conflict with their spouse at home.

> *If I sit at home, she [my wife] would not like me being in the way.* (M65M1)

Current working experience

While the current working experiences of participants are diverse, they discuss certain common topics. Working arrangements and working hours, difficulties faced, competence, social relations at work, work-life balance/family support and challenges brought by the COVID-19 pandemic arise as sub-themes.

Most participants with medium SES have flexible work arrangements and working hours. Many are self-employed and arrange their daily routine according to their workload, family obligations, social relations and hobbies. Some of those who work for others have an understanding or contract with their employers, which provides them with greater freedom. F72M1 works at a private hospital:

> *They do not force us to work particular hours … Our starting time depends on our agreement with the administration. Some work part-time, some full.* (F72M1)

On the other hand, except for those with precarious "free-lance" jobs such as painting and cleaning, most participants with lower SES cannot arrange their work times and conditions. For instance, F62L1 works as a live-in nursemaid and does not have defined working hours. Her working day starts with breakfast and ends after the kids go to sleep.

Regarding work difficulties participants face, physical challenges are most frequently voiced, especially among participants with lower SES. Tasks associated with physical endurance or using physical force, such as carrying, painting or commuting, become harder for participants as they age. Yet, age-related physical problems are not at a level that prevent them from continuing to work. F67L1, a farmer, states that:

> *We used to carry sacks full of vegetables. At old age, it has become harder. We can carry buckets only.* (F67L1)

While many participants do not express or describe emotional difficulties, two truck drivers M61L1 and M61L2, stress emotional and physical difficulties related to their working conditions.

My job is hard. I work at a construction site. I always stay away from home. I could only take 8 days of leave every two months. I used to travel to and from home for 2 days. I used to stay home for 6 days. Why would I run away from home? I love home … Some drink tea, coffee in the morning at home and return home at night. Our job is not like that. Day and night, winter, summer we are on the road. I cried a lot. My hands froze. I encountered risk of freezing several times … . How much I had to endure. (M61L2)

Albeit very rare, participants with medium SES also voice physical difficulties. The limited difficulties they face are primarily non-physical. A dentist complains about the cost of dentistry materials. An academic, who works full-time, describes having an excessive workload from time to time. A couple discuss legal responsibilities associated with their job. M75M1, a physician, talks about the responsibility of giving health clearance for licences such as driving and navigation.

You only report what you observe and detect in the patient … . The burden, responsibility is high. But once you don't get into funny business, you are fine. (M75M1)

Some of the participants who work for others are concerned about the difficulty of finding a new job if they lose their current job.

It is very hard to find a job. It is even hard for those who are younger. (M69M1)

Experience-related competence is also a subject discussed by some of the participants. They emphasise that the maturity and experience brought by years of working and age are an advantage. Working in the hospital as a psychiatrist, F72M1 speaks of the importance of experience as a psychiatrist.

There is no discrimination between young and old doctors. Of course, not. Yet, sometimes patients prefer more experienced doctors. Young doctors also know the work well, but some come looking for experience. (F72M1)

Participants also socialise at their workplace, both with colleagues, customers and friends. Many have good relationships with their younger co-workers and enjoy being with them. The relationship most portrayed is mainly non-professional and underlines the age difference and the closeness of the relationship. For instance, working as a security guard, M70L1 describes the relationship with the workers in the construction site and compares it to a father-son relationship. F67M1, a female realtor, also stresses strong bonds.

There is love [attachment] in the office. I am the oldest in the office. I am not saying that I am old. I am older than most of their [co-workers'] parents … I love them all. They also love me. (F67M1)

Some participants report adverse interactions with other individuals at the workplace. However, according to the same participants, this situation can always be encountered and does not affect them negatively in terms of social adaptation, in general.

Many participants do not face problems with work-life balance, especially those with flexible working arrangements. In most cases, their families are supportive of their work, both because of the benefits of being active and because of the financial rewards. Participants whose spouses also work organise working time accordingly. On the other hand, those participants with long working hours or rarely at home express their discontent. F61L2, who works as a nursemaid, states that her children want her to quit her job as soon as they find a job.

> *I will quit when my son starts working. More precisely, I want to quit. My family do not want me to work also.* (F61L2)

While many express their positive working experience and affection for working and job satisfaction (see above on motivation), others have negative experiences. Among the participants, M61L1 and M61L2, with low SES, shared their negative feelings about working under challenging conditions, especially those working long hours in physically demanding jobs. These negative feelings do not pertain only to working conditions in later life but during the whole life course. As M61L1, a truck driver put it:

> *I get tired. I come home. I thank God I have a wife I love. … I have been married for so many years. But I could not take my wife out to dinner. We did not have a vacation. I did not have a weekend or annual leave. I did not have a job which would start at 8 o'clock in the morning and end at 5 in the afternoon. I was on the road for days and months away from home. That also wore me out.* (M61L1)

The COVID-19 pandemic and restrictions limiting freedom of movement for the older population is another issue passionately discussed concerning their current working experience. Only a few worked online or continued working during the COVID-19 pandemic restrictions. Many of the participants interrupted their working lives. Participants experienced a continuous and long-term non-active, isolated life at home. With the easing of lockdown measures, participants returned to work. For some, this return meant lowering the intensity of work. Lockdown experience reminded them of the important role that work played in their lives and in terms of their quality of life. F65M1, who is engaged in marketing, explains that she gave up the idea of stopping work after her experience of lockdown:

> *Before the Pandemic, I was considering stopping working … I wanted to buy a caravan and travel with my friends. But during the Pandemic, I felt trapped. I felt disconnected from people … No, I will continue my job. This is the best thing*

I can do. ... During the lockdown, I felt as if I was burying myself alive in the grave. (F65M1)

Outcomes of working

Regarding the outcomes of working, participants speak of active living and improvement of physical and mental health, being useful, autonomy and independence, self-realisation and socialisation.

For most participants, working is a way of living actively, and it brings them vitality and vigour. Many of them state that if they had not been working, they would feel much older. Physical activity and engagement through working improve their mental and physical health. For instance, M65M1, who gives advertising services to tourism firms, expresses that he is versatile and happy to work. He thinks engaging both the body and brain helps to preserve vigour.

I have a job where I brainstorm. In other words, working gives vitality. (M65M1)

According to F65M1, a marketing specialist, her physical health would have been worse if she had not been working.

Feeling useful is another theme that comes up in relation to the outcomes of working later in life. Some state that being productive, sharing their experiences with others, and solving problems makes them feel useful, giving them meaning and purpose. A truck driver M61L2 states that

When you work, you feel peaceful. To put it correctly, you feel useful in old age. (M61L2)

An illiterate female study participant employed in the agricultural sector illustrates her competence and takes pride in being useful in her job.

Nobody can catch up to me. I work very well. Of course, if the novice workers come, they bring them to me. I teach them too. The engineer asks me and says whether I like the way he [the new worker] is doing his job – should we hire him? They ask me. If I say "No", they don't hire him. (F66L1)

Enhanced autonomy and independence are also cited as consequences of working in older age. For the participants, work provides financial independence. Earning additional salaries on top of their pension facilitates attaining a more comfortable life, where they can travel and consume whatever they want or support their children.

While the participants do not directly use the expression, self-realisation is a common theme throughout the interviews regarding work.

I feel my "existence", when I work. (M70L1)

Socialising is also another subject discussed in connection with outcomes of present working experiences. Working provides the participants with opportunities to meet people from every walk of life and to build new relationships. Most of the time, these new relations bring positive energy to the participants, as M75M1 puts it:

> *They make you laugh; you make them laugh. You give them happiness. You get happy. You meet your positive energy needs, and you support them by giving positive energy.* (M75M1)

Plans for future

Most participants from both socio-economic backgrounds would like to work until they encounter impediments, especially regarding health. Accordingly, being healthy surfaces as a precondition in the decision to work in later life. Gardening and travel are the most common subjects discussed concerning plans once the working life ends. Nonetheless, most participants with medium SES are especially eager to work.

> *I will continue to work as long as my health permits.* (M67M1)

On the other hand, some participants with lower SES gave an exact date for quitting their jobs. The most important reason among these is the decrease in economic need, the working-age limit in some professions and retirement for non-retired people. F66L1 started working late and worked in different and sometimes precarious jobs. She has not retired yet. When she is entitled to her pension, she will continue working for just a year.

Those with severe working conditions or heavy workloads and participants who do not like their jobs especially talk about quitting. M61L1 and M61L2, who work as truck drivers, stated that they do not like their job; they do it out of necessity. They said that they plan to stop working when they reach the age limit of 65, that is, when their truck driving license is cancelled.

> *It is not because it's a heavy burden. I don't like being a truck driver. I did not like it because I had accidents. But I was obliged to work.* (M61L2)

Gender-based experiences

All themes are common to both genders except motivation to extend working life. Male participants were more enthusiastic talking about motivation compared to females. Getting out of the house and working as a habit are most often cited by men for extending working life. Job satisfaction and financial relief are the prime reasons to extend working life for both genders. However, male participants were more expressive about financial concerns. The traditional role of men as the breadwinner is most probably why men were more vocal about financial concerns. This manifests itself in the words of M61L1:

> *I have a son, whom I am responsible for. There is his mother. Others [referring to his other children] can take care of themselves ... I will work until my children can take care of themselves. I also bought a house (with debt). I hope to leave my wife at least a pension, so that she can be independent when I am gone.* (M61L1)

Further, as activities and social gatherings are limited for men, they feel there are few social opportunities other than work. M70L1 puts it:

> *I don't like going to (all men) cafes. I don't like [to] saunter about. I got used [to] working from childhood.* (M70L1)

As to current working experiences and future plans, there are no apparent differences in the discourse. On the other hand, while sub-themes relating to outcomes of working reported by both men and women were similar, there were differences in the ways in which they expressed them. Females were more likely to talk about being useful. Male participants speak more of active living and health effects as well as self-realisation. The focus of female participants on being useful might be associated with the perspectives regarding the distinction between paid professional work and unpaid domestic work. Women participate in public life and the labour market at a lower rate than men in Turkey. They mainly deal with household work. On the other hand, domestic work is seen as worthless because it is unpaid and is not seen as a job. For this reason, both society and women themselves may regard work done at home as useless and worthless. Accordingly, paid work is seen as a valuable contribution to society and gives women a feeling of self-worth.

On the other hand, the expressiveness of male participants regarding active living and health effects again pertains to the traditional gender roles. Women in Turkey actively perform domestic activities throughout their life course. On the other hand, when men end their work life, their activity levels decrease. For this reason, for men, physical decline occurring with age becomes more common. Male participants were aware of the physical and cognitive implications of ageing and expressed the view that they compensated for these by working.

Self-realisation is also discussed differently by men and by women. Self-realisation for women is associated with achievements in work life and family life, probably due to traditional gender roles. However, for men, their professional achievements become more prominent. Hence, we find that male participants are more expressive regarding self-realisation.

Another subtheme where there is a difference is autonomy and independence. Women more frequently emphasise independence in making a living, getting away from housework and getting out of the house.

> *It is good for me not to be dependent on my child.* (F67M1)
>
> *Thanks to this job, I travelled to Dubai, the Far East, Russia twice with 14-storey ships. I travelled and visited all of them.* (F65M1)

For male participants, work-induced independence is expressed in terms of getting out of the house and easing the stress of living alone with their spouse. Accordingly, working prevents spousal conflicts.

> *When I'm not working, my wife and I fight like we are at war … Working is beneficial because of that. When I work, I spend less time at home.* (M70L2)

In terms of gender-based discrimination, most of the female participants stated that they had not experienced such discrimination.

> *I have never looked at the issue as gender discrimination … . I have not encountered such a thing personally. There may not have been an incident important enough to leave a mark.* (F67M1)

Despite this overt statement regarding gender equality, sexist discourses are observed in the discussions of the participants. Significantly, among male participants, the idea that women should be protected and glorified because they are more vulnerable and weaker than men is dominant.

> *We live in an apartment building by the seaside. Retired governors also live in the building. We insisted on hiring a female concierge. It does not matter if the concierge is male or female. Outside, there are female concierges at schools. There are female police officers. There are female judges. Why not let the concierge be female? This year we will push it to the agenda again. We will try to make the apartment manager be a woman. That is why women are in everything. They should be in everything: The beauty of the building is with women. It is possible with women. When we push them away with the back of our hand, you can't be successful.* (M83M1)

On the other hand, some female participants emphasised the difficulty of working as a woman when they were younger. Housework and childcare that women do outside of work increased their burden. For example, F66L1, who has worked as an agricultural worker since her youth, has four children.

> *Of course, being a woman is difficult in everything. When my children were small, there was no washing machine, no dishwasher. You used to wash them by hand. There was no single use diaper. You used to make your own bread. I was both working and doing all of these things. Now I take my shower and go in front of the TV. Everything is ready.* (F66L1)

However, such burden arising from domestic engagements is not expressed concerning their later life.

Discussion and conclusion: SWB and working in later life

Many of the themes and sub-themes identified relate to both hedonic and eudemonic well-being. Following Vanhoutte (2014)'s discussion of eudemonic well-being based on works of Ryff and Keyes (1995), Ryan and Deci (2000) and Hyde et al. (2003), autonomy as well as competence and self-realisation is among the dimensions of eudemonic well-being. These dimensions surface in our study in connection with discussions relating to present working experience and outcomes of working. Furthermore, based on Diener (1984), Vanhoutte (2014) identifies two aspects of hedonic well-being: affective and cognitive. While our study does not delve much into the affective aspect, it finds results related to domain-specific cognitive well-being, specifically regarding work (Diener et al., 1999). Using a bottom-up approach, satisfaction in work-life and financial satisfaction are significant contributors to life satisfaction (Schimmack, 2008).

Beyond the general concept of work, sub-themes that come up under motivations to extend working life and outcomes of working are related to other life domains or other aspects taken together with SWB. Financial relief is provided by supplementary income, especially for the pensioners and getting out of the house and socialising (Kahneman & Deaton, 2010; Pinquart and Sörensen, 2000; Axelrad et al., 2020; Leung et al., 2011), active living (Sagherian et al., 2021; Parra-Rizo and Sanchis-Soler, G., 2020) and health (Okun et al., 1984) are related to SWB.

Plagnol and Scott (2011) find that priorities attached to life domains shift over time, and employment loses its prominence. While we cannot compare working life with other life domains, our study finds that working is still an important life domain, at least for participants who do not give a time indication for termination of working life. The COVID-19 pandemic, which has led to an interruption of most participant's working life and negative self-evaluations, triggered a desire to go back to work. This alone illustrates the importance of working for the participants and their positive SWB. Nonetheless, health seems to be more important in line with Plagnol and Scott's (2011) finding, as good health is put forth as a precondition to extend working life.

Recent research finds a positive relationship between working in later life and SWB. Yet, not all employment at old age is positively correlated. For instance, Axelrad et al. (2020) find that employment in old age is associated with SWB, provided there is room for one's development. Nikolova and Graham (2014) find that the relationship is valid if the employment is voluntary. However, Dingemans and Henkens (2014) argue that workers who extend their working life for financial reasons find their SWB decreased. Our research supports these findings.

The themes discussed by participants illustrate their perspectives on working in later life, hence their subjective evaluations. We observe that motivations, experiences, outcomes and future plans interact and reinforce each other.

Positive experiences and outcomes overlap with future plans, such that positive experiences motivate participants to work. On the other hand, negative experiences especially accumulated through the life course, as in the truck driver example, lead participants to determine a time to quit working.

Our findings suggest that, through self-realisation, competence, autonomy and independence, being useful, active living, perceived positive health outcomes, job satisfaction, financial relief, socialising and taking part in the public sphere (getting out of the house) contribute to SWB either directly or through working experience. The interplay of these aspects manifests itself in the subjective evaluations of workers well-being. In this regard, if the evaluation is positive, workers decide to continue to work. If the evaluation is negative, they set a time to quit, provided they do not need the supplementary income.

Many of the participants in our sample with lower SES do not have a date in mind to stop working. However, this tendency is not that prevalent for the participants with medium SES. Three main differences between the socioeconomic groups are (1) ability to make flexible work arrangements and time schedules, (2) priority attached to financial relief and (3) the physical endurance requirement of the occupation. Accordingly, our findings support Golden et al. (2013) and Okulicz-Kozaryn and Golden (2018), who find that flexible work arrangements are associated with well-being. It is also in line with Nikolova and Graham (2014), who finds workers working voluntarily fare better than retirees. Furthermore, as self-employment would provide such flexibility, it also supports Binder and Coad (2011) and Wahrendorf et al. (2017).

Gendered differences emerge in the motivation for working. These differences are mostly related to domestic life and the public sphere. Due to gender roles, the burden of making a living in the public sphere has been felt heavily by men and many participants worked earlier than women; working has become a routine habit in the life course. At the same time, financial concerns were expressed more by the male participants.

The effects of gender roles also surface in outcomes of working. Compared to males, higher female engagement in unpaid domestic work means that female participants evaluate working more in terms of being useful. On the other hand, as men's activity level is related to working in a public space throughout their adulthood until later life, the end of working life for men signifies a decline in activity. Consequently, working male participants are more expressive in being active and reporting positive health effects in evaluating outcomes. Gender roles also affect the interpretation of self-realisation. The self-realisation of female participants does not only pertain to achievements in working life but also in family life. In comparison, male participants are more likely to focus on professional achievements. In terms of autonomy and independence, while female participants underline getting away from domestic space, for male participants, it means independence and getting away from the house and spouse.

In line with previous research, our findings suggest that not all employment contributes to a positive assessment of SWB. Working conditions and time schedules that the older workers can arrange according to their preferences and employment opportunities enabling workers to demonstrate their competence and fulfil their potential would be most beneficial in terms of SWB. This is an important finding to take into account when considering any policy intervention to extend working life. In the light of the limited social policy targeting older adults in Turkey, especially in terms of active ageing, financial incentives should be devised for employers to employ older adults with flexible time arrangements at jobs that are not physically demanding, where they can use accumulated work-life experiences.

Note

1 In Turkey high socio-economic status (SES) usually is achieved by successful self-employed because of the societal structure. People with high-status occupations such as medical doctors and engineers are usually not in the top of socio-economic ladder, because of lower wages compared to their European counterparts. Among those with paid employment, only senior managers at large corporations make it to high SES. Accordingly, medical doctor and engineer participants in our study are classified as belonging to medium SES.

References

Axelrad, H., Sherman, A. and Luski, I. (2020). The effect of employment on the SWB of 60–80 years old people. *International Journal of Social Economics*, 47(12), doi:10.1108/IJSE-04-2020-0212

Bardo, A. R. (2017). A life course model for a domains-of-life approach to happiness: Evidence from the United States. *Advances in Life Course Research*, 33, 11–22.

Biggio, G. and Cortese, C. (2013). Well-being in the workplace through interaction between individual characteristics and organisational context. *International Journal of Qualitative Studies on Health and Well-being*, 8(1), 19823.

Binder, M. and Coad, A. (2011). From Average Joe's happiness to Miserable Jane and Cheerful John: Using quantile regressions to analyse the full SWB distribution. *Journal of Economic Behavior & Organization*, 79(3), 275–290.

Braun, V. and Clarke, V. (2014). What can "thematic analysis" offer health and well-being researchers? *International Journal of Qualitative Studies on Health and Well-being*, 9, 26152. 10.3402/qhw.v9.26152

Çağlayan, Ç., and Etiler, N. (2015). Health of older workers in Turkey: A further analysis of a national sampla. *Turkish Journal of Geriatrics/Türk Geriatri Dergisi*, 18(4), 285–292.

Demirbilek, T. and Özgür, A. Ö. (2017). Gümüş Ekonomi ve Aktif Yaşlanma Bağlamında Yaşlı İstihdamı. *Yaşlı Sorunları Araştırma Dergisi*, 10(1), 14–28.

Diener, E. (1984). Subjective well-being. *Psychological Bulletin*, 95(3), 542–575.

Diener, E., Scollon, C. N. and Lucas, R. E. (2009). The evolving concept of subjective well-being: The multifaceted nature of happiness, In: E. Diener (ed.). *Assessing Well-Being: The Collected Works of Ed Diener*. Springer, 67–100.

Diener, E., Suh, E. M., Lucas, R. E. and Smith, H. L. (1999). Subjective well-being: Three decades of progress. *Psychological bulletin*, 125(2), 276.

Dingemans, E. and Henkens, K. (2014). Involuntary retirement, bridge employment, and satisfaction with life: A longitudinal investigation. *Journal of Organisational Behavior*, 35(4), 575–591.

Frey, B. S. and Stutzer, A. (2010). *Happiness and economics: How the economy and institutions affect human well-being*. Princeton University Press.

Glick, P. and Fiske, S. T. (1996). The ambivalent sexism inventory: Differentiating hostile and benevolent sexism. *Journal of Personality and Social Psychology*, 70(3), 491–512.

Golden, L., Henly, J. R. and Lambert, S. (2013). Work schedule flexibility: A contributor to happiness?. *Journal of Social Research & Policy*, 4(2), 107.

Gomez, V., Krings, F., Bangerter, A. and Grob, A. (2009). The influence of personality and life events on SWB from a life span perspective. *Journal of Research in Personality*, 43(3), 345–354.

Graham, C. (2014). Late-life work and well-being. *IZA World of Labor*, 107, 1–10.

Guest, G., MacQueen, K. M. and Namey, E. E. (2012). Validity and reliability (credibility and dependability) in qualitative research and data analysis. *Applied thematic analysis*. London: Sage Publications, 79–106.

Hsieh, C. M. (2005). Age and relative importance of major life domains. *Journal of Aging Studies*, 19(4), 503–512.

Hyde, M., Wiggins, R. D., Higgs, P. and Blane, D. B. (2003). A measure of quality of life in early old age: The theory, development and properties of a needs satisfaction model (CASP-19). *Aging & Mental Health*, 7(3), 186–194.

Kadefors, R., Nilsson, K., Rylander, L., Östergen, P. O. and Albin, M. (2018). Occupation, gender and work-life exits: A Swedish population study. *Ageing & Society*, 38(7), 1332–1349.

Kahneman, D. and Deaton, A. (2010). High income improves evaluation of life but not emotional well-being. *Proceedings of the National Academy of Sciences, 107*(38), 16489–16493.

Kansky, J. and Diener, E. (2021). Science of well-being: Notable, In. A. Kostic and D. Chadee (eds.). *Positive Psychology: An International Perspective*. Willey, 43.

Korkut, G. and Bulduk, M. F. (2021). Sektörler İtibariyle İşverenlerin Yaşlı İstihdamına İlişkin Tutumlarının Belilenmesine Yönelik Bir Araştırma. *Süleyman Demirel Üniversitesi İktisadi ve İdari Bilimler Fakültesi Dergisi*, 26(1), 51–63.

Leung, A. S. M., Ha Cheung, Y. and Liu, X. (2011). The relations between life domain satisfaction and subjective well-being. *Journal of Managerial Psychology*, 26(2), 155–169.

Lucas, R. E. and Diener, E. (2015). Personality and subjective well-being: Current issues and controversies, In M. Mikulincer, P. R. Shaver, M. L. Cooper and R. J. Larsen (eds.). *APA handbooks in psychology- APA handbook of personality and social psychology, Vol. 4. Personality processes and individual differences*. Washington, DC. American Psychological Association, 577–599.

Lux, T. and Scherger, S. (2017). By the sweat of their brow? The effects of starting work again after pension age on life satisfaction in Germany and the United Kingdom. *Ageing and Society*, 37(2), 295.

Mercan, M. A. (2020). Turkey, In Ní Léime, Á., Ogg, J., Rašticová, M., Street, D., Krekula, C., Bédiová, M. and Madero-Cabib, I. (eds). *Extended Working Life Policies: International Gender and Health Perspectives*. Cham: Springer Open, 459–468.

Nikolova, M., & Graham, C. (2014). Employment, late-life work, retirement, and well-being in Europe and the United States. *IZA Journal of European Labor Studies*, 3(1), 1–30.

Okbay, A., Baselmans, B. M., De Neve, J. E., Turley, P., Nivard, M. G., Fontana, M. A., Meddens, S. F. W., Linnér, R. K., Rietveld, C. A., Derringer, J. and Gratten, J. (2016). Genetic variants associated with subjective well-being, depressive symptoms, and neuroticism identified through genome-wide analyses. *Nature Genetics*, 48(6), 624–633.

Okulicz-Kozaryn, A. and Golden, L. (2018). Happiness is flextime. *Applied Research Quality Life*, 13, 355–369.

Okun, M. A., Stock, W. A., Haring, M. J. and Witter, R. A. (1984). Health and subjective well-being: A meta-analysis. *The International Journal of Aging and Human Development*, 19(2), 111–132.

Parra-Rizo, M. A. and Sanchis-Soler, G. (2020). Satisfaction with life, SWB and functional skills in active older adults based on their level of physical activity practice. *International Journal of Environmental Research and Public Health*, 17(4), 1299.

Plagnol, A. (2010). SWB over the life course: Conceptualisations and evaluations. *Social Research: An International Quarterly of the Social Sciences*, 77(2), 749–768.

Plagnol, A. C. and Scott, J. (2011). What matters for well-being: Individual perceptions of quality of life before and after important life events. *Applied Research in Quality of Life*, 6(2), 115–137.

Pinquart, M. and Sörensen, S. (2000). Influences of socio-economic status, social network, and competence on SWB in later life: a meta-analysis. *Psychology and Aging*, 15(2), 187.

Rowe, J. W. and Kahn, R. L. (1997). Successful aging. *The Gerontologist*, 37(4), 433–440.

Ryan, R. M. and Deci, E. L. (2000). Self-determination theory and the facilitation of intrinsic motivation, social development, and well-being. *American Psychologist*, 55(1), 68.

Ryff, C. D. and Keyes, C. L. M. (1995). The structure of psychological well-being revisited. *Journal of Personality and Social Psychology*, 69(4), 719.

Sagherian, K., Rose, K., Zhu, S., Byon, H. D. and Crawford, K. (2021). Productive activities but not paid work relate to well-being in older adults. *Research in Gerontological Nursing*, 14(1), 24–32.

Schimmack, U. (2008). The structure of subjective well-being, In M. Eid and R. J. Larson (eds.) i *The Science of Subjective Well-being*. New York: Guilford Pres., 97–123.

Sığın, A. (2016). Çalışma Hayatı ve Emeklilik Bağlamında Türkiye'de Yaşlılık. *Pamukkale Üniversitesi Sosyal Bilimler Enstitüsü Dergisi*, (Ek1), 7–101.

Taylor, P. (2019). Working longer may be good public policy, but it is not necessarily good for older people. *Journal of Aging & Social Policy*, 31(2), 99–105.

T.C. Cumhurbaşkanlığı Strateji ve Bütçe Başkanlığı (2019). *On Birinci Kalkınma Planı 2019–2023*. https://www.sbb.gov.tr/wp-content/uploads/2019/07/OnbirinciKalkinmaPlani.pdf

Vanhoutte, B. (2014). The multidimensional structure of SWB in later life. *Journal of population ageing*, 7(1), 1–20.

Walker, A. and Maltby, T. (2012). Active ageing: A strategic policy solution to demographic ageing in the European Union. *International Journal of Social Welfare*, 21, S117–S130.

Wahrendorf, M., Akinwale, B., Landy, R., Matthews, K. and Blane, D. (2017). Who in Europe works beyond the state pension age and under which conditions? Results from SHARE. *Journal of Population Ageing*, 10(3), 269–285.

Winkelmann R. (2009). Unemployment, social capital, and subjective well-being. *Journal of Happiness Studies*, 10(4), 421–430.

Yelboğa, N. (2018). Yaşlı ayrımcılığı ve kadının dışlanması. *Sosyal Çalışma Dergisi*, 2(1), 51–64.

Appendix

Table A9.1 Characteristics of participants

Code	*Age*	*Education*	*Present job*	*Sex*	*No. of children*	*Marital status*	*Occupation*	*Socio-economic status*	*Interruption in working*
M61L1	61	Secondary school	Truck driver	M	3	Married	Truck Driver	Low	No
M75M1	75	Graduate	Ophthalmologist	M	2	Married	Ophthalmologist	Medium	No
F61L1	61	Primary school	Entrepreneur	F	5	Married	Entrepreneur	Low	No
F67L1	67	Illiterate	Farmer	F	3	Married	Farmer	Low	No
M70L1	70	Primary school	Security guard	M	3	Married	Painter	Low	No
F67M1	67	Secondary school	Realtor	F	1	Widow	Government official	Medium	No
M83M1	83	Under-graduate	Building contractor	M	3	Married	Soldier	Medium	No
M69M1	69	Under-graduate	Engineer	M	1	Married	Engineer	Medium	No
M73M1	73	Under-graduate	Realtor	M	3	Married	Teacher	Medium	No
M70L2	70	Primary school	Painter	M	1	Married	Painter	Low	No
F62L1	62	Illiterate	Nursemaid	F	4	Married	Housewife	Low	Yes
F66L1	66	Illiterate	Agricultural worker	F	4	Widow	Agricultural worker	Low	No
M61L2	61	Primary school	Truck driver	M	3	Married	Truck driver	Low	No
M65M1	65	Secondary school	Graphic designer	M	-	Married	Photographer	Medium	No
F65M1	65	Under-graduate	Marketing specialist	F	3	Divorced	Government official	Medium	No
F72M1	72	Graduate	Psychiatrist	F	2	Married	Psychiatrist	Medium	No
F71L1	71	Primary school	Housekeeper	F	1	Married	Housekeeper	Low	Yes
F61L2	61	Primary school	Nurse maid	F	3	Married	Housewife	Low	Yes
F66M1	66	Under-graduate	Dentist	F	1	Divorced	Dentist	Medium	No
M67M1	67	Graduate	Academic	M	2	Married	Academic	Medium	No

10 Gender Differences in Working Conditions in France

Sabrina Aouici, Jim Ogg, and Julie Rochut

Introduction

As in many other European countries, gender differences related to employment in France have been dominated throughout the 20th century by patterns of lower labour force participation by women and discriminatory policies and practices that disadvantage them. However, as Meurs and Pora (2019) have shown, in a long-term perspective much progress has been made. In 2020, women participate massively in the labour market across a wide spectrum of professions, with a participation rate approaching that of men: in 2018, 68 per cent of women aged 15 to 64 were economically active, whether employed or unemployed, 8 percentage points less than men, compared to 31 percentage points less in 1975 (Bernard, 2019).

Women's education levels have also risen considerably and since the 1990s they have, on average, attained higher levels than men. For example, during the period 2014–16, among young people completing their education, 40 per cent of men and 49 per cent of women were higher education graduates, compared to 32 per cent and 33 per cent respectively in the period 1990–92 (Couppié and Epiphane, 2019). Many gender equality policies have been introduced and they have been increasingly put into place in industry and businesses.

Despite these positive trends, the average salary of women has stagnated for the past 30 years and in 2017 women employees in the private sector earned on average 16.8 per cent less than men in full-time equivalent, i.e. for the same amount of work (Georges-Kot, 2020). The factors behind this phenomenon are well known: the differences between women and men in terms of working hours and access to higher-paid jobs explain most of the gap. In 2017, in France (excluding Mayotte), 29.6 per cent of employed women aged 15 to 64 were working part-time, compared with 7.7 per cent of men[1] and in 2018, 18 per cent of private-sector employees were working part-time and 78 per cent of them were women (Mourlot & Yildiz, 2020). Even if male part-time employment is steadily increasing, the part-time employment of women has fluctuated only slightly since the early 2000s. For women, the probability of working part-time increases with the number of dependent children, especially when children are young (Insee, 2019). Women, young people and seniors are more likely to work part-time:

DOI: 10.4324/9781003145325-10

31 per cent of women, 24 per cent of adults aged under 26 years and 28 per cent of employees aged 55 and above have a part-time job (Dares, 2020). Among older women who work part-time, a distinction can be made between those who declare that they would prefer to work full-time but are unable to find a full-time job, and those women who choose to work part-time (Pak, 2013). Although almost one in three part-time employees declare that they work part-time because they have not been able to find a job, these workers are more likely to be found among younger age groups (Pak, 2013). Older women who work part-time are more likely to report that they "choose" this working arrangement, and more than 40 per cent of them report that they work part-time to look after their children or another member of their family (Pak, 2013).

The persistence of the gender pay gap now appears to be mainly linked to the consequences of motherhood. A child's arrival results in a loss of annual income for women largely due to adjustments in their working time such as career breaks and difficulties related to re-entering the labour market. This penalty is higher for mothers who are at the bottom of the wage distribution (Meurs & Pora, 2019) and it has long-term consequences since retirement pensions are computed on a mean salary basis. In 2016, the average state retirement pension for women was €1,005 whereas it was €1,627 for men (Nortier-Ribordy, 2019) and the average retirement age in 2019 was 63.0 years for women and 62.5 years for men (CNAV, 2020). These gender pension gaps reflect career differences between women and men, but also the rules for calculating pension entitlements in pension systems. Mechanisms including attributing periods of retirement insurance for mothers and survival pensions exist in France to correct the gender income gap both during working life and in retirement, but these do not suffice to eradicate gender income inequalities.

As in most European countries, French women are more implicated in caring tasks within the family. Older working women therefore often have to balance obligations towards their elderly parents as well as grandparenting tasks such as looking after their grandchildren during school holidays (Attias-Donfut 2007). Combining private and public lives differs also according to social class and professions. Older women in managerial or non-manual professions often have more flexible working arrangements that allow them to combine paid work and family obligations. In manual work and the service industries, older women are more likely to resort to taking on part-time jobs, sometimes with different employers, in order to find time to care for their dependent family members.

Finally, older French women are more likely to experience discrimination based on gender in the workplace compared to men (Carcillo & Valfort, 2018). Citing data from the 2015 Eurobarometer survey, Carcillo and Valfort (2018) note that the majority (53%) of the French population believe that French women experience discrimination based on gender whereas a third of the general European population believe that this is the case. Older women therefore are exposed to gender discrimination as well as age discrimination. Many have not been able to acquire professional skills due to their earlier family obligations and temporary withdrawal from the labour market, and additionally they are less likely to receive training than younger workers.

In this chapter, we present some of the key literature that explains the characteristics of the French labour market participation of women and specifically older women and the mechanisms resulting from labour market components, focusing on the recent consequences of the COVID-19 pandemic. The first section presents a description of the gendered segmentation of the labour market. The second section details the over-exposure of labour market risk faced by older women, namely unemployment and harsh working conditions. Finally, we complete our literature review by considering the COVID-19 pandemic and the specific consequences that relate to the participation of older women in the labour market and their working conditions.

The employment of (older) women

At the end of the 20th century, and specifically during the period 1981–1995, the economic activity rate of men between 50 and 64 years of age significantly decreased as a result of a lowering of the state pension age and policies facilitating early retirement. During the past 25 years, rates of economic activity for both men and women between the age of 50 and 64 years have steadily risen, in part due to specific policies to extend working life but mostly due to an increase in the employment rates of older women. In 2017, 69.1 per cent of women between the age of 55 and 59 years were employed compared to 74.8 per cent of men (Figure 10.1).

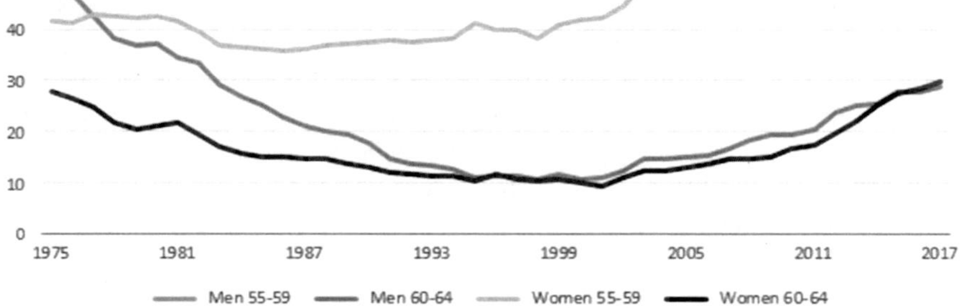

Figure 10.1 The employment rate (%) of men and women aged 55–64 during the period 1975–2017.

Source: Insee employment surveys.

Above the age of 65, employment rates of both men and women are very low but gender differences are notable, since these older women are mostly single and with low qualification levels compared to highly qualified men.

The similar employment rates of older men and women mask an important gender difference in the number of weekly hours worked. Older women are significantly more likely to work part-time: in 2017, the proportion of women aged 55–64 working part-time was 33.7 per cent compared to only 11 per cent for men (CSEP, 2019). For the over-60s, part-time work accounts for 43.3 per cent of employment for women and 25.9 per cent for men (CSEP, 2019). Moreover, whereas part-time employment rates among younger women have been decreasing, among older women they are increasing (CSEP, 2019).

Older working women are more likely to be employed in short-term contracts than men. The proportion of short-term contracts for older workers has steadily increased since the 1990s for both men and women: in 2017, 7.4 per cent of women aged between 55 and 64 years were employed on a short-time contract compared to 5.1 per cent of men. This gender difference has increased in recent years, reflecting the greater instability in the labour market experienced by older women. The differences in the characteristics of older French workers bear witness to the greater difficulties that women have in accessing employment, job training and securing wage parity.

In addition to being over-represented in part-time work and short-term job contracts, older women workers face other difficulties such as sexist attitudes in the workplace and, as the main carers of their elderly parents, managing conflicting roles in public and private life. There are an estimated 1.1 million female carers aged between 55 and 64 years in France (CSEP, 2019). Women caring for an elderly parent or another family member can experience difficulties combining this role with participation in the labour market and some older women leave their jobs to resolve these issues. Others remain in paid work but work shorter hours – it is estimated that among employed female carers aged 55 to 64, 12 per cent report having made adjustments to their professional activity in order to provide care for family members (CSEP, 2019).

In summary, although women have entered the labour market in large numbers over the past 50 years, compared to men they are more likely to occupy lower-skilled jobs that are concentrated in the tertiary sector.[2] These gender differences are accentuated for older workers, who are less likely to participate in job training and re-skilling. Older women workers have lower levels of job training than men and fewer educational qualifications which combine to place them at a disadvantage in the labour market.

The professions where (older) women are more represented than men

The distribution of older women across the professions mirrors that of younger women. As noted above, during the past 50 years women have entered the

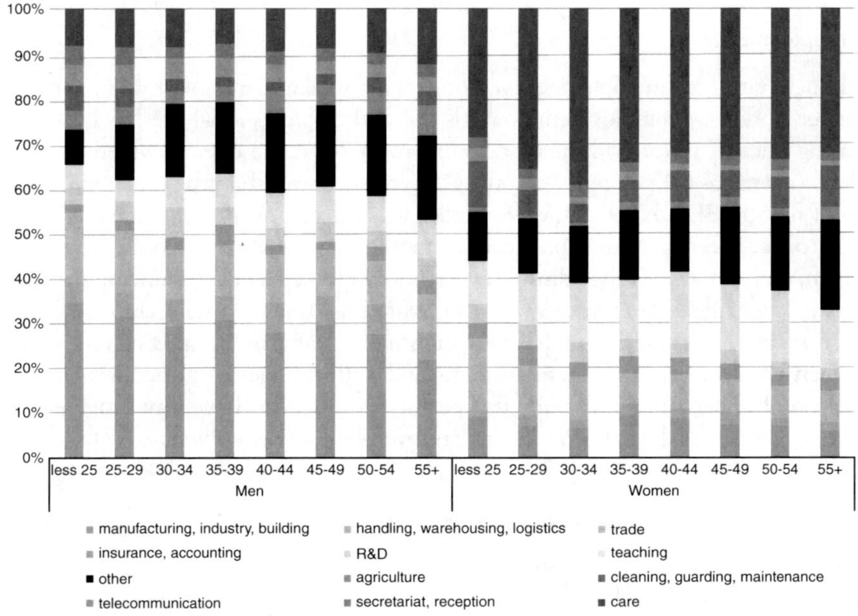

Figure 10.2 Main sector of activity by age group and gender.

Source: CT-RPS Dares 2016.

French labour market in large numbers. In 2017, men and women were active in the total labour market in almost equal proportions – 48.1 per cent of women compared to 51.9 per cent of men. Among those women who were in paid employment, 13.8 per cent worked in industry, 6.5 per cent in construction, 2.6 per cent in agriculture and 75.9 per cent in the service sector. Figure 10.2 shows the distribution of men and women by age across the different occupations and professions in the labour market.

The occupational distribution of jobs for older women and men (aged between 50 and 64 years) is markedly unequal and on the same scale as the average for all ages: 87.7 per cent of older women and 87.5 per cent of women as a whole work in the tertiary sector (CSEP, 2019). This is the case for 65.5 per cent of women and 65.2 per cent of men. With the exception of intermediate occupations (clerical, sales, services) the distribution of jobs by socio-professional category differs greatly by gender. Women are much less likely to be self-employed than men. For example, 43 per cent of employed women are employees, compared to 13 per cent of men.[3] Conversely, 32 per cent of men are blue-collar workers, compared to 9 per cent of women. Men are more often managers than women (20% compared to 15%). They are also more likely to be farmers as well as artisans, traders or entrepreneurs (Insee, 2019: p. 38).

Exposure to risks and well-being

Unemployment

Although rates of unemployment among older workers are lower than among younger workers, unemployment towards the end of professional life has been increasing since 2010 for both men and women. In 2017, the unemployment rate of older women was 6.4 per cent and only 0.3 per cent lower than the unemployment rate of men (CSEP, 2019). However, older women who work part-time are more likely to face the risk of unemployment. Importantly, many older people, especially women, do not meet all the administrative criteria to be eligible for unemployment benefits (and therefore are not officially counted as "unemployed") (Insee, 2019). Older women are therefore more often than men caught in an unrecognised state between employment and unemployment and with no source of income. Such a situation of uncertainty, especially if it persists in time, can have a negative effect not only on careers but also on health and well-being (Letroublon, 2017).

Gender gap in health status and well-being

In common with many European countries, women rate their health as poorer than men in all age groups below the age of 75 years, but this gap narrows considerably after the age of 75 years (Drees, 2015). As far as the effect of working conditions on health is concerned, little research exists on gender differences among older workers on exposure to hazardous risks and length of working hours (Chappert & Théry, 2016). However, women are less likely than men to have had an ascending career and are more likely to have been employed in professions with high risks of musculoskeletal disorders and stress (nursing and caring professions, night work and unsociable hours). A survey that examined gender differences in a range of businesses found that the majority of women had been in the same job longer than men, which is a factor known to be associated with stress and burn-out (CSEP, 2019: p. 99). Work stress due to a low degree of decision-making latitude and high psychological demands of the job is more common among older women than men (Bouffartigue and Bouteiller, 2015). The "overexposure" of women to psychosocial risks at work compared to men is true for all socio-professional categories, even if it is slightly less marked in the category of employees and managers. However, it is blue-collar workers and employees who are most exposed to stress at work, not managers as one might think. For example, data on working conditions from the French EU-SILC survey (2018) for workers aged 55 years and above show that the proportion of women reporting that work is always repetitive and under time constraints is twice that of men (11.5% compared to 5.6%). Higher rates of physically demanding work are reported for older women as compared to older men (21% compared to 15%).

In professions where the proportion of women dominates, there is an increased risk of over-exposure to psychosocial risks and impaired mental health. The seven occupations with the most impaired mental health status are predominantly female.

Four are blue-collar or white-collar occupations: postal workers, industrial workers, cleaners and bank employees. Two are intermediate administrative occupations in the civil service and banking management (CSEP, 2019).

Overall, women are less concerned (31% of them) than men (46%) by exposure to these hardship factors; while the proportion of employees exposed to at least one of ten recognised hardship factors associated with jobs decreases overall with age, and older employees are still largely concerned. However, the proportion of employees exposed to at least one of the ten hardship factors decreases much less sharply with age for women than for men (Rivallin & Sandret, 2014).

According to Bahu et al. (2012: p. 124) "among people aged 50–59 who have worked for at least ten years, those who have been exposed to at least one of the following risk factors – night work, repetitive work, physically demanding work, working with harmful products – are more likely to report that they are physically limited in their daily activities (23%) than those who have not been exposed to at least one of the risk factors studied". Among women, activity limitations are particularly associated with night work (ibid).

In summary, older women workers rate their health as worse than men, although as Cambois (2016) notes, this may be due to factors outside the workplace and in particular the combination of family and work roles.

Effects of the COVID crisis on the labour market and the professional situation of (older) women in France

One of the primary factors associated with a severe form of Coronavirus infection is age. Although serious health complications can arise from COVID-19 in all age groups (Groupe CES-COVID, 2020), from a public health perspective serious and fatal forms of the disease are very heavily concentrated in subpopulations according to age and degree of co-morbidities. Recent research in France shows that older workers are more vulnerable to illness and to the deadly and debilitating effects of COVID-19 (Riou et al., 2020). According to recent French unemployment data, older workers are relatively protected compared to younger workers (9% of people who were working before the first lockdown aged 15 to 24 years old lost their job compared to less than 2% of the working population between the ages of 40 and 65 years) (Givord & Silhol, 2020), whereas in the United States of America, older workers are more likely to have become unemployed during the COVID-19 lockdown than younger workers (Bui et al., 2020). As Alon et al. (2020) suggest "compared to 'regular' recessions, which affect men's employment more severely than women's employment, the fall in employment related to social distancing measures has a large impact on sectors with high female employment shares. In addition, closures of schools and day care centres have massively increased childcare needs, which has a particularly large impact on working mothers" (p. 2). The COVID pandemic has exacerbated existing inequalities in working conditions as well as generating new ones. Whether in terms of employment or working conditions, during the first lockdown workers in higher professional categories appeared to be less affected than those in other occupations: by the seventh week of lockdown, 86 per cent of workers in higher professional occupations had maintained their professional activities and two-thirds were working from home (Lambert et al., 2020).

Inequalities relating to a decline in economic activity

The labour market has been deeply affected by the COVID-19 crisis. France has witnessed a significant fall in production, restructuring or closure of companies, and the destruction of thousands of jobs (including the termination of short-term employment contracts and redundancies) and a major rise in unemployment. Certain sectors have been particularly hard hit and these mostly relate to industries which have regular contact with the public such as restaurants, public services and the caring professions, and jobs that are related to the arts and entertainment (Dares, 2020). The different waves of the survey on employment conditions and access to labour (Acemo) carried out by Dares during the COVID-19 crisis found that at the height of the epidemic at the end of March 2020, a quarter of employees were working on-site and a quarter on building sites, a quarter were working from home and a quarter were on short-time working. Regarding the introduction of full-time working from home where possible, several difficulties have been revealed. Due to the lack of technical and ergonomic facilities provided by the employer or a quiet space at home, many employees report the occurrence of musculoskeletal pain, mental health risks, feelings of isolation and lack of interaction with colleagues. The Coconel survey (COronavirus and CONfinement: Longitudinal Survey – COronavirus et CONfinement: Enquête Longitudinale in French) carried out by the French National Demographic Institute, (INED) states that the feeling of isolation is stronger among women (41% compared to 35% of men), poor households (45%) and young people (44%) (May 2020).

Despite some improvement since the outbreak of the crisis in the spring of 2020, more than four out of five companies have had recourse to help provided by public authorities, including the short-time working scheme (70% of companies), to face the sudden fall in activity (Dauvin et al, 2020). These figures are also confirmed by the SHARE survey (COVID-19 Wave 8 module) where 37 per cent of workers reported having been made completely redundant or having to work shorter hours (partial unemployment). The sectors taking advantage of this scheme are mostly the restaurant/hosting industries, for which 45 per cent and 20 per cent of employees in the sector were in this situation in October 2020. The same is true of breaches of employment contracts or collective redundancy procedures for economic reasons, which increased in 2020 in the sectors of trade and automobile repairs, manufacturing industry, restaurant/hosting industry (Dares, 2020). Again, women represent a significant proportion of employees in these affected sectors. These initial observations therefore raise questions about the possible consequences of the COVID crisis at the end of the career stage for older women workers: we may assume that many of them found themselves in a situation of partial unemployment from the first lockdown in March 2020 and that this sudden and unforeseen cessation of activity will have consequences on their retirement conditions and the extension of their working lives.

Inequalities in activity and employment have therefore increased in certain sectors of activity and for certain categories of the active population with the health, social and economic crisis. At the end of November 2020, the French Parliament voted to create a specific "CDI inclusion" (full-time permanent jobs) for individuals above 57 years who are unemployed, in order to counteract the rise in unemployment of people aged 55 and over observed in recent years. This measure is not directly linked to the COVID-19 crisis but it takes into account the current context. Unfortunately, it is too early to evaluate its impact and to identify which groups are using this measure and whether older women will benefit from it.

Finally, the COVID crisis seems to mark the return of early retirement in France: several major groups have set up early retirement plans for their older employees. Although early retirement used to concern men more than women (Martin-Houssart & Roth, 2002; Rapoport, 2012), their re-introduction poses questions about the end of women's careers and their possibility of remaining in employment.

The impact of COVID-19 on the professions of older women

What are the consequences of COVID-19 for the careers of women, who, along with young people, are known, even before the pandemic, to be more likely to have precarious jobs? In France, there is currently limited data to analyse this phenomenon. In general, poor working conditions of older women employed in jobs characterised by physical and/or psychological constraints have been exacerbated by the crisis because of an increase in work intensity, time pressures and stress. In the labour force, women are more likely to be exposed to the COVID-19 virus on account of their over-representation in certain occupations (Dubost et al., 2020). Between mid-March and July 2020, the lockdown imposed by the French government in the face of the COVID-19 outbreak forced a partial or total shutdown of jobs deemed to be "non-essential", while others were mobilised in the face of the crisis. It was estimated that this latter comprised 10.4 million workers directly or indirectly on the "front line", mostly in the professions of healthcare, health education, cleaning and domestic jobs, food and its distribution, and public sector jobs (Flamand et al., 2020; OECD, 2020). These professions are over-exposed to health risks and moreover they are mostly occupied by women (teachers, nurses and midwives, care assistants, home helpers, childcare workers and care-workers for frail older people). In addition to these jobs characterised by a social utility, women are over-represented in certain professions in the private sector such as work in supermarkets and cleaning industries. The COVID-19 pandemic has intensified the workload of older women in these professions thereby increasing their exposure to health risks.

The first publications of the Coconel survey[4] show that women and the working classes are dropping out of the labour market and the data reveal the emergence of new inequalities linked to working from home (Lambert et al., 2020). The "Acemo spéciale COVID" survey provides valuable information on how jobs have been affected since the first lockdown and the main difficulties that workers have encountered since March 2020, such as working shorter hours, having recourse to temporary work and the implementation of barrier measures in the workplace.[5] Although the gender dimension is not discussed, the analyses by sector of activity nevertheless provide a certain amount of information on temporary work, catering or service activities, where women have a strong presence. Finally, the TrEpid survey conducted by the trade union Ugict-CGT and CGT-ministères sociaux (Social Ministries)[6] representing engineers, managers and technicians on working conditions during lockdown periods indicates that women are particularly exposed during these periods, thus putting their jobs and working conditions at risk.

The work status most affected by the disappearance of jobs in France is that of temporary work, which mainly affects workers from lower social class groups. The number of workers in temporary work fell to an all-time low in the first quarter of 2020 (Insee, 2020). During this period, an unusual rise in the unemployment rate was also observed. Working from home became the norm for many, but in employment sectors where women are overrepresented, many have had to continue to work on-site, thus being exposed to higher risk of contracting the virus as well as accumulating stress related to travelling to work during a period of health crisis. The majority of older women work in occupations in contact with the public (particularly in the health sector, shops and personal services) and have in fact been more exposed to the risk of infection since the start of the health crisis. The main contribution of these studies for understanding how older workers and particularly women are experiencing the COVID-19 crisis in France is dealt with below.

According to a survey undertaken on the economic consequences of the COVID-19 pandemic during the first lockdown (Givord & Silhol, 2020), a higher proportion of women reported that their working time had increased (23% of women compared to 15% of men). The reasons for this increase can be explained in part by the over-representation of women among professions that were mobilised during the lockdown such as health care professions, shop-workers and teachers. Moreover, older women are particularly associated with these professions. A further consequence of the COVID-19 pandemic for older female workers has been the increase in demand for childcare due to school closures. According to UNESCO, in March 2020 at the height of the first worldwide lockdown, more than 1.5 billion children were not attending school. As grandparents, many older women increased the amount of time they spend looking after their grandchildren.

Women are also more likely than men to mention a deterioration in their working conditions due to changes in their profession or due to working from home (TrEpid survey 2020; Lambert et al., 2020). In many shops and establishments in the care and personal services sector (which mainly concerns women), it has indeed been necessary to review procedures in order to comply with COVID-19-related instructions such as disinfection, distancing, visits, etc. In many cases, the procedures have been revised in order to comply with the public health measures associated with COVID-19. According to the "Acemo spéciale COVID" survey, some employees declared that they worked in companies that had not implemented certain prevention measures due to a lack of equipment (43%), because it was not necessary (43%) or not possible (23%) given the nature of the activity (43%) (Dares, 2020).

But beyond the specific characteristics of the labour market, the tense context has also led to the resurgence of inequalities linked to the reconciliation of work and family life. Among those in employment, mothers are twice as likely as fathers to give up work to care for their children (21% versus 12%) (Albouy and Legleye, 2020). Similarly, women's and men's living conditions at home have not been affected in the same way from one social category to another. Indeed, it is for women that the situation has deteriorated most markedly: among those who were in employment on March 1, 2020, only two out of three continue to work two months later, compared with three out of four men.

Although the proportion of women working from home is approximately the same as men, conditions for these women are worse since they are more likely to report having to look after their children at the same time. The Coconel survey shows that women working from home were more often in lockdown with one or more children at home (48% compared with 37% of men) and had a dedicated room less often (25% compared with 41% of men). Most of the time, therefore, they have to share their workspace with their children or other household members. The gender gaps reach maximum levels within the managers group: 29 per cent of female managers have a specific room dedicated to work compared to 47 per cent of male managers.

The TrEpid study also found that more women reported having to look after their children at the same time and devoting more time to them: the closure of schools resulted for 47 per cent of them in more than four hours of additional domestic chores per day (compared with 26% for men); this situation particularly affects women working from home compared to their male counterparts. Furthermore, those looking after their children while working from home report being frequently anxious (38%), and women report higher rates than men (respectively 44% versus 34%). Finally, while employees state that on average they perceive a feeling of autonomy and freedom when working from home, this is less the case for women (38% compared to 47% of men), which shows that the situation is more restrictive for women, who are typically responsible for domestic and family activities. Finally, the TrEpid study shows a double penalty for women, since not only is childcare still often dependent on them, but in addition, lockdown has generated tensions and domestic violence (physical or verbal) (Ugict-CGT et CGT-ministères sociaux, 2020).

The successive lockdowns of the COVID-19 pandemic are leading to the loss of work for some of the active population and its redevelopment for others, with home working disrupting the private sphere and reinforcing gender inequalities. Early research on the consequences of this pandemic on working conditions thus shows an increase in precariousness (loss of income, partial unemployment, intensification of work, particularly in the workplace, fears for employment) and an increase in inequalities among women in front-line work because of their professions being more exposed to health risks and precarious working conditions. These studies also underline the consequences of this crisis on women's place in the family: still very often at the heart of family structures, they are more often faced with the double constraint of working from home while having to take care of their children or grandchildren during lockdown, juggling more than men between professional life and family/domestic responsibilities. As the Coconel (2020) survey points out, "after half a century of gradual reduction of these inequalities, the health crisis has caused women to return to the home, reinforced their assignment to domestic and parental tasks, and made their incomes more fragile than those of men. At home, women also work in worse conditions than their male counterparts, and have less personal space" (Lambert et al., 2020: p. 5).

Conclusion

The significant gains that women have made during the latter part of the 20th century regarding their participation in the labour force risk being compromised by the COVID-19 pandemic, which has had a profound effect on the French labour market (Dauvin et al., 2020). During the eight weeks of the first lockdown, gross domestic product (GDP) contracted by 32 per cent and the loss of GDP represented 165 billion euros. By the end of 2020 France's GDP had fallen by 8.3 per cent.[7] This major upheaval will lead to tremendous change in French society and in the labour market. As far as the specific impact of COVID-19 on older workers is concerned, protection measures should be introduced by institutions through appropriate legislation, notably through paid sick leave (Ghilarducci & Farmand, 2020).

In France, as in the United States of America, calls have been made to address the compulsory waiting period of two days before receiving paid sick leave. Mothers have particularly been impacted by the COVID crisis, in terms of working conditions but also in terms of living conditions since they were generally the ones who managed homeschooling, care, household tasks and work. A decree published in the Official Journal on November 15, 2020 provides that the waiting period does not apply until December 31, 2020. Under these conditions, even with gender parity in retirement ages, many women may be obliged to work past retirement age to secure an adequate income in old age. Moreover, current trends suggest that they will also continue to be implicated in caring tasks within the family, and balancing private and public lives will be a major challenge for the future.

Notes

1 The part-time rate in France (19% in 2017) is close to the European Union average (20%) but below that of the United Kingdom (27%), Germany (28%) and the Netherlands, which peaks at 51 per cent. As in Europe as a whole, part-time work is predominantly female in France.
2 In France, the tertiary sector of professional occupations covers a wide range of activities from commerce to administration, transport, financial and real estate activities, business and personal services, education, health and social work.
3 The term "employé" in French refers to a person who works under someone's orders in the non-productive spheres of the economy (commerce, administration, etc.) and whose work is of an intellectual rather than manual nature (as opposed to a business head, head of department or blue-collar worker).
4 The COCONEL survey was conducted via the internet during the period March 27, 2020 to April 9, 2020. Once a week, a sample of a thousand people, representative of the adult population residing in France, answered a questionnaire covering various aspects of the COVID-19 crisis.
5 https://dares.travail-emploi.gouv.fr/publications/activite-et-conditions-d-emploi-de-la-main-d-oeuvre-pendant-la-crise-sanitaire-119550 Consulted October 18, 2021.
6 https://luttevirale.fr/enquete/rapport/ Consulted May 31, 2021.
7 Consulted May 31, 2021.

References

Alon, T., Olmstead-Rumsey, J., Doepke, M. and Tertilt, M. (2020). *The impact of COVID-19 on gender equality*. NBER Working Paper No. 26947. Available at: https://www.nber.org/system/files/working_papers/w26947/w26947.pdf

Albouy, V. & Legleye, S. (2020).Conditions de vie pendant le confinement : les écarts selon le niveau de vie et lacatégorie socioprofessionnelle. Insee Focus No197. Available at http://acdc2007.free.fr/inseecamme620.pdf. Accessed 14 July 2022.

Attias-Donfut, C. & Segalen, M. (2007). *Grands-parents. La famille à travers les générations*. Paris: Odile Jacob.

Bahu, M., Mermilliod, C. and Volkoff, S. (2012). Conditions de travail pénibles au cours de la vie professionnelle et état de santé après 50 ans. *Revue française des affaires sociales*, 106–135. 10.3917/rfas.124.0106. Accessed 29 November 2020.

Bernard, J. (2019). Femmes et hommes sur le marché du travail: des écarts moins marqués en début de vie active. *Insee Focus*, 168.

Bouffartigue, P. & Bouteiller, J. (2015). Les «RPS» au regard du genre : Le cas d'une profession mixte, en relation avec lepublic : Factrices et facteurs de la Poste. [Rapport de recherche] DEB13-952 du 28/06/2013, Laboratoire d'économie et sociologie du travail (LEST). Available at https://halshs.archives-ouvertes.fr/halshs-01306678/document Accessed 14 July 2022.

Bui, T. T. M., Button, P. & Picciotti, E. G. (2020). *Early evidence on the impact of COVID-19 and the recession on older workers*. National Bureau of Economic Research, Working Paper 27448. Available at http://www.nber.org/papers/w27448. Accessed 28 November 2020.

Cambois, E. (2016). Des inégalités sociales de santé moins marquées chez les femmes que chez les hommes: une question de mesure? *Rev Epidemiol Sante Publique*, 64, S75–S85. doi:10.1016/j.respe.2016.02.007

Carcillo, S. & Valfort, M.-A. (2018). *Les Discriminations au travail. Femmes, éthnicité, réligion, âge, apparence, LGBT*. Paris: Sciences Po.

Chappert, F., and Théry, L. (2016). Égalité entre les femmes et les hommes et santé au travail. Comment le genre transforme-t-il l'intervention sur les conditions de travail? [Equality between men and women and occupational health]. *Perspectives interdisciplinaires sur le travail et la santé*. 10.4000/pistes.4882.

CNAV (2020). *Age de depart à la retraite [Retirement age]*. Figures available at https://www.statistiques-recherches.cnav.fr/age-de-depart-a-la-retraite.html Accessed 30 November 2020.

Conseil Supérieur de l'égalité professionnelle (CSEP) entre les femmes et les hommes, (2019). *Les femmes seniors dans l'emploi*. Etats des lieux, Paris France Stratégie.

Couppié, T. & Epiphane, D. (2019). Et lesfemmes devinrent plus diplômées que les hommes, Céreq Bref n°373. Available at https://hal.archives-ouvertes.fr/hal-03184644/document. Accessed 14 July 2022.

Dares (2020). Activité et conditions d'emploi de la main-d'oeuvre pendant la crise sanitaire COVID-19. *Synthèse des résultats de l'enquête flash* – Octobre 2020.

Dauvin, M., Ducoudré, B., Heyer, E., Madec, P., Plane, M., Sampognaro, R. & Timbeau, X. (2020). *Evaluation au 26 juin 2020 de l'impact économique de la pandémie de la COVID-19 et des mesures du confinement et du déconfinement en France*. Revue de l'OFCE N)166 2020/2. Available at https://www.ofce.sciences-po.fr/pdf/revue/166/revue-166.pdf#page=111. Accessed 28 November 2020.

Dubost, C., Pollak, C. & Rey, S. (2020). *Les inégalités sociales face à l'épidémie de COVID-19. État des lieux et perspectives*. Paris: Dossier de la Drees No. 62. Available at https://drees.solidarites-sante.gouv.fr/publications/les-dossiers-de-la-drees/les-inegalites-sociales-face-lepidemie-de-COVID-19-etat-des. Accessed 15 February 2020.

Drees (Direction de la recherche, des études, del'évaluation et des statistiques). (2015). L'état de santé de la populationen France. Available at https://drees.solidarites-sante.gouv.fr/sites/default/files/2021-1/rappeds_v11_16032015.pdf

Epiphane D. and Couppié T. (2019). *Et les femmes devinrent plus diplômées que les hommes … Céreq Bref*, n° 373, Mars 2019, 4.

Flamand, J., Jolly, C. and Rey, M. (2020). Les métiers au temps du corona. *La note analyse* no. 88 de France Stratégie.

Georges-Kot, S. (2020). Écarts de rémunération femmes-hommes: surtout l'effet du temps de travail et de l'emploi occupé. *Insée Première*, No. 1083, Insee, Paris.

Ghilarducci T. and Farmand A. (2020). Older Workers on the COVID-19-Frontlines without Paid Sick Leave. *Journal of Aging & Social Policy*, 32(4–5), 471–476.

Gilles, C. (2012). L'emploi des femmes et des hommes dans la crise: les effets de la segmentation du marché du travail. *Note d'analyse*, Centre d'analyse stratégique no 312.

Givord, P. and Silhol, J. (2020). Confinement: des conséquences économiques inégales selon les ménages. *Insee Première*, No. 1822. Available at http://www.epsilon.insee.fr/jspui/bitstream/1/135765/1/ip1822.pdf. Accessed 28 November 2020.

Groupe CES-COVID (2020). Quelles sont les populations fragiles à risque de formes graves de COVID-19 et en emploi? Available at https://www.ces-asso.org/sites/default/files/st_note_florence_jusot_populationsfragiles_fin3.pdf Accessed 28 November 2020.

Insee (2019). *Tableau de l'économie française, édition 2019*. Paris: Insee Références.

Lambert, A., Cayouette-Remblière, J., Guéraut, É., Le Roux, G., Bonvalet, C., Girard, V. and Langlois, L. (2020). Le travail et ses aménagements: ce que la pandémie de COVID-19 a changé pour les français. *Population et Société*, 2020/7(579), 1–4.

Letroublon, C. (2017). Les seniors au travail. La durée du travail est-elle plus faible à l'approche de la retraite? *Dares Analyses*, 50.

Martin-Houssart, G. and Roth, N. (2002). Activité et emploi après 50 ans. *Retraite et société*, 2(2), 9–27. 10.3917/rs.036.0009

Meurs, D. and Pora, P. (2019). Gender equality on the labour market in France: A slow convergence hampered by motherhood. *Economie et Statistique/Economics and Statistics*, 510-511-512, 109–130. Available at 10.24187/ecostat.2019.510t.1990. Accessed 15 February 2021.

Mourlot L. & Yildiz H. (2020). *Quelles sont les conditions d'emploi des salariés à temps partiel? Dares Analyses*, No. 25. Available at http://www.epsilon.insee.fr/jspui/bitstream/1/132865/1/2020-25.pdf. Accessed 1 December 2020.

Nortier-Ribordy, F. (2019). *Les inégalités entre les femmes et les hommes à la retraite*. Paris: Conseil d'orientation des retraites. Available at https://www.cor-retraites.fr/sites/default/files/2019-12/2019_12_02_FNR_court.pdf. Accessed 1 December 2020.

OECD. (2020). *Women at the core of the fight against COVID-19 crisis*. Available at https://www.oecd.org/coronavirus/policy-responses/women-at-the-core-of-the-fight-against-COVID-19-crisis-553a8269/. Accessed 15 February 2021.

Pak, M. (2013). Le temps partiel en 2011: des profils et des conditions d'emploi très contrastés selon que le temps partiel est choisi ou subi. *Dares Analyses*, 5. Available at https://dares.travail-emploi.gouv.fr/IMG/pdf/2013-005-2.pdf. Accessed 1 December 2020.

Rapoport, B. (2012). Des fins de carrière toujours marquées par l'inactivité pour les femmes. *Retraite et société*, 2(2), 79–108. 10.3917/rs.063.0079

Riou, B., Cariou, A., Duranteau, J., Langeron, O., Crestani, B., Adnet, F., and Raux, M. (2020). Retour d'expérience sur la direction médicale de crise à l'Assistance Publique-Hôpitaux de Paris pendant la crise COVID-19. *An Fr Med Urgence*, 10, 340–349.

Rivallin, R. and Sandret, N. (2014). L'exposition des salariés aux facteurs de pénibilité dans le travail. *Dares Analyse*, 095.

TrEpid (2020). Le travail sous épidémie : 100questions, 34 000 réponses, et 60 propositions pour sortir de la crise. Report available at https://luttevirale.fr/enquete/rapport/ Accessed 14 July 2022.

Ugict-CGT et CGT-ministères sociaux (2020). *Le travail sous épidémie (TrEpid)*. une enquête nationale.

Addendum

COVID surveys in France with data on employment

Attitudes of citizens towards COVID-19

The data used in this light are mainly drawn from public data from the second wave of the French survey of the project "Citizens' Attitudes Under COVID-19 Pandemic", whose research team is composed of Sylvain Brouard (Sciences Po, CEVIPOF/LIEPP), Michael Becher (Université Toulouse 1 Capitole, IAST), Martial Foucault (Sciences Po, CEVIPOF), Pavlos Vasilopoulos (University of York) and Eric Kerrouche (Sciences Po, CEVIPOF). The data were collected by Ipsos from March 23 to 25, 2020 from a sample of 2,000 individuals representative of the French population aged 18 and over. A total of 984 respondents were employed before the confinement (working people excluding the self-employed and farmers). Among them, 623 respondents continued to work during the confinement and 361 stopped working on or after March 17, 2020. The data are available at https://data.sciencespo.fr/dataset.xhtml?persistentId=doi:10.21410/7E4/EATFBWU15T

The Coconel "Housing and Living Conditions" survey

This survey was carried out by the Institut national d'études démographiques (INED), in partnership with the Coconel consortium (VITROME IHU Méditerranée Infection, CIC Cochin-Pasteur, EHESP, ORS Paca), ANR, IRD and IFOP. A sample of 2,003 people, representative of adults residing in metropolitan France, was drawn using the quota method (age, sex, education, socio-professional group, region and category of municipality). The survey was conducted via the Internet from April 30 to May 4, 2020. It focused on the situation before and during confinement, and addressed different themes: housing and living conditions; employment and working conditions; children and educational continuity; neighbourhood and feelings of isolation.

EpiCOV: Tracing the immune status of the population to guide public decision-making

Quantifying the proportion of people who have developed antibodies in response to the SARS-CoV2 virus and documenting the effects of this epidemic on the living conditions of French citizens are major challenges in order to support the development of the most appropriate deconfinement and prevention strategies, to enable the early detection of any outbreak and, in the longer term, to monitor the effectiveness of the measures taken. The EpiCOV project is a large-scale epidemiological study carried out by Inserm and the Department of Research, Studies, Evaluation and Statistics (DREES) of the Ministry of Solidarity and Health, in conjunction with their partners (INSEE, Public Health France, CNRS, INED, Paris-Saclay University), backed by a major statistical survey, providing a global and scientifically reliable mapping of the population's immune status and its dynamics, throughout the territory, via the collection of biological samples coupled with questionnaires. The first wave of the survey took place between May 2 and June 2, 2020, tracking the period of the lockdown of the population. A total of 135,000 people aged 15 or over on January 1, 2020, took part in the survey. The survey was carried out mainly on the Internet but also by telephone: the use of this second method made it possible to increase the participation rate and to interview people without Internet access or with limited use of it, thus ensuring the representativeness of the responses collected. The objective of the EpiCOV project is to provide, on the one hand, a precise mapping of the population's immune status, health, living conditions and social inequalities, and on the other hand, a monitoring of the epidemic dynamics in the short, medium and long term.

11 (Active) Ageing, Gender and Social Policy Reforms: The Case of Pension and Eldercare Reforms in Croatia

Ivana Dobrotić and Siniša Zrinščak

Introduction

Ageing is a global phenomenon that brings significant social transformations and has implications for all aspects of society, including the welfare state. The appropriate policy response is increasingly seen in "active ageing", often referring to the World Health Organisation's (WHO) conception of active ageing, which sees it as a "process of optimizing opportunities for health, participation and security in order to enhance quality of life as people age" (WHO, 2002: 12). While the WHO's notion of active ageing has become an integral part of the European union's (EU) social policy discourse, the remit of active ageing policy remains unclear and is often limited to economic aspects of ageing (Walker and Maltby, 2012; O'Brien, 2017). Extending working life is promoted as a kind of panacea for addressing low employment and the financial sustainability of social systems such as pensions or healthcare. Such a policy practice tends to extend to the EU Member States, resulting in a lack of coherent and integrated active ageing strategies, and even more so in active ageing policies that may fail to put the issue of gender equality at the centre of interest (Walker, 2008; Foster and Walker, 2013).

Whether and how active ageing ideas shape social policy reforms in a specific context can be illustrated by the Croatian example, which depicts a story of a profound social transformation that has indeed created "new" social risks and can, therefore, be particularly sensitive to new solutions offered elsewhere. Yet radical political and social changes in the post-communist period have not created an ideational vacuum, raising the question of how existing ideas (e.g. on ageing or gender) mix with new ones and how they are contextualised in different social policy programs. As pointed out by Béland (2005, 2019), ideas matter; however, to fully understand policy outputs, it is also important to pay attention to policy legacies and formal institutional rules.

Against this backdrop, this chapter explores whether and how social policy reforms in Croatia have been legitimised through "active ageing" ideas. More specifically, combining insights on ideas (e.g. Hall, 1993; Cox, 2001; Béland, 2005) with insights from active ageing (e.g. Walker, 2008; Walker and Maltby, 2012; Foster and Walker, 2013) and welfare state literature (e.g. Hemerijck, 2012, 2018;

DOI: 10.4324/9781003145325-11

Jenson, 2012), the chapter analyses to what extent pensions and eldercare reforms are informed by an active ageing perspective. It seeks to explore how "active ageing" is understood and utilised by political actors in the process of legitimising reforms, with additional attention being given to the gender aspects of ageing, that is, the extent to which social welfare systems address gender differences in the experience of ageing.

The chapter starts with a brief literature review providing a conceptual framework, which outlines ideational perspectives that can be expected to have been influential in social policy reforms and how they relate to "active ageing". Following this, developments in pensions and eldercare systems in the last three decades are discussed in order to understand how ideas on (active) ageing have been used in reforms. In conclusion, there is a discussion of the findings and gender implications of the reforms.

(Active) ageing, welfare state and gender: A conceptual framework

In recent decades – followed by the impetus of international organisations (e.g. WHO, EU) – policies for older people in Europe have become increasingly framed within a more positive paradigm, shifting from the idea of old age being characterised by dependency and need towards healthy and active ageing (Walker, 2008; Walker and Maltby, 2012; Zaidi and Howse, 2017). These developments have challenged a dependency narrative that dominated the post-World War II welfare state, providing a new "set of values that should shape and underpin policies for promoting well-being in later life" (Zaidi and Howse, 2017: 3) and stressing a need for a multidimensional social policy approach with a strong life course perspective and rights-based orientation (cf. Walker, 2008; Zaidi and Howse, 2017).

It is well established that the emergence of new policy ideas may affect the character of social policy reforms (Seeleib-Kaiser and Toivonen, 2011; Blum, Formánková and Dobrotić, 2014). "Ideas" play an important role in policy-making. They are used to frame a problem, argue for change and legitimise desirable policy solutions (Cox, 2001; Schmidt, 2002; Béland and Cox, 2016). Broader ideational frameworks, often referred to as policy paradigms, are central here. They serve as "prisms" through which policymakers see the world and specify the nature of the problems and policy goals, including the instruments needed to address them (Hall, 1993: 279). The process by which new ideas come to the fore does not consist of "definitive stages – failure of an old idea followed by a period of uncertainty and then consolidation of a new one" (Mehta, 2011: 32). New ideas usually compete with (pre-)existing ideas and expectations, which may also be resilient and deeply embedded in institutions and, therefore, act to limit particular policy options (Béland, 2005; Jacobs, 2009).

The latter point is particularly important in the context of this chapter. When given prominence at the European social policy agenda, "active ageing" was confronted with the "pension-heavy and insider-biased welfare provision" legacy in many countries (Hemerijck, 2018: 814). That is, welfare systems that were initially developed within the traditional Keynesianism, an ideational paradigm that favoured protection oriented welfare state and aimed at "passive" risk protection with social insurance policies based on the traditional (male) life-course perspective education-work-retirement being central (Hemerijck, 2012; Jenson, 2012). Dependency and need in old age was the main normative image of a social contract postulating "a view of old age as a time of life when people step back from all kinds of commitments and social roles, including work" (Zaidi and Howse, 2017: 5), providing legitimacy for investments in pension systems (Walker and Maltby, 2012). As this perspective favoured the traditional family and gendered division of care (Jenson, 2012), these would typically include survivors' pensions that women could access through a relationship with a male breadwinner.

"Active ageing" emerged together with the social investment paradigm, seen as a response to the period of gender-blind neoliberal critique of the welfare state. Both neoliberalism and social investment share an orientation towards activation; however, they differ in many aspects (see Hemerijck, 2012; Jenson, 2012). When it comes to ageing, neoliberalism opened a space to portray "large cohorts" of pensioners as a burden for pension and healthcare systems' sustainability, asking for a (more) limited state involvement and growing individual and community responsibility (Hemerijck, 2012, 2018). Contrary to neoliberalism, the social investment paradigm sees social policy as a necessary precondition for (future) economic growth, with a comprehensive active ageing policy being one of the central components (cf. Hemerijck, 2018; Walker and Maltby, 2012; Zaidi and Howse, 2017). Still, when it comes to the (practical) policy level, the social investment perspective has been criticised for privileging market-oriented objectives (e.g. Saraceno, 2015). This coincides with "active ageing" literature stressing that policy framing and instruments for older populations continued to centre around economic aspects of ageing and were predominantly focused on a narrow "productivist" dimension, asking for changes to the pension systems and labour market policies that will seek to extend working lives (Walker and Maltby, 2012). As argued by Foster and Walker (2013: 7), "where productivist approaches to the notion of active ageing are dominant, this has led to measures predominantly based on the male trajectory of work and retirement which largely ignore the different needs of older men and women". A more comprehensive social policy approach supported by WHO, going beyond the promotion of paid work and acknowledging other areas of life such as unpaid work, independent and autonomous living, care provision or voluntary activities, has received less prominence (Zaidi et al., 2017).

The latter may be particularly the case in countries where the welfare system has not followed a coherent policy paradigm, such as Croatia, resulting in "ad-hoc, uncoordinated and ill-advised reforms" (Dobrotić, 2016b:320) and became sensitive to new solutions offered from outside (e.g. Deacon and Stubbs, 2007). Namely, as is the case with other post-communist countries, the literature on Croatian social policy development underlines the challenges of its classification according to the generally known ideal-type welfare state models (Stubbs and Zrinščak, 2009; 2015). Similarly, labels such as "post-communist", "hybrid", "neo-corporatist" or "welfare patchworks" indicate the complex nature of social policy reforms and changes; however, they do not help much in understanding the nature of changes, the actors involved and the motives behind a particular reform or the overall setup of the Croatian welfare regime. A recent attempt to use a so-called agency, structure, institutions and discourses or ASID model (Moulaert, Jessop and Mehmood, 2016) in three post-Yugoslav countries (Bosnia and Herzegovina, Croatia and Serbia) demonstrates the need for an analytical frame wide enough to capture quite specific elements of the post-Yugoslav space (Stubbs and Zrinščak, 2019). In the Croatian case, these elements cover the communist legacy and post-communist social circumstances, which heavily influenced how social policy reforms had been designed and implemented.

Therefore, to shed light on whether and how "active ageing" ideas enter the Croatian social policy debates, further analysis must closely examine both policy legacies and a broader context. The analysis in this chapter is focused on reforms in pension and eldercare systems as they could be particularly telling in assessing whether a productivist or comprehensive approach to the notion of "active ageing" is present in social policy debates, as well as of the extent to which the notion of "active ageing" is gender-equality-oriented. While the pension system is crucial for setting the preconditions for older people's participation in the labour market and recognising gender differences across the life course, the eldercare system shapes the conditions needed for independent and autonomous living and recognises care work. The in-depth analysis covers the 2007–2020 period and draws on existing literature, national legislation proposals, policy statements and parliamentary debates. This time frame provides ample room for identifying and gaining insight into possible "ideational turns" behind the reforms.

(Active) ageing, gender and social policy reforms in Croatia

Communist and early post-communist social policy legacy

In relation to (active) ageing policy and gender, Croatia inherited the Bismarckian pension system, which has its roots in the late 19th and early 20th centuries when Croatia belonged to the Austro-Hungarian Empire (Puljiz, 2007). It was fully developed in communist Yugoslavia and was based on employees and employers' contributions. It was run as a part of the state administration, lacking autonomy and efficiency. The latter became apparent in the 1980s, at a time of economic crisis and the deteriorating ratio of insured to retired persons, which dropped from 8.75:1 in 1950 to 2.83:1 in 1990 (Puljiz, 2019: 17). Despite that, the system remained quite generous in terms of pension replacement rate and eligibility criteria. Men were entitled to a full pension at the age of 60 and women at age 55, while the pension amount was calculated based on the best ten years of earnings (Puljiz, 2008: 103). From a gender perspective, pensions calculated in this way were less detrimental to women as the level of pensions was less affected by childbirth-related career breaks. Nevertheless, although the communist regime promoted the dual-earner model and facilitated women's participation in the labour market through investments in childcare policies, female employment was moderate (Puljiz and Zrinščak, 2002). Survivors' pensions that women could access through marriage, therefore, formed an important element of the pension system (Puljiz, 2007). This legacy has remained very influential in debates on pension reforms since 1990.

By contrast, the state did not emerge as a strong actor in eldercare, leaving care predominantly to the family, that is, women burdened with the gendered division of care work and household responsibilities. The foundations of the eldercare system were indeed built in the communist period; however, the eldercare sector was developed within the social care system characterised by social assistance orientation and remained marginal. It relied heavily on state-owned residential homes, while community-based care was almost non-existent and supported by cash benefits rather than community services. The limited capacities of institutional care can be illustrated by the fact that only 1.8 per cent of persons over the age of 65 had a place in residential homes in the late 1980s (Dobrotić, 2016a: 28), which is much lower than the provision that would cover at least 5 per cent of 65+ population required to meet residential care needs. Therefore, the provision for older people in that period was established within the "protection" oriented paradigm prevailing at the time in many European countries, emphasising dependency and disengagement in old age and assuming a gendered division of labour (Zaidi and Howse, 2017).

In the 1990s, social policy had been fully conditioned by the circumstances surrounding the dissolution of Yugoslavia. That period did not witness many reform attempts, but it set a social agenda for future changes. This mainly refers to the enormous economic and social consequences of the war against Croatian independence (from 1991 to 1995) and the state- and nation-building process accompanied by high centralisation and a semi-authoritarian political regime (Stubbs and Zrinščak, 2009). The change from a state to a market economy was entirely controlled by the ruling party. It resulted in quite ineffective and unfair privatisation of the economy as such conditions created a "clientelistic capture", a regime where the state has remained the leading distributor of goods and services, largely directed towards powerful or politically loyal interest groups (Stubbs and Zrinščak, 2015). An additional consequence of the collapse of the economy was a deteriorating pension system and the use of early retirement to mitigate rising unemployment, while eldercare services have remained on the margins of the social policy agenda. The ratio of insured to retired persons dropped further to only 1.38:1 in 1999 (Stubbs and Zrinščak, 2007: 91). Simultaneously, the value of pensions has fallen significantly, especially after the 1993 government decision not to adjust pensions to wage growth, which the Constitutional Court later proclaimed unconstitutional (Puljiz, 2019). These developments constituted pensioners as the largest interest group highly dissatisfied with their position and a so-called pension debt – named as such by the Constitutional Court decision – was one of the main controversial public issues.

In addition to the already mentioned traditional division of gender roles in the private sphere and the minimal role of the state in care provision, women's position in the 1990s had been conditioned by a neo-conservative turn. The newly acquired public role of religion, the process of nation- and state-building in wartime circumstances and the population decline nurtured ideas about the role of women as mothers and protectors of the nation's spirit (see Dobrotić et al., 2013). While most of the proposed policy measures seeking to assign women primarily a reproductive and caring function (e.g. withdrawal of nurseries, cash-for-care benefits) were never realised due to lack of funds, such a narrative has grown and strengthened, which was largely evident in the 1996 National Programme of Demographic Development (Puljiz and Zrinščak, 2002). Moreover, through various cost-containment measures (e.g. in leave benefits) and non-investments in care services – backed up by gender-blind conditionalities attached to the World Bank and International Monetary Fund's loans – the early transition period weakened the defamilialising potential of policies inherited from the socialist period (cf. Dobrotić et al., 2013; Dobrotić, 2020). Therefore, employment-oriented gender equality ideas inherited from the socialist period and later strengthened by the Europeanisation process have had some influence on future reforms. Still, the mixture of opposing narratives and the reality of care being left primarily to the family, i.e. especially women (Kamenov and Jugović, 2011; Dobrotić, 2017) has been influencing whether and how a gender dimension is taken into account in social policymaking, as discussed further in the cases of pension and eldercare reforms.

Croatian pension debates and developments

In addition to the communist legacy and a steady collapse of the pension system in the 1990s, the comprehensive and radical reform implemented in the 1999–2002 period created a framework for all future changes and accompanying narratives within the pension system. The reform has been labelled radical for two reasons. First, the implementation of profound changes, including the increase in retirement age (from 60 to 65 years for men and 55 to 60 years for women by 2008), the extension of the reference salary period included in pension calculation to cover the whole employment period, a new pension formula discouraging early retirement, a new indexation formula and stricter eligibility criteria for the disability pension. Second, the shift from the inherited PAYGO towards a three-pillar pension system in which the second (obligatory) and the third (voluntary) pillars based on capitalised savings were added to the first PAYGO pillar (Stubbs and Zrinščak, 2007; Puljiz, 2007, 2019; Dobrotić, 2020). These changes were packed in an entirely new neoliberal discourse stressing activation and individual responsibility for old age, heavily influenced by the World Bank and International Monetary Fund. The inherited pension system was accused of inappropriate collectivistic (i.e. communist) traits and as being financially unstable. At the same time, ageing was portrayed as a problem seeking new solutions such as individual responsibility for security in old age and the need to rely on market solutions to make the system financially sustainable. Extending working life and individual responsibility, along with predicted economic growth, were described as magical solutions for all pension's setbacks (Stubbs and Zrinščak, 2007: 91–96).

The 2007/2008 reform aimed to address pension adequacy, that is, a low real value of pensions and "pension debt". The pension formula introduced with the 1999–2002 reform caused inequalities as pensioners with similar qualifying conditions ended with quite different pensions. In response, the 2007/2008 reform diminished penalisation for early retirement, introduced a pension supplement to reduce differences in pension values and raised the minimum pension and (in specific cases) disability pensions. In addition, there was a change in the pension formula for part-time workers and – following a Constitutional Court decision – a right to survivor pension for unmarried couples was regulated (HS, 2007, 2008). Contrary to the 1999–2002 reform, the central underlying rhetoric was social security, that is, protection in old age. Corrective measures introduced with this reform aimed to protect various categories of pensioners and were a purely passive response to a very fragmented and, therefore, non-functional pension system. The (de)activation discourse was used only in a "negative" sense, as "forced" or "pragmatic" deactivation. The argument used by the right-wing government, and widely shared by MPs from different political parties and spectrum, was that the decision to retire earlier is, for the majority, the only real solution while facing unemployment in old age or simply avoiding the diminution of their pension due to announced changes in the pension formula. The gender aspect was mentioned only in relation to the equalisation of married and unmarried couples' rights, which was seen as a positive change. It was emphasised that women are overrepresented among the survivor's pension recipients (HS, 2007, 2008).

In 2010, under the right-wing government and as the response to the 2008 economic crisis which hit Croatia hard, privileged pensions were reduced. Financial stability and solidarity (e.g. diminishing pension to those who were privileged and those with higher pensions) were central arguments. The other change – more telling from the perspective of active ageing – implemented another Constitutional Court decision to equalise the retirement age for men and women (at the age of 65). Although the first government proposal envisaged equalisation by 2020, it encountered strong resistance, setting 2030 as a milestone for full implementation. Activation elements within the pension system were strengthened in two ways. First, through the penalisation of early retirement – the penalty level increased and became more strongly connected with working-age period duration, and not only with retirement age. Second, through higher pensions for those who continue to work after acquiring the right to a pension. The main arguments put forward by the right-wing government were again financial sustainability (to discourage earlier retirement), activation (the penalisation of early retirement; higher pensions for extended working life) and gender equality (equalisation of retirement age for men and women, though over a 20 year period) (cf. HS, 2010; Puljiz, 2019; Dobrotić,

2020). However, the parliamentary debate revealed another set of arguments. Although retirement age equalisation was endorsed as a general principle, the rejection of the proposal was based on the fact that, in reality, there is no gender equality, and equalisation will actually deepen discrimination against women who are burdened with two jobs (professional and domestic) and will have to work even longer with this change. It was also argued that this could stimulate early retirement as women will try to avoid stricter eligibility criteria for a full pension. These gender-related arguments were expanded by those against longer working lives in general, especially for some professions. High unemployment and generation-related arguments (high unemployment of youth) were also listed against longer work in old age. Notions of activation (i.e. activity or longer work in old age) were therefore completely overshadowed by the vision of early deactivation and passive social protection. At the same time, the pension system was accused of financial instability and failure to offer decent protection in old age (HS, 2010).

Another set of changes followed in the 2013–2015 period, this time under the left-wing government. As there were many doubts about whether all pension rights – particularly those connected with war veterans' pensions – were obtained according to rules, the government became preoccupied with control and introduced mechanisms for better monitoring and revision of rights. Cheating, misuse and control were the main arguments used (HS, 2013, 2014). When observed from the active ageing perspective, reforms were ambivalent. On the one hand, though in the long run, another extension of the working age was passed – 67 years for both sexes by 2037 for a full pension. In addition to this, activation elements were strengthened by regulating part-time work after retirement to allow for this combination. On the other hand, "passive" elements were emphasised. More precisely, few measures – presented as fair or as a correction to various anomalies of the system – allowed early retirement. For instance, 60-year-olds with longer working histories (41 years or more) received the right to claim the full pension, while early retirement without penalisation was allowed for workers meeting the criteria for early retirement who were unemployed for two years due to the bankruptcy of their companies (cf. HS, 2014; Puljiz, 2019; Dobrotić, 2020).[1] All changes were framed as contributing to pension system sustainability, especially by extending working life. Similarly, as with the previous reform, parliamentary debate put forward other reasons, such as not to accept the increase in retirement age. It was argued that 67 years is an unrealistic goal, particularly for some professions and for women, and that, in reality, the possibility to work longer is available to only a minority of workers. Therefore, as with previous reforms, the gender aspect was raised only in opposition to extended working life. Still, the proposal to differentiate the penalisation of early retirement for women was rejected based on the formal gender equality argument stressing that "differences based on the sex are not allowed". Also, the proposal to provide mothers with additional pension insurance period based on the number of children was not accepted, arguing that this would stimulate early retirement and undermine the basic pension system principle of pensions being based on contributions paid (HS, 2013, 2014). Finally, in 2015, the right to a survivor's pension for life-time (same-sex) partners was introduced due to a need to harmonise with the newly passed Act on Life-Time Partnership (HS, 2015).

Under the right-wing government, a more extensive reform of the pension system was undertaken in 2018 addressing the financial sustainability of the pension system (e.g. the ratio of insured to retired persons fell to only 1.20:1 by 2017), combining elements of "control", protection and activation. In particular, mechanisms of "control" continued to target disability pensions. Although the radical 2002 reform – which introduced the second pillar based on capitalised savings – promised financial stability of the pension system and better social protection in old age, the net pension replacement rate fell to 37.35 per cent in 2018, thereby putting pension adequacy among the central issues of the 2018 reform. Recalling a need to improve pensioners' material and social security, a low level of pensions was addressed by extending the pension supplement – initially introduced in 2008 to compensate for the "pension debt" – to "new" pensioners insured within a two-pension-pillar system. The need to extend working life has been emphasised more than with the previous reforms, which was clearly reflected in a number of new activation elements such as a faster increase in retirement age (67 years in 2033 and not in 2037) and gender equalisation in retirement age (65 years for both sexes in 2027 and not in 2030), higher penalty level for early retirement and higher pensions for those who continue to work after reaching retirement age, as well as relaxed rules related to pensioners' continuous participation in the labour market (e.g. the possibility to work part-time while keeping the right to a full pension) (HS, 2018, 2019). The latter set of changes was highly controversial, recalling the arguments from previous reforms on the non-functional labour market and (gender) inequalities in the labour market, which eventually led to the referendum initiative "67 is too much". To avoid the referendum, the government withdrew provisions related to the increase in retirement age and a higher penalty for early retirement (HS, 2019). A gender dimension was strengthened by providing mothers (or fathers if they used maternity leave in case the mother transferred the right to them) with an additional six months of pension insurance period for each child. However, it was argued that this was a demographic measure and not per se implemented to improve gender equality (HS, 2018).

Similarly, in 2020 a means-tested "national benefit for elderly" was introduced, referring to international instruments (e.g. ILO Recommendation No. 202 convention, European Pillar of Social Rights). It was argued that it would improve the social protection of those without any income in old age, particularly women in rural areas who did not have equal opportunities to participate in the labour market (HS, 2020). However, this benefit amounts to the same amount as social assistance and differs from social assistance only in eligibility criteria that are less strict. Therefore, it does not greatly improve older people's situation.

The Croatian eldercare debates and developments

The eldercare system, inherited from the communist period, continued to operate under the social care system characterised by a social assistance orientation and remained unchanged in its basic features during the 1990s. The main novelty was the opportunity given to non-state actors to act as care providers. This change was based on the premise that non-state actors' involvement in care provision will relieve the state of the growing social costs of institutional care (Balaband, 1997). As a result, the late 1990s witnessed an increase in privately-owned residential facilities and, to a lesser extent, adult foster care beneficiaries (Jurčević, 1999; Puljiz, 2001). In the early 2000s, a comprehensive welfare reform plan prepared by the left-centre government under the financial and expert assistance of the World Bank served as the context for eldercare system development. The main ideas promoted were decentralisation, deinstitutionalisation, pluralisation and individualisation (Puljiz, 2004), while the main reform proposals sought to introduce market elements into eldercare provision (e.g. vouchers). However, most of the changes introduced were never implemented. Moreover, the eldercare sector continued to form part of the social care system preoccupied with social benefits reforms and has never gained importance on the agenda as an independent issue. Therefore, over the last two decades, the expansion of eldercare capacity in Croatia has continued to rely primarily on the entry of private service providers into the system, within a sub-regulated institutional framework and a non-transparent subcontracting process (e.g. undefined service charges, absence of public calls for new service providers) (Dobrotić, 2016a). The overarching narrative behind these changes was based on neoliberal elements, emphasising that pluralisation of service providers will relieve the state from the high social costs of residential care (Dobrotić, 2016b), enable cost rationalisation and reduced state responsibility, as well as greater "freedom of choice" in choosing a caregiver which will also improve the service quality (Puljiz, 2004; Dobrotić, 2016a).

In the mid-2000s, with a new right-wing government, planned changes in the eldercare system's governance were put aside (e.g. public tenders to new providers), and emphasis started to be placed on community-based services as reflected in two main developments. The first is the professionalisation of adult foster care and the growth of "family homes" (small care units for up to 20 people). The second is the development of a policy and legislative framework for home-care services. The latter change was argued for by relying on active ageing ideas, stressing the importance of social inclusion and active participation by older people in society, but also a work-life balance. Still, neoliberal elements of "freedom of choice" and cost-effectiveness, as well as the framing of ageing as a "problem" that affects economic development, puts pressure on public finances and "burdens" on social systems have remained present (VRH, 2007; Hrvatski Sabor, 2007a). While growth in community-based services was evident, bringing in 15,550 new beneficiaries (VRH, 2013), home-care services – together with "day-stay" programs and community-based multidisciplinary gerontological centres – were developed as parallel systems which functioned on a project basis outside the social care system. The unstable, project-based funding resulted in the withdrawal of home-care services in the 2008 economic crisis period.

In 2013, with a new centre-left government, these project-based home-care services were integrated into the social care system and became subject to stricter needs-testing, but also a means-testing what was not the case before. One of the arguments put forward stressed a need for a more "just" system, which will enable all users to access the services under the same eligibility criteria. Still, the reform's general aim was a stricter targeting and "rationalisation" of public spending and a growing individual responsibility (Hrvatski Sabor, 2013a). That was clearly reflected in the sharp drop in the number of beneficiaries. A year after the reform was implemented, only around 1,500 new beneficiaries entered the social care system, which was much less than 15,500 project-funded beneficiaries (Dobrotić, 2016a).

These developments created a gap and uncertainty in home-care services provision, which, since the mid-2010s, has been predominantly addressed by EU funds. Home-care services mainly became provided through the program "Zaželi". In the first programming period (2017–2020) 29,707 older people were supported (Europski socijalni fond, 2020a). This program, therefore, brought important improvements in eldercare coverage rates, especially in rural areas; however, this program had weaknesses if considered from a gender perspective and the perspective of the long-term sustainability of services. The program was framed within employment-oriented goals, explicitly targeting long-term unemployed (older) women of lower education as care providers; while long-term unemployed men cannot be employed as carers under this program (Europski socijalni fond, 2020b). Therefore, the program has not only been gender-unaware, but it also facilitated gender inequalities in the labour market by pushing long-term unemployed women exclusively towards the precarious and undervalued care sector. They could not be paid more than the state-level defined minimum wage (ibid), while the dependence on project-to-project funding brought uncertainty and career breaks. Moreover, in the periods between the projects, older people in need of care have been exposed to a risk of being left without any services. Therefore, although increasingly framed as invoking active ageing ideas (VRH, 2017), the eldercare system remains underfinanced, fragmented, underdeveloped and characterised by a lack of services (cf. Dobrotić, 2016a).

Conclusion

This chapter analysed pension and eldercare systems reforms in Croatia from both "active ageing" and gender perspectives. In addition to the influence of the communist legacy and profound subsequent social changes under different democratically chosen governments, which affected both systems heavily, the analysis reveals several factors that shaped the reforms.

In relation to the pension system, the notion of extending working life came primarily from two sources. One was related to the 1999–2002 radical reform that – mainly through the role of the World Bank – brought ideas of demographic ageing and changes in the working life cycle as a "problem" and "burden", which made the inherited pension arrangements unsustainable. Such a view continued to shape public debates. The second was related to the basic features of the pension system, which due to economic reasons and an extremely unfavourable ratio of insured to retired persons failed to offer basic social security. In that sense, new ideas, whether they came from abroad or were inspired by the phenomenon of longer life expectancy and the inevitable crisis of the pension system or both, became fully conditioned by the pension system's crisis and its basic malfunctioning. The Croatian case is an example not only of how new ideas can compete with existing ideas and existing institutions and rules but also how larger structural conditions can cause disruption of ideas and policies. Basic expectations of social security in old age, which the system had not been able to fulfil, conditioned the dominance of narratives of dependency and need in old age, which – together with the clientelistic nature of the state – caused a series of inconsistent reforms in which the ideas of active ageing in a full sense and quality of life were absent or unrecognisable.

The development of the eldercare system had a slightly different trajectory; however, it ended in similar disarray. Here, the legacy had a greater impact as the system remained marginal and anchored exclusively inside the social care framework preoccupied with social benefits reforms. New ideas in terms of pluralisation, deinstitutionalisation, individualisation and activation came in the course of the comprehensive welfare reform, influenced again by the World Bank but also through knowledge from various international and national experts. However, the reform has never been implemented, and changes in eldercare provision became connected with the expansion of the private sector and, to some extent, the EU-funded home-care services that were not properly integrated into the eldercare system. Features of the latter program and a general lack of eldercare services pose a risk of deepening gender inequalities in the labour market. Gender inequalities associated with the division of work and care have not been widely acknowledged in any of the reform attempts, which is reflected in the growing gender pension gap, which reached 29.7 per cent in 2018 and higher at-risk-of-poverty rates of women in old age, at 33.6 per cent of women compared to 24.9 per cent of men during the same year (Eurostat, 2020).

It may be concluded that "active ageing" ideas have entered social policy debates in Croatia mainly as a part of a narrow, labour market-oriented framing of reforms bringing changes to the pension system that seek to extend working lives. Gender equality arguments have not been central and were typically purely instrumental, used either to "defend" features of the "old" system (e.g. when opposing the increase in retirement age) or argue for policy instruments that could serve employment-oriented or demographic goals. Moreover, while "protection" in old age was a central argument in many reforms seeking adequate pensions, it was not used as an integral part of a more comprehensive, coherent and rights-based approach to active ageing. Part of the answer may be found in the ambiguous nature of "active ageing", allowing policymakers to "pick-up" aspects that serve their interests and indeed posing a risk for an economically-oriented understanding of working longer to become the dominant narrative and policy solution (cf. Walker and Maltby, 2012).

Note

1 There were some other changes, but these are less central for arguments in this chapter, including a further reduction of privileged pensions, the regulation of the possibility to purchase a supplementary and the introduction of a new indexation formula.

References

Balaband, A. (1997). Socijalna skrb i nezaposlenost u Republici Hrvatskoj. *Revija za socijalnu politiku*, 4(3), 253–263.

Béland, D. (2005). Ideas and social policy: An institutionalist perspective. *Social Policy and Administration*, 39(1), 1–18.

Béland, D. and Cox, R. H. (2016). Ideas as coalition magnets: Coalition building, policy entrepreneurs, and power relations. *Journal of European Public Policy*, 23(3), 428–445.

Béland, D. (2019). Narrative stories, institutional rules, and the politics of pension policy in Canada and the United States. *Policy and Society*, 38(3), 356–372.

Blum, S., Formánková, L. and Dobrotić, I. (2014). Family policies in "Hybrid" Welfare States after the crisis: Pathways between policy expansion and retrenchment. *Social Policy and Administration*, 48(4), 468–491.

Cox, R. H. (2001). The social construction of an imperative: Why welfare reform happened in Denmark and the Netherlands but not in Germany. *World Politics*, 53(3), 463–498.

Deacon, B. and Stubbs, P. (eds.) (2007). *Social Policy and International Interventions in South East Europe*. Cheltenham: Edward Elgar.

Dobrotić, I., Matković, T. and Zrinščak, S. (2013). Gender equality policies and practices in Croatia: The interplay of transition and late Europeanization. *Social Policy & Administration*, 47(2), 218–240.

Dobrotić, I. (2016a). Razvoj i poteškoće sustava skrbi za starije osobe u Republici Hrvatskoj. *Društvena istraživanja*, 25(1), 21–42.

Dobrotić, I. (2016b). Crisis and Croatian welfare state: A new opportunity for welfare state retrenchment? In Schubert, K., de Villota, P. and Kuhlmann, J., (Eds), *Challenges to European Welfare Systems*. Springer Publishing, 301–324.

Dobrotić, I. (2017). *Posao ili obitelj? Uloga i važnost politika usklađivanja obiteljskih obaveza i plaćenog rada*. Zagreb: Ured pravobraniteljice za ravnopravnost spolova.

Dobrotić, I. (2020). The Croatian welfare system: A lack of coherent policy paradigm followed by inconsistent policy reforms?. In Blum, S., Kuhlmann, J. and Schubert, K., (Eds). *Routledge Handbook of European Welfare Systems*. Abingdon: Routledge, 237–256.

Europski socijalni fond (2020a). *Zaželi - program zapošljavanja žena – faza II; UP.02.1.1.13, initial version*. [online] Available at: http://www.esf.hr/wordpress/wp-content/uploads/2020/02/ND-Za%C5%BEeli-faza-II.zip [Accessed 8 March 2021].

Europski socijalni fond (2020b). *Zaželi - program zapošljavanja žena – faza II; UP.02.1.1.13, revised version*. [online] Available at: http://www.esf.hr/wordpress/wp-content/uploads/2020/02/UZP-ZA%C5%BDELI-II_22.12.2020_pro%C4%8Di%C5%A1%C4%87eni-tekst.pdf [Accessed 8 March 2021].

Eurostat (2020). Closing the gender pension gap? [online] Available at: https://ec.europa.eu/eurostat/web/products-eurostat-news/-/DDN-20200207-1 [Accessed 8 March 2021].

Foster, L. and Walker, A. (2013). Gender and active ageing in Europe. *European Journal of Ageing*, 10, 3–10.

Hall, P. A. (1993). Policy paradigms, social learning, and the state: The case of economic policymaking in Britain. *Comparative Politics*, 25(3), 275–296.

Hemerijck, A. (2012). Two or three waves of welfare state transformation?. In Morel, N., Palier, B. and Palme, J., (Eds), *Towards A Social Investment Welfare State?: Ideas, Policies and Challenges*. Policy Press, 33–60.

Hemerijck, A. (2018). Social investment as a policy paradigm. *Journal of European Public Policy*, 25(6), 810–827.

Hrvatski Sabor. (2007). Prijedlog paketa zakona o mirovinskom osiguranju – prijedlozi zakona ifonogram rasprava. Information and Documentation Department of Croatian Parliament. Available at: https://www.sabor.hr/hr/sjednice/pregled-dnevnih-redova [Accessed 8 December 2020].

Hrvatski Sabor. (2007a). Prijedlog zakona o izmjenama i dopunama Zakona o socijalnoj skrbi –prijedlog zakona i fonogram rasprava. Information and Documentation Department of Croatian Parliament. Available at: https://www.sabor.hr/hr/sjednice/pregled-dnevnih-redova. [Accessed 8 December 2020].

Hrvatski Sabor. (2008). Prijedlog Zakona o izmjenama i dopunama Zakona o mirovinskom osiguranju– prijedlog zakona i fonogram rasprava. Information and DocumentationDepartment of Croatian Parliament. Available at: https://www.sabor.hr/hr/sjednice/pregled-dnevnih-redova [Accessed 8 December 2020].

Hrvatski Sabor. (2010). Prijedlog Zakona o izmjenama i dopunama Zakona o mirovinskom osiguranju– prijedlog zakona i fonogram rasprava. Information and Documentation Department of Croatian Parliament. Available at: https://www.sabor.hr/hr/sjednice/pregled-dnevnih-redova. [Accessed 8 December 2020].

Hrvatski Sabor. (2013). Prijedlog Zakona o izmjenama i dopunama Zakona o mirovinskom osiguranju– prijedlog zakona i fonogram rasprava. Information and DocumentationDepartment of Croatian Parliament. Available at: https://www.sabor.hr/hr/sjednice/pregled-dnevnih-redova [Accessed 8 December 2020].

Hrvatski Sabor. (2013a). Prijedlog Zakona o socijalnoj skrbi – prijedlog zakona i fonogram rasprava. Informationand Documentation Department of Croatian Parliament. Available at: https://www.sabor.hr/hr/sjednice/pregled-dnevnih-redova [Accessed 8 December 2020].

Hrvatski Sabor. (2014). Prijedlog Zakona o izmjenama i dopunama Zakona o mirovinskom osiguranju– prijedlog zakona i fonogram rasprava. Information and Documentation Department of Croatian Parliament.Available at: https://www.sabor.hr/hr/sjednice/pregled-dnevnih-redova [Accessed 8 December 2020].

Hrvatski Sabor. (2015). Prijedlog Zakona o izmjenama i dopunama Zakona o mirovinskom osiguranju– prijedlog zakona i fonogram rasprava. Information and Documentation Department of Croatian Parliament.Available at: https://www.sabor.hr/hr/sjednice/pregled-dnevnih-redova [Accessed 8 December 2020].

Hrvatski Sabor. (2019). Prijedlog Zakona o izmjenama Zakona o mirovinskom osiguranju –prijedlog zakona i fonogram rasprava. Information and Documentation Department of Croatian Parliament. Available at: https://www.sabor.hr/hr/sjednice/pregled-dnevnih-redova [Accessed 8 December 2020].

Hrvatski Sabor. (2020). Prijedlog Zakona o nacionalnoj naknadi za starije osobe – prijedlogzakona i fonogram rasprava. Information and Documentation Department ofCroatian Parliament. Available at: https://www.sabor.hr/hr/sjednice/pregled-dnevnih-redova [Accessed 8 December 2020].

Jacobs, A. M. (2009). How do ideas matter? Mental models and attention in German pension politics. *Comparative Political Studies*, 42(2), 252–279.
Jenson, J. (2012). Redesigning citizenship regimes after neoliberalism: Moving towards social investment. In Morel, N., Palier, B. and Palme, J., (Eds), *Towards a Social Investment Welfare State?: Ideas, Policies and Challenges*. Policy Press, 61–88.
Jurčević, Ž. (1999). Socijalna skrb u Hrvatskoj u 1998. godini. *Revija za socijalnu politiku*, 6(2), 133–146.
Kamenov, Ž. and Jugović, I. (2011). Percepcija, iskustvo i stavovi o rodnoj (ne)ravnopravnosti u obitelji. In Kamenov, Ž. and Galić, B., (Eds), *Rodna ravnopravnost i diskriminacija u Hrvatskoj*. Zagreb: Ured za ravnopravnost spolova Vlade RH, 120–142.
Mehta, J. (2011). The varied roles of ideas in politics: From "Whether" to "How". In Béland, D. and Cox, R. H., (Eds), *Ideas and Politics in Social Science Research*. Oxford: Oxford University Press, 23–46.
Moulaert, F., Jessop, B. and Mehmood, A. (2016). Agency, structure, institutions, discourse (ASID) in urban and regional development. *International Journal of Urban Sciences*, 20(2), 167–187.
O'Brien, E. (2017). Planning for population ageing: The rhetoric of 'active ageing': theoretical shortfalls, policy limits, practical constraints and the crucial requirement for societal interventions. *International Planning Studies*, 22(4), 415–428.
Puljiz, V. (2001). Reforme sustava socijalne politike u Hrvatskoj. *Revija za socijalnu politiku*, 8(2), 159–180.
Puljiz, V. and Zrinščak, S. (2002). Hrvatska obiteljska politika u europskom kontekstu. *Revija za socijalnu politiku*, 9(2), 117–137.
Puljiz, V. (2004). Socijalna prava i socijalni razvoj Republike Hrvatske. *Revija za socijalnu politiku*, 11(1), 3–20.
Puljiz, V. (2008). Mirovinski sustav. *Socijalna politika Hrvatske*. Zagreb: Pravni fakultet, 73–118.
Puljiz, V. (2019). Mirovinski sustav. In Bežovan, G., (Ed), *Socijalna politika Hrvatske*. Zagreb: Pravni fakultet, 109–158.
Saraceno, C. (2015). A critical look to the social investment approach from a gender perspective. *Social Politics: International Studies in Gender, State & Society*, 22(2), 257–269.
Schmidt, V. (2002). Does discourse matter in the politics of welfare state adjustment? *Comparative Political Studies*, 35(2), 168–193.
Seeleib-Kaiser, M. and Toivonen, T. (2011). Between reforms and birth rates: Germany, Japan, and family policy discourse. *Social Politics: International Studies in Gender, State & Society*, 18(3), 331–360.
Stubbs, P. and Zrinščak, S. (2007). Croatia. In Deacon, B. and Stubbs, P., (Eds), *Social Policy and International Interventions in South East Europe*, Cheltenham: Edward Elgar, 85–102.
Stubbs, P. and Zrinščak, S. (2009). Croatian social policy: The legacies of war, state-building and late Europeanization. *Social Policy & Administration*, 43(2), 121–135.
Stubbs, P. and Zrinščak, S. (2015). Citizenship and social welfare in Croatia: Clientelism and the limits of "Europeanization". *European Politics and Society*, 16(3), 395–410.
Stubbs, P. and Zrinščak, S. (2019). Reforming welfare assemblages in semi-peripheral spaces: Understanding "drivers of inertia" in Bosnia-Herzegovina, Croatia and Serbia. In An, S., Chubarova, T., Deacon, B. and Stubbs, P., (Eds), *Social Policy, Poverty, and Inequality in Central and Eastern Europe and the Former Soviet Union. Agency and Institutions in Flux*. Stuttgart: Ibidem-Verlag, 285–305.

VRH (2007). Program razvoja usluga za starije osobe u sustavu međugeneracijske solidarnosti od 2008. do 2011. godine. *Official Gazette*, 90/2007.

VRH (2013). *Izvješće o provedbi zajedničkog memoranduma o socijalnom uključivanju Republike Hrvatske (JIM) u 2012. godini.* [online] Available at: http://www.vlada.hr/hr/naslovnica/sjednice_i_odluke_vlade_rh/sjednice_i_odluke_vlade_rh/107_sjednica_vlade_republike_hrvatske [Accessed 15 May 2015].

VRH (2017). Strategija socijalne skrbi za starije osobe u Republici Hrvatskoj za razdoblje od 2017-2020. *Official Gazette*, 97/2017.

Walker, A. (2008). Commentary: The emergence and application of active aging in Europe. *Journal of Aging & Social Policy*, 21, 75–93.

Walker, A. and Maltby, T. (2012). Active ageing: A strategic policy solution to demographic ageing in the European Union. *International Journal of Social Welfare*, 21, S117–S130.

WHO (2002). *Active Ageing: A Policy Framework*. [online] Available at: https://www.who.int/ageing/publications/active_ageing/en/ [Accessed 12 February 2021].

Zaidi, A. and Howse, K. (2017). The policy discourse of active ageing: Some reflections. *Population Ageing*, 10, 1–10.

Zaidi, A., Gasior, K., Zolyomi, E., Schmidt, A., Rodrigues, R. and Marin, B. (2017). Measuring active and healthy ageing in Europe. *Journal of European Social Policy*, 27(2), 138–157.

Index

Note: Italicized and bold page numbers refer to figures and tables. Page numbers followed by "n" refer to notes.